Corruption and Government

D0032458

High levels of corruption limit investment and growth and lead to ineffective government. Developing countries and those making a transition from socialism are particularly at risk, but corruption is a worldwide phenomenon. Corruption creates economic inefficiencies and inequities, but reforms are possible to reduce the material benefits from payoffs. Corruption is not just an economic problem, however; it is also intertwined with politics. Reform may require changes in both constitutional structures and the underlying relationship of the market and the state. Effective reform cannot occur unless both the international community and domestic political leaders support change. No single "blueprint" is possible, but the primary goal should be to reduce the gains from paying and receiving bribes, not simply to remove "bad apples."

Susan Rose-Ackerman is Henry R. Luce Professor of Law and Political Science, Yale University, and Co-director of the Law School's Center for Law, Economics, and Public Policy. She holds a Ph.D. in economics from Yale University and has held fellowships from the Guggenheim Foundation and the Fulbright Commission. Professor Rose-Ackerman was a Visiting Research Fellow at the World Bank in 1995–96. She is the author of *Controlling Environmental Policy: The Limits of Public Law in Germany and the United States, Rethinking the Progressive Agenda: The Reform of the American Regulatory State*, the landmark analysis *Corruption: A Study in Political Economy*, and joint author of *The Uncertain Search for Environmental Quality* and *The Nonprofit Enterprise in Market Economies*. She has also published widely in law, economics, and policy journals. Her current research interests include comparative regulatory law and policy, the political economy of corruption, public policy and administrative law, and law and economics.

Corruption and Government

Causes, Consequences, and Reform

SUSAN ROSE-ACKERMAN

CAMBRIDGE
UNIVERSITY PRESS

PUBLISHED BY THE PRESS SYNDICATE OF THE UNIVERSITY OF CAMBRIDGE
The Pitt Building, Trumpington Street, Cambridge, United Kingdom

CAMBRIDGE UNIVERSITY PRESS
The Edinburgh Building, Cambridge CB2 2RU, UK   http://www.cup.cam.ac.uk
40 West 20th Street, New York, NY 10011-4211, USA   http://www.cup.org
10 Stamford Road, Oakleigh, Melbourne 3166, Australia

© Susan Rose-Ackerman 1999

This book is in copyright. Subject to statutory exception
and to the provisions of relevant collective licensing agreements,
no reproduction of any part may take place without
the written permission of Cambridge University Press.

First published 1999

Printed in the United States of America

Typeface Times Roman 10/12 pt.   *System* QuarkXPress [BTS]

A catalog record for this book is available from the British Library.

Library of Congress Cataloging-in-Publication Data

Rose-Ackerman, Susan.
    Corruption and government: causes, consequences, and reform/
Susan Rose-Ackerman.
        p.   cm.
    Includes bibliographical references.
    ISBN 0-521-63293-5 hb. – ISBN 0-521-65912-4 pb
    1. Political corruption.   2. Political corruption – Economic aspects.
    I. Title.
    JF1081.R675   1999
    364. 1'323 – dc21   98-43631
                                                                          CIP

ISBN   0 521 63293 5   hardback
ISBN   0 521 65912 4   paperback

For my mother, with love

CONTENTS

PREFACE

Economics is a powerful tool for the analysis of corruption. Cultural differences and morality provide nuance and subtlety, but an economic approach is fundamental to understanding where corrupt incentives are the greatest and have the biggest impact. In an earlier book, *Corruption: A Study in Political Economy* (1978), I made this point for an audience of economists and technically trained political scientists. Twenty years later I hope to broaden my audience and deepen my analysis with a new book that focuses on the way corruption affects developing countries and those in transition from state socialism.

The growing interest in institutional issues among development economists encouraged me to make this effort. The study of corruption forces scholars and policy makers to focus on the tension between self-seeking behavior and public values. Those worried about the development failures common throughout the world must confront the problem of corruption and the weak and arbitrary state structures that feed it.

In 1995–1996 I was a Visiting Research Fellow at the World Bank in Washington, D.C. Since I previously had focused on public policy problems in the United States and Western Europe, a year at the World Bank was a transformative experience. I learned a tremendous amount, not just by reading whatever was at hand, but also by using the Bank's e-mail system to track down lunch partners with complementary interests. For a scholar used to sitting alone before a computer, the year in Washington was a welcome and energizing change. It was fascinating to work on a topic – corruption – that the Bank had treated with indirection in the past. I began to collect euphemisms. People told me that when a review of a program mentioned "governance problems," "unexplained cost overruns," or "excessive purchase of vehicles," this meant that corruption and simple theft were a problem. A World Bank staffer pointed out that complaints about "excessive capital–labor ratios" in a report on Indonesia meant that corruption was not only rife but costly.

My current work on corruption began before I arrived at the World Bank and was completed after I left, but my understanding was deepened by talking to Bank staff who were living with the problem. Among the many supportive and helpful staffers, I particularly wish to thank Ladipo Adamolekun, William Easterly, Daniel Kaufmann, Petter Langseth, John Macgregor, Boris Pleskovic, Neil Roger, Sabine Schlemmer-Schulte, Frederick Stapenhurst, and Michael Stevens. At the International Monetary Fund I also had useful discussions with Nadeem Ul Haque, Paolo Mauro, Vito Tanzi, and Caroline Van Rijckegham. All of them were helpful sounding boards, but should not, of course, be implicated in any of my conclusions. Obviously, the World Bank itself bears no responsibility for my analysis and conclusions. I owe a special debt to Estelle James for suggesting that I apply to the Bank as a Visiting Research Fellow and to Michael Klein and his staff for providing me with a congenial institutional home at the Bank's unit on the Private Provision of Public Services located in the Private Sector Development Department.

Soon after I arrived in Washington, James Wolfensohn, the World Bank's new president, sought to put the corruption issue openly on the Bank's agenda. Because my economic perspective fit well with the Bank's own efforts to define its role in this area, I was pleased to contribute something to the internal debate – a debate that generated a 1997 paper, *Helping Countries Combat Corruption* (World Bank 1997a), stating the Bank's position.

After leaving the Bank, I continued to work with Bank staff on the corruption section of the *World Development Report 1997, The State in a Changing World* (World Bank 1997c), and I wrote a paper entitled "Corruption and Development" for the Annual World Bank Conference on Development Economics in May 1997 (Rose-Ackerman 1998b). Both Brian Levy and Sanjay Pradhan of the World Development Report team were helpful critics and colleagues. In the spring of 1997 I presented the Philip A. Hart Memorial Lecture at Georgetown Law School on the topic of "The Role of the World Bank in Controlling Corruption" (Rose-Ackerman 1997c). I also wrote a background paper for the Management Development and Governance Division of the Bureau for Policy and Programme Support of the United Nations Development Programme (UNDP). The UNDP issued this report as a discussion paper, entitled "Corruption and Good Governance" (United Nations Development Programme 1997a), and the UNDP has used this paper to develop its own thinking on the topic. Finally, in 1998 I prepared a paper for the

World Bank's Operations Evaluation Department (OED) to help guide its review of the Bank's anticorruption efforts. Anwar Shah and his staff at the OED provided me with helpful background information and suggestions.

In 1994 I joined the board of the United States chapter of Transparency International (TI), an international nonprofit organization devoted to fighting corruption worldwide. This association has given me a valuable opportunity to be on the inside of a growing international movement and to keep up to date on worldwide developments. TI–USA's executive director Nancy Boswell has been a strong moral supporter of my research efforts, as has Fritz Heimann, the chair of TI–USA's board. The international organization – based in Berlin, but with chapters worldwide – has become a global force and a clearinghouse for information on corruption. This is due to the tireless efforts of TI's chairman, Peter Eigen, and TI's first managing director, Jeremy Pope. Their success in raising the issue of corruption to international consciousness has corresponded to my own scholarly and policy concerns. I thank TI for its interest in my own work, but obviously do not implicate them in any of my specific proposals.

Several collaborative papers have contributed to the arguments I develop here. Within the World Bank Group, I collaborated with Jacqueline Coolidge of the Foreign Investment Advisory Service on a paper on corruption in Africa and with Andrew Stone of the Private Sector Development Department on a paper that analyzed World Bank surveys in the Ukraine and Pakistan. At Yale University, I collaborated with Silvia Colazingari, an advanced graduate student in political science, on a paper on the Italian case. I thank all three coauthors for bringing their own knowledge and insights to bear on topics that I could never have tackled on my own.

Two Yale political science graduate students, Jonathan Rodden and Sarah Dix, provided indefatigable research assistance on all manner of diverse topics. I an extremely grateful for their help, patience, and good humor. I thank my assistant, Barbara Mianzo, for excellent assistance at all stages of this project, and Gene Coakley and the Yale Law Library staff for tracking down sources and checking references. I am also grateful to my husband, Bruce Ackerman, who gave the manuscript a careful and critical reading as it neared completion.

Over the last several years, as my thinking developed, I have presented my work in a variety of places. I gave seminars at a number of universities and colleges, including the universities of Iowa, Michigan, Ottawa, and Pennsylvania; the Kennedy School at Harvard University; New York University; Northeastern University; Swarthmore College;

Trinity College; Yale University; and the Jerome Levy Institute at Bard College. Several workshops at the World Bank and the International Monetary Fund were especially helpful. The Comparative Law and Economics Forum, of which I am a member, was a congenial place to present several early draft papers. I also presented papers at the American Economics Association Annual Meeting in San Francisco; a workshop in Dakar, Senegal, sponsored by the U.S. Agency for International Development; the Annual Meeting of the American Society for International Law in Washington, D.C.; a conference organized by the Institute for International Economics; several seminars and workshops in Santiago, Chile, and Buenos Aires, Argentina, during a visit sponsored by the United States Information Agency; a meeting in Paris sponsored by the Organization for Economic Cooperation and Development and the UNDP; a conference on institutional reform held at the Autonomous Technical Institute in Mexico City; the Latin American Law and Economics Association Meeting in Buenos Aires; and a conference at the Yale Center for International and Area Studies sponsored by the UNDP.

My research on this book was made possible by research stipends provided by Yale Law School and by the Visiting Research Fellows program of the World Bank. I am grateful to both institutions for their support without implying any responsibility for the results.

1

Introduction: The Costs of Corruption

Poverty, poor health, low life expectancy, and an unequal distribution of income and wealth are endemic throughout the world. Many countries have very low or negative growth rates. Even some countries that are well endowed with natural resources have poor growth records and low per capita incomes. Others, especially in the former Soviet bloc, have weak economic records in spite of a well-educated labor force.

Yet a paradox exists. International lending organizations, such as the World Bank, often have difficulty locating acceptable projects. How can this be so when the need is obviously so great? One root of the problem is dysfunctional public and private institutions. Poorly functioning governments mean that outside assistance will not be used effectively. Low-income countries and those with weak growth records are often in difficulty because they are unable to use their human and material resources effectively.[1] They need institutional reform, but such reform is difficult. Constructing dams, highways, and port facilities is technically straightforward. Reforming government and nurturing a strong private sector are more subtle and difficult tasks that cannot be reduced to an engineering blueprint.

The tension between the capacities of developing countries and the requirements of international aid and lending organizations arises from

---

[1] Phillip Keefer and Stephen Knack (1995) examine the impact of government institutions on investment and growth for 97 countries over the period 1974 to 1989. Their measure of government quality combines indices of corruption, expropriation risk, rule of law, risk of contract repudiation by the government, and the quality of the bureaucracy. The authors show that measures of the quality of government institutions do at least as well as in explaining investment and growth as measures of political freedoms, civil liberties, and the frequency of political violence.

1

sources as multitudinous as the histories and cultures of the countries involved. To critics, the international organizations do not appreciate local customs and institutions and fail to adapt their programs to fit individual country's special circumstances. Although this is undoubtedly true in some cases, that is not all there is to it. Some countries' institutions are poorly adapted to their own stated development goals.

Other critics question the goals of the international community, arguing that economic growth is a narrow and incomplete measure of well-being. But even accepting that criticism, wide differences remain across and within countries in health, education, economic opportunity, and environmental quality. Whatever seems universally valuable – be it higher per capita income, longer life expectancy, or reduced infant mortality – varies widely around the world and is rising and falling at different rates.

Obviously, subtle differences in culture and basic values exist across the world. But there is one human motivator that is both universal and central to explaining the divergent experiences of different countries. That motivator is self-interest, including an interest in the well-being of one's family and peer group. Critics call it greed. Economists call it utility maximization. Whatever the label, societies differ in the way they channel self-interest. Endemic corruption suggests a pervasive failure to tap self-interest for productive purposes.

We can go a good way toward understanding development failures by understanding how self-interest is managed or mismanaged. The best case is provided by the archetypal competitive market where self-interest is transmuted into productive activities that lead to efficient resource use. The worst case is war – a destructive struggle over wealth that ends up destroying the resource base that motivated the fight in the first place. In between are situations where people use resources both for productive purposes and to gain an advantage in dividing up the benefits of economic activity – called "rent seeking" by economists (Bhagwati 1974; Krueger 1974).

I explore the interaction between productive economic activity and unproductive rent seeking by focusing on the universal phenomenon of corruption in the public sector. In recent studies, high levels of corruption are associated with lower levels of investment and growth. Corruption reduces the effectiveness of industrial policies and encourages business to operate in the unofficial sector in violation of tax and regulatory laws.[2] Foreign direct investment (FDI) is discouraged by

---

[2] Paolo Mauro (1995, 1998) demonstrates that high levels of corruption are associated with lower levels of investment as a share of Gross Domestic Product

high corruption levels. Asian economies are not an exception – those with high corruption levels would have attracted more FDI if corruption had been lower, and their industrial policies would have been more effective.[3]

Even when corruption and economic growth coexist, payoffs introduce costs and distortions. Corrupt high-level officials support too much unproductive public investment and under-maintain past investments. Corruption reduces total investment and limits FDI, but it encourages excessive public infrastructure investment (Tanzi and Davoodi 1997). In a corrupt regime, economic actors with few scruples, such as those engaged in illegal businesses, have a comparative advantage. A country is poorer overall if corruption levels are high. It may be caught in a corruption trap where corruption breeds more corruption and discourages legitimate business investment.

Cross-country empirical work has confirmed the negative impact of corruption on growth and productivity, but it is of little use in designing anticorruption strategies. The research shows that corruption is harmful but does not identify the precise mechanisms by which corruption affects

(GDP). The corruption indices are highly correlated with other measures of bureaucratic efficiency, such as the level of red tape and the quality of the judiciary. As a consequence, Mauro was unable to measure the marginal effect of any one of these measures. Putting the separate indices together in a measure of bureaucratic efficiency (that ranges from one to ten), "if Bangladesh [with a score of 4.7] were to improve the integrity and efficiency of its bureaucracy to the level of that of Uruguay [score 6.8] . . . its investment rate would rise by almost five percentage points and its yearly GDP growth rate would rise by over half a percentage point" (Mauro 1995: 705). Mauro also demonstrates that highly corrupt countries tend to underinvest in human capital by spending less on education (Mauro 1998). He argues that this occurs because education provides less lucrative corruption opportunities than other types of more capital-intensive public spending.

Alberto Ades and Rafael di Tella (1997a) argue that an aggressive industrial policy may be partly motivated by the corrupt gains the policy makes available. In such cases, the direct positive effect of the policy can be undermined by its role in increasing corruption and, hence, discouraging investment. Their empirical results demonstrate that in the presence of corruption, the positive impact of industrial policy is halved. East Asian economies are not immune from this effect. Simon Johnson, Daniel Kaufmann, and Pablo Zoido-Lobatón (1998: 389–391) find that higher levels of corruption are associated with a larger unofficial economy.

[3] Shang-Jin Wei (1997) shows that corruption acts like a tax on FDI. An increase in the corruption level from relatively clean Singapore to relatively corrupt Mexico is the equivalent of an increase in the tax rate of over 20 percentage points. The statistical result holds for East Asian countries as well as for the others in his sample.

economic performance. In fact, it is not even clear what it means for a country to rank highly on a corruption index. Does it mean that bribes are a large share of the value of contracts and government services? Does it mean that the proportion of deals influenced by bribery is high? Does it mean that bribery has an especially distortionary impact on economic and political life? The surveys give no information that would help one understand their underlying meaning, and in fact, such information does not appear to exist. Further complicating matters, the correlation between corruption and poor economic performance is not absolute. High levels of corruption are more destructive under some conditions than others (Wedeman 1997: 459).

The level of bribes is not the critical variable. One wants to know not just how much was paid, but also what was purchased with the payoff. For that, one needs detailed country-by-country and sector-by-sector analyses. This book is an attempt to set the agenda for such efforts and to draw lessons from the work that already exists. Only if one looks at the fine structure of political and economic systems can one go beyond a showing that corruption is harmful to an understanding of the way it operates in different contexts.[4] Given that knowledge, reform programs can attack corruption where it has the worst effects. I draw on existing work in individual countries to illustrate my arguments concerning the causes and consequences of corruption and to recommend reforms. However, the existing collection of cases is not sufficient. We need more systematic knowledge of just how corruption and self-dealing affect the operation of government programs and private markets.

I analyze the problem of corruption along four dimensions. The first takes the background organization of state and society as given and asks how corrupt incentives arise within public programs. I show that corruption can create inefficiencies and inequities and is, at best, inferior to legally established payment schemes. Reforms can reduce the incentives for bribery and increase the risks of corruption. The goal is not the elimination of corruption but an improvement in the overall efficiency, fairness, and legitimacy of the state. The total elimination of corruption will never be worthwhile, but steps can be taken to limit its reach and reduce the harms it causes.

---

[4] As an example of the kind of detailed understanding needed for concrete proposals in particular cases, consider Judith Tendler's 1979 report to the World Bank on graft in rural works programs in Bangladesh. The paper is an admirable analysis of the impact of graft on different aspects of a development project and a discussion of the conditions under which local people can be used as monitors of others' honesty.

The second recognizes that corruption has different meanings in different societies. One person's bribe is another person's gift. A political leader or public official who aids friends, family members, and supporters may seem praiseworthy in some societies and corrupt in others. My aim is not to set a universal standard for where to draw the legal line between praiseworthy gifts and illegal and unethical bribes. It will be enough to isolate the factors that should go into the choice. Culture and history are explanations, not excuses. As an economist, I cannot provide an in-depth analysis of the role of culture and history, but I can point out when the legacy of the past no longer fits modern conditions.

The third approach considers how the basic structure of the public and private sectors produces or suppresses corruption. I consider the relationship between corrupt incentives and democratic forms and discuss the relative bargaining power of public and private organizations and individual actors. Reform at this level may well require changes in both constitutional structures and the underlying relationship between the market and the state.

The final section of the book considers the difficult issue of achieving reform. First, I discuss the role of the international community, both aid and lending organizations, and multinational economic and political bodies. For some countries, especially those at low levels of development, the role of multinational businesses is critical. If these firms collaborate in maintaining corrupt regimes, they undermine development goals. I assess recent efforts to enlist business in helping limit corruption in developing countries and in those making a transition from socialism.

Second, proposals for reform lead to the problem of domestic political will. Good ideas are useless unless someone is willing to implement them. The book concludes with lessons drawn from successful and sustainable policies carried out in the past. Although no two countries face the same set of background conditions, modern-day reformers can learn something from the historical record.

This book does not present a blueprint for reform; it does not end with a compilation of "best practices." Instead, it suggests a range of alternatives that reformers must tailor to the conditions in individual countries. There is one fundamental lesson, however. Reform should not be limited to the creation of "integrity systems." Instead, fundamental changes in the way government does business ought to be at the heart of the reform agenda. The primary goal should be to reduce the underlying incentives to pay and receive bribes, not to tighten systems of ex post control.

Enforcement and monitoring are needed, but they will have little long-term impact if the basic conditions that encourage payoffs are not reduced. If these incentives remain, the elimination of one set of "bad apples" will soon lead to the creation of a new group of corrupt officials and private bribe payers.

PART I

Corruption as an Economic Problem

2

The Economic Impact of Corruption

All states, whether benevolent or repressive, control the distribution of valuable benefits and the imposition of onerous costs. The distribution of these benefits and costs is generally under the control of public officials who possess discretionary power. Private individuals and firms who want favorable treatment may be willing to pay to obtain it. Payments are corrupt if they are illegally made to public agents with the goal of obtaining a benefit or avoiding a cost. Corruption is a symptom that something has gone wrong in the management of the state. Institutions designed to govern the interrelationships between the citizen and the state are used instead for personal enrichment and the provision of benefits to the corrupt. The price mechanism, so often a source of economic efficiency and a contributor to growth, can, in the form of bribery, undermine the legitimacy and effectiveness of government.

This chapter isolates the most important situations where widespread corruption can determine who obtains the benefits and bears the costs of government action.

- The government may be charged with allocating a scarce benefit to individuals and firms using legal criteria other than willingness to pay. *Bribes clear the market.*
- Officials in the public sector may have little incentive to do their jobs well, given official pay scales and the level of internal monitoring. They may impose delays and other roadblocks. *Bribes act as incentive bonuses.*
- Those engaged in legal pursuits seek to reduce the costs imposed on them by government in the form of taxes, customs duties, regulations. *Bribes lower costs.*
- Illegal businesses frequently purchase corrupt benefits from the

9

state. In extreme cases illegal businesses and organized crime bosses dominate the police and other parts of the state through corruption and intimidation. *Bribes permit criminal activity.*

These categories are not mutually exclusive. A bribe that acts as an incentive payment, for example, might also allocate a scarce benefit or provide a tax exemption. Nevertheless, each raises enough distinctive issues so that it is worth considering each one separately.

Payments that Equate Supply and Demand

Governments frequently provide goods and services for free or sell them at below market prices. Often dual prices exist – a low state price and a higher free market price. Firms will then pay off officials for access to below-market state supplies. In China, for example, some producer goods were sold at both state-subsidized prices and on the free market. Although the price differences have shrunk in recent years, they were once very large. Chinese researchers reported that in 1989 the market price of coal was 674 percent of the subsidized price. The market prices of seven other producer goods were from 250 percent to 478 percent of the prices fixed by the state. Not surprisingly, payoffs to obtain supplies at state prices were reportedly very common.[1] In Nigeria when oil prices were set artificially low relative to the market price in neighboring Benin, smuggling facilitated by corruption was apparently widespread. The price difference provided benefits both to the smugglers and to the officials who were paid to overlook the illegal trade.[2]

If the supply of credit and the rate of interest are controlled by the state, bribes may be paid for access. Interviews with business people in Eastern Europe and Russia indicate that payoffs are frequently needed to obtain credit (De Melo, Ofer, and Sandler 1995; Webster 1993; Webster and Charap 1993). In Lebanon a similar survey revealed that loans were not available without the payment of bribes (Yabrak and Webster 1995). Personal influence and corruption lead banks into high-risk lending – sometimes to "borrowers" with no intention of repaying the funds. In Kenya, for example, one well-placed observer estimated that a third of banking assets were close to worthless in 1992 as a result of political

---

[1] Data from the Price Reform Group of the Finance and Trade Institute of China's Academy of Social Science, printed in *Zhongguo Wujia (China Price)*, Beijing, October 1990. For an example, see "China's Paragon of Corruption," *New York Times*, March 6, 1998. On corruption in China, see Gong (1993), Hao and Johnston (1995), and Johnston and Hao (1995).

[2] "Camel Through the Needle's Eye," *Newswatch*, February 3, 1991. Excerpts reprinted in World Bank (1993b, Annex 26).

interference in the financial system (Bigsten and Moene 1996: 191). A similar situation existed at the National Bank of Fiji where political influence was apparently widespread (Findlay 1997: 54). In Korea bank loans continued to be made to well-connected companies after they experienced serious financial difficulties. The companies had made substantial payoffs to powerful politicians, and these same officials pressured the banks to continue making loans. The bankers themselves were also bribed.[3] In Pakistan well-informed researchers calculated that it would cost the government 10 to 15 percent of 1996–1997 gross domestic product to deal with a banking crisis based on nonperforming loans provided to friends of the regime (Burki 1997: 9).

Exchange rates often do not reflect underlying economic fundamentals, thus producing incentives to pay bribes to get scarce foreign exchange at favorable rates. For example, Paraguay's multiple exchange rate system led to corruption before it was reformed (World Bank 1994b). South Africa's twin currency system was a source of payoffs. The financial rand was abolished in March 1995, a policy change that removed one set of corrupt incentives.[4]

The allocation of scarce import and export licenses is a frequent source of payoffs and patronage with bribes linked to the value of the benefits conferred. In the Philippines in the early 1950s both methods operated. Those with political connections could easily obtain licenses so long as they paid a 10 percent commission (Hutchcroft 1998: 73). In Nigeria, the regime in power in the early 1980s resisted free trade reforms favored by the International Monetary Fund (IMF) apparently because the existing system of import licensing was a major source of payoffs and patronage (Herbst and Olukoshi 1994: 465). By the late 1980s the import licensing system had become so discredited that it was abolished. Apparently the Manufacturers Association of Nigeria, whose members had paid bribes without complaint in earlier years, began to see that they would be better off without the system. Furthermore, at the same time that the import licensing system ended, the state introduced other new rent-seeking opportunities (Faruqee 1994: 246; Herbst and Olukoshi 1994: 481–482).

The incentives to make payoffs are clear enough in these cases, but

---

[3] "Yet Another Shock to South Korea's System," *The Economist*, May 24, 1997; "Hanbo Group Founder Is Jailed for 15 Years," *Financial Times*, June 3, 1997.

[4] *Transparency International Newsletter*, June 1995; "South African Economy in Global Firing Line," *Financial Times*, March 13, 1995; and "Strong Debut for Unified Rand," *Financial Times*, March 14, 1995. According to the March 13 article, however, South Africans still face tough controls on taking funds abroad, a situation that could encourage illegal attempts to circumvent the controls.

what are their efficiency and distributive consequences? Do they simply equate supply and demand, functioning much like prices in a legal market? I consider three cases. First, the public benefit is scarce and fixed in supply. The officials charged with its allocation have no discretion to increase or decrease total supply. Second, the benefit is scarce, but officials themselves can influence the quality and quantity available. Third, the service is available to all who qualify, but officials have discretion to determine who meets the requirements.

Fixed Supply

In the first case, where the official must allocate a fixed number of licenses or benefits, the number of people qualified to obtain the service exceeds the supply. If the corrupt market operates efficiently, the service will be provided to the applicants with the highest willingness to pay. If there is no price discrimination, the "market clearing" bribe will be equivalent to the price in an efficient market. The state could have legally sold the service with the same result except for the distribution of the revenue. Bribes increase the incomes of civil servants. Legal payments go into the government's treasury. But even that difference may be illusory. If the labor market is competitive, the government can reduce the pay of civil servants to below private sector wages because of the payoffs available to public officials (Besley and McLaren 1993; Flatters and MacLeod 1995). In short, if competitive conditions exist both in the corrupt market and in the labor market, illegal payoffs are like market prices. The winners are those willing to pay the most in bribes; the losers are those willing to pay in other forms such as time spent in a queue or persistence in petitioning officials.

Consider, however, the ways in which inefficient or unfair results can arise even in this simple case. To begin, suppose allocation to those with the highest willingness to pay is acceptable. Then one must ask whether corrupt markets are likely to differ much from open competitive ones. In general, they will not work as efficiently as legal markets (Bardhan 1997; Cartier-Bresson 1995; Gambetta 1993; Rose-Ackerman 1978). The illegality of bribery induces participants to spend resources keeping the transaction secret. This, in turn, means that information about bribe prices will not be widely available. Prices may be relatively sticky because of the difficulty of communicating market information. Some potential participants may refuse to enter the market because of moral scruples and fear of punishment, and public officials may limit their dealing to insiders and trusted friends and relations to avoid disclosure (della Porta and Vannucci 1997a). For all these reasons, a corrupt system will be not only less competitive but also more uncertain than a legal market.

Furthermore, payoffs may undermine the goals of a program. In Great Britain in the eighteenth century many officials were legally remunerated by retaining a portion of the fees they collected. Reformers, urging a shift to fixed salaries, claimed that officials unfairly focused on the most "profitable" parts of their jobs (Chester 1981: 139). In particular, services designed to benefit the needy or the well-qualified will go instead to those with the highest willingness to pay. Thus the sale of import and export licenses or restaurant licenses could be efficient, but the allocation of subsidized credit, housing, or university admissions by price would undermine the programs' distributive goals even if those admitted are nominally "qualified" under the law.

Consider the allocation of subsidized housing. Corruption has occurred in public housing programs in the United States where the number of qualified households far outstrips the number of places in subsidized units. In one Connecticut town, officials operated two lists – one for the honest and another, faster moving queue for those who made payoffs (cited in Rose-Ackerman 1978: 96). In Washington, D.C., two city officials were convicted of accepting bribes to certify unqualified people for subsidized housing and to give applicants higher priority on the waiting list than they deserved [*United States v. Gatling*, 96 F. 3d 1511 (1996)]. Similar corruption has arisen in the allocation of public housing in Hong Kong and Singapore where demand also exceeds supply (Lee 1986: 98). In Hong Kong the amounts paid were a function of the value of the benefit disbursed (Alfiler 1986: 54).

The allocation of irrigation water or land is another case where allocation to the high bribers is inconsistent with the programs' distributive goals. In irrigation projects, payoffs from upstream farmers to public officials may mean that little or no water reaches the farmers at the bottom of the system. In some irrigation systems in India and Pakistan, downstream farmers obtain too little water even for subsistence farming, and some ditches run dry before the end of the system is reached (Murray-Rust and Vander Velde 1994; Vander Velde and Svendsen 1994; Wade 1982, 1984). When land reform is designed to benefit poor farmers, corrupt payments for the best plots will favor the more well-to-do and those with connections to the officials administering the program (Bunker and Cohen 1983: 109).

Variable Supply

Consider now the second and third cases where officials can influence the quantity and quality of services provided and the identity of beneficiaries. In these cases, corruption is almost certain to lead to inefficiency. A single individual may have authority to issue permits or subsidies, overlook violations of the law, or grant contracts (Findlay 1991; Klitgaard 1988; Rose-Ackerman 1978; Shleifer and Vishny 1993).

In the second case, where the quantity is scarce but variable, the official, like a private monopolist, may distribute less than the officially sanctioned level to increase the economic rents available for division. In contrast, if the government has set the supply below the monopoly level, the corrupt official will seek to provide an increased supply of the service. The official seeks to maximize his or her gains, not set the optimal level of services. The official's behavior depends not only on the total economic rents but also on the share that the official can extract in dealing with corrupt beneficiaries. If several officials have authority over the allocation of scarce benefits, the problems can multiply as each tries to extract a share of the gains.

Consider, for example, the market for commercial real estate in Russia. Local government councils hold ownership rights, but the head of the administration has a great deal of personal discretion in deciding how much real estate to supply to the private sector. Real estate allocation does not follow commercial principles. Existing occupants are favored, and rental rates are far below market prices. The low rents create "a huge economic rent which accrues to local officials" (Harding 1995: 10) and creates pervasive excessive demand. The ambiguity and inconsistency of federal requirements have left room for corrupt and self-seeking maneuvering by local agencies. The lack of a rule of law leads to rent seeking by officials. This process is exacerbated in Russian cities by the existence of overlapping authorities, each of which tries to extract benefits from its strategic situation. The result is an inefficient, unfair, and corrupt system.

In the third case, a public service – such as a passport, a driver's license, or an old age pension – is not scarce, but is available to all who "qualify." Unqualified people and firms frequently pay bribes to obtain such benefits. For example, in Thailand individuals paid to pass the entrance exam for the Police Cadet Academy and to obtain driver's licenses without taking any tests (Alfiler 1986: 37, 56). In Korea officials were accused of accepting bribes to fake the qualifying scores of nursing students, to issue a license to an unqualified bonesetter, and to conduct inspections of food corporations and polluting firms (ibid.: 38, 47). In the United States officials of the Immigration and Naturalization Service have been bribed to issue fraudulent working papers.[5] In Brazil massive fraud in the processing of workmen's compensation claims involved the

---

[5] "Immigration Department's Eyes Are Still on Newark Office," *New York Times*, August 18, 1996.

corruption of social security officials, politicians, prosecutors, and judges (Fleischer 1997: 309–310). Andrei Shleifer and Robert Vishny (1993: 601) call this case "corruption with theft" because their archetypal example is a firm that bribes to be excused from paying customs duties, but the range of examples also includes cases in which a qualifications process is undermined or a regulation violated. Clearly, the unqualified will often be those with the highest willingness to pay because they have no legal way to obtain the service.

Even those who are qualified may pay, however, if officials have sufficient monopoly power to create scarcity either by delaying approvals or withholding them unless paid bribes (Paul 1995). Attempts to create scarcity can successfully generate bribes if applicants have no alternative source of the service and no effective means of appeal. Another strategy is to maintain vague and uncertain qualification standards. Then officials can withhold services from anyone who does not make a payoff, but it will be difficult for anyone to prove that they have been unfairly treated.

The greater the discretion of officials and the fewer the options open to private firms and individuals, the higher the costs of a system that condones corruption even if all who obtain the service are, in fact, qualified. The costs are the time and trouble suffered by potential beneficiaries as a result of officials' efforts to extract bribes (Bardhan 1997; Klitgaard 1988).

Bribes as Incentive Payments for Bureaucrats

Since time is money, firms and individuals will pay to avoid delay. In many countries a telephone, a passport, or a driver's license cannot be obtained expeditiously without a payoff. Sometimes the service is available only to the corrupt, but not to the patient but honest citizen.

An Indian newspaper published a list of the standard "fees" for a range of routine public services.[6] In St. Petersburg in 1992 the going rate for a telephone installation was $200 (Webster and Charap 1993). A study of the informal economy in the Ukraine lists the payoff levels for a range services needed by private businesses. Most firms reported paying fees in connection with importing and exporting. Phone lines almost invariably involved an "informal payment." Payments to tax, fire, and health inspectors were common, as were unofficial lease fees and payments for access to credit. The high cost of dealing with state officials through bribery induces many firms to operate in the informal sector

---

[6] "Bribe Index," *Sunday Times of India*, December 17, 1995. For example, a driver's license cost 1000 to 2000 rupees, and installation of an electric meter cost 25,000 to 30,000 rupees.

and many others to underreport sales, costs, and payroll to the authorities. The losses to the state are large, and, in addition, the level of payoffs discourages investment and the entry of new firms (Kaufmann 1997).

Similar corrupt incentives exist if the government does not pay its bills on time. In Argentina, for example, a scheme in which insurance companies bribed to get delayed claims paid by a state-run reinsurance company degenerated into a system of outright fraud against the state organized by corrupt state officials and intermediaries (Moreno Ocampo 1995).

In highly corrupt countries managers spend many hours dealing with state officials. In surveys of business people from a number of countries, Ukraine is an extreme case. In 1996 proprietors and senior managers spent an average of 30 percent of their time dealing with officials. Elsewhere the percentages range from 7 percent in El Salvador to 15 percent in Lithuania and Brazil (Kaufmann 1997).

Some scholars have constructed economic models where bribes have desirable incentive properties. For example, payoffs to the managers of queues can be efficient (Lui 1985). The payments give officials incentives both to favor those who value their time highly and to work quickly. The provision of telephone services in India illustrates the point. Officially, an egalitarian norm prevails, but businesses pay bribes to obtain preferential treatment in placing calls (Rashid 1981). Some argue that in developing countries the corruption of tax collectors can be efficient so long as the government can impose a binding overall revenue constraint (Flatters and MacLeod 1995). The minister sets a revenue target, a nominal tax liability schedule, and the wage rate of the tax collector. Corruption gives the tax collector an incentive to seek tax revenue, and the government tolerates bribery so long as the collector turns in an amount equal to the revenue target. The larger the difference between nominal tax liabilities and the revenue target, the higher the corruption.

The authors of some of these studies conclude that routine corruption may be tolerable. I disagree. First, toleration of corruption in an important agency, such as tax collection or the provision of public utilities, may encourage its spread to other areas with harmful consequences. Second, the authors assume that officials have only limited discretion. For example, the tax collector "discovers" the tax liabilities of citizens and firms. In reality, he or she might "create" tax liabilities as a bribe extraction device. If firms' and individuals' vulnerability to corrupt demands varies, the result is an arbitrary and unfair pattern of payments. The sum of taxes and bribes would vary across taxpayers in a way that reflects the collector's leverage, not the underlying tax rules. If taxpayers differ in their propensity and willingness to bribe and if the tax breaks given in return for payoffs are not publicized, the result can be a system based on special favors given to some, but not others. Similarly, officials may create corrupt opportunities that harm the government. For example, in India telephone operators moved from expediting calls to failing to bill customers (Rashid 1981: 456–458). In Italy, where long bureaucratic delays are the rule, officials often ask for bribes just to do their job. As a consequence, the rest of the public suffers even longer holdups (della Porta and Vannucci 1997a: 525–526).

Third, corruption can contribute to an uncertain business climate. Firms pay bribes to obtain certainty,[7] but the certainty may be illusory because they cannot enforce corrupt deals. In the short term, bribes may enhance efficiency in tax collection or the provision of services, but difficulties arise in the longer term. Payments made to increase certainty for individual firms result in a wide variance in conditions across firms. For example, although they present no direct evidence of corruption, Lant Pritchett and Geeta Sethi (1994), using data from Jamaica, Kenya, and Pakistan, show how higher tariff rates are associated not only with lower proportional collections, but also with greater variance in the rates actually paid. Surveys of business people in Pakistan and Ukraine indicate high interfirm variability in reported bribes (Rose-Ackerman and Stone 1998). Nominal tax liabilities are poor predictors of actual tax liabilities for the firm itself and for its competitors. Individualized attempts to reduce uncertainty can, at the level of society, increase uncertainty. As a consequence, potential entrants will view the economic environment as risky and unpredictable.

Ingrained corruption can also hold back state reform. Firms that have benefited from payoffs will resist efforts to increase the clarity of rules and laws. Their allies within the state apparatus will also oppose reform efforts designed to make the economy more open and competitive (Bigsten and Moene 1996). In short, although bribes can sometimes be characterized as incentive payments to public officials, a policy of active tolerance will undermine the prospects for long-term reform. It will also tend to delegitimate government in the eyes of its citizens. Payoffs that are widely viewed as acceptable should be legalized, but not all "incentive pay" schemes will improve bureaucratic efficiency. Some may simply give officials an incentive to create more delays and red tape and to favor the unscrupulous and the well-off.

---

[7] Legal and regulatory uncertainty is frequently mentioned by business people interviewed in surveys in developing countries. See, for example, Economisti Associati (1994), Webster (1993), Webster and Charap (1993).

Bribes to Reduce Costs

Governments impose regulations and levy taxes. Individuals and firms may pay for relief from these costs. I first consider corrupt incentives in regulatory programs followed by corruption in the collection of taxes and duties. I then consider the economic and political impact of this type of corruption.

Regulatory Programs

Under public regulatory programs, firms may pay to get a favorable interpretation of the rules or to lighten the regulatory load. Rules and regulations can be used by corrupt officials as a means of enriching themselves. Everywhere rules are bent in return for payoffs. The loci of payoffs are remarkably similar throughout the world considering the large differences in culture, economic conditions, and political organization. Payoffs occur in business licensing, in the inspection of construction sites and buildings, and in the regulation of environmental hazards and workplace safety. Whenever regulatory officials have discretion, an incentive for bribery exists.

For example, in Korea after a department store collapsed in 1995, it was revealed that the contractors used substandard concrete and that city officials had taken bribes to allow the violation of safety rules.[8] In Turkey, after earthquakes destroyed many buildings in late June 1998, construction deficiencies were revealed. Government-built schools and hospitals were especially hard-hit, leading many people to suspect that building inspectors and other government officials had been corrupted.[9] These allegations will sound familiar to anyone knowledgeable about the corruption of inspectors of construction projects in New York City or of housing authorities in Russia (Anechiarico and Jacobs 1996: 26–28; Harding 1995).

In Mexico payoffs have been common in regulatory agencies that issue permits and licenses (Morris 1991: 51). The same is true in Kenya where companies connected with the president enjoy a regulatory advantage.[10]

---

[8] Other Korean examples include an apartment house that collapsed, killing 28 people, and a bridge in Seoul that fell apart, killing 31. See "Owner, Son Jailed in Fatal South Korea Store Collapse; City Officials Also Found Guilty of Accepting Bribes," *The Baltimore Sun,* December 28, 1995; "Grease That Sticks," *Far Eastern Economic Review*, March 23, 1995.

[9] John Barham, "Political Aftershocks Rumble on after Turkish Earthquake," *Financial Times,* July 6, 1998.

[10] Bigsten and Moene (1996: 182); "American, Other Foreign Companies Selling Off Holdings: Kenya Corruption Overwhelms Investors," *Los Angeles Times,* June 25, 1989.

In Indonesia connections are important (Robison 1986), and less well-connected small businesses experience high bribery demands. One study claimed that small entrepreneurs make payments that range from 5 to 20 percent of annual gross income.[11] In Pakistan control over the implementation of environmental rules has been viewed as a source of rents (Burki 1997: 16–17).

Regulations that surround the exploitation of natural resources are particularly open to corruption since bending the rules will often produce high profits. Studies of the forestry industry, for example, indicate that corrupt payoffs have frequently been used to enhance the profitability of forestry concessions (Roodman 1996). Similarly, corrupt incentives are high for newly privatized state enterprises dealing with fledgling regulatory agencies without a track record. Squeezed by a competitive bidding process, a firm may try to increase its gains ex post by using bribes to secure a favorable business climate.

Taxes and Customs Duties
Paying taxes and customs duties is always burdensome. In addition, customs agents control something that firms value – access to the outside world. Thus businesses and individuals may collude with tax collectors and customs agents to lower the sums collected and to expedite services. As a result, revenue collection may be both inadequate and distributed unfairly. For example, in Pakistan one study estimated that if the leakages caused by corruption and mismanagement could be reduced by 50 percent, the tax to Gross Domestic Product (GDP) ratio would increase from 13.6 to over 15 percent (Burki 1997: 16). In New York City workers used their computer skills to reduce or eliminate tax liability for hundreds of property owners. The officials generally collected bribes equal to 10 percent of the tax liability eliminated, but sometimes their share was as high as 20 to 30 percent. Using a similar technique a city water-meter reader collected bribes in return for reducing water bills.[12]

The experience of a number of African countries illustrates the magnitude of the problem. In Gambia, in the early nineties, forgone revenue from customs duties and the income tax was 8 to 9 percent of GDP (six to seven times the country's spending on health). Income tax evasion alone was 70 percent of revenue due. Only 40 percent of small- and medium-sized enterprises paid taxes, and many individuals did not file

---

[11] Hetifah Sjifudian, "Graft and the Small Business," *Far Eastern Economic Review,* October 16, 1997.
[12] "29 Arrested in Tax Fraud Scheme Described as New York's Largest," *New York Times,* November 22, 1996; "20 Arrested in Scheme to Cut Water Bills," *New York Times,* October 22, 1998.

returns. Underpayment of customs was facilitated by the lack of clear guidelines and of published tariffs. The extensive discretion of officials encouraged corrupt payoffs designed to evade tariffs. Of course, a well-working system would have been able to reduce tax and tariff rates, but the distortionary effect of such a high level of evasion is clear (Dia 1996: 46–47, 94–100). A study of tariff exemptions in Zambia, Tanzania, and Mali estimated that exemptions, both justified and unjustified, produced a revenue shortfall of close to 50 percent (Low 1995). In Mozambique in 1995 the customs service collected 49 percent of the revenue it would have collected if no exemptions had been given. This total includes validly granted exemptions, but it excludes false declarations of value. Customs officials had discretion to grant exemptions without guidelines. Officials added extra delays, overestimated the value of goods, and applied higher rates in an attempt to extract payoffs (Stasavage 1996). In Zaire, much of the country's output was smuggled out with the complicity of customs officials. Corruption was also pervasive in evading import duties and controls. A study of cross-border trade reported how importers would undervalue their load by half and divide the resulting benefit with customs officials. The Anti Fraud Brigade was also paid off (MacGaffey 1991).

Taxpayers and corrupt officials divide the savings in taxes and duties. The costs are born by those taxpayers who are poorer and less well-connected and by the general public in the form of reduced services. In Africa, for example, studies of Gambia, Mozambique, and Ghana suggest that corruption permits the rich to avoid taxes (Dia 1996; Stasavage 1996). Tax avoidance in the Philippines reputedly means that the poor contribute twice as much as the rich, and 63 percent of imports pay no duty.[13]

New corrupt opportunities are one of the growing pains of economic and political transformation and can undermine otherwise promising reforms by reducing their legitimacy and fairness. A corrupt tax and customs system that favors some groups and individuals over others can destroy efforts to put a country on a sound fiscal basis and discredit reform. For example, in Mozambique interviews carried out in 1996 indicated that corruption had grown since the beginning of reform efforts in 1986. Overall taxes fell from 20 percent of GDP in 1993 to 17.6 percent in 1994 with import taxes falling from 5.1 percent to 3.9 percent of GDP (Stasavage 1996). Corruption is especially common when nominal tax rates are very high, as in the transitional states in Eastern Europe and the former Soviet Union (De Melo, Ofer, and Sandler 1995; Novitzkaya,

---

[13] *Far Eastern Economic Review,* April 20, 1996.

Novitzky, and Stone 1995; Webster and Charap 1993). High nominal tax rates lead to bribes and other types of tax avoidance which lead to even more avoidance, and so forth in a vicious spiral.

Economic Impact and Political Legitimacy

The economic impact of bribes paid to avoid regulations and lower taxes depends on the efficiency of the underlying programs that are subject to corrupt distortions. Suppose a state has many inefficient regulations and levies burdensome taxes on business. Then, given the existing inefficient legal framework, payoffs to avoid regulations and taxes may increase efficiency (Leff 1964). Bribes can overcome excessive regulation, reduce tax payments, and allocate scarce goods (Rashid 1981). Even if the corrupt "market" has some of the problems outlined above, the result may still be superior on efficiency grounds to compliance with the law. This defense of payoffs is commonly espoused by investors in developing countries and appears in discussions of investment in Eastern Europe and the former Soviet Union as well. It is a pragmatic justification that grows out of frustration with the existing legal order. This argument is important because it attempts to justify corruption to obtain benefits to which one is *not* legally entitled. Bribers are better off than they would be in an honest system in which they had to comply with the law.

But are individuals and firms obligated only to obey laws that they judge to be efficient and just? Clearly, in industrialized countries such conduct would not be tolerable. American and European firms do not generally try to bribe their way out of environmental and health and safety rules or enlist the help of criminals to evade the law. Instead, such firms work to change the laws, make legal campaign contributions, lobby public agencies, and bring lawsuits that challenge laws and regulations. One can complain about the importance of wealth and large corporations in the political life of developed countries, but at least well-documented lobbying activities and campaign contributions are preferable to secret bribes in maintaining democratic institutions.

Some of these same firms, however, feel less constraint about violating laws in developing and transitional economies. Because the United States outlaws bribes paid abroad to obtain business, American companies face domestic legal sanctions.[14] But the perceived importance of that constraint suggests that multinationals do not always feel an obligation to obey the law in the developing countries where they operate. Survey

---

[14] The act is the Foreign Corrupt Practices Act, 15 U.S.C. §§ 78m(b) & (d)(1) & (g)–(h), 78dd-1, 78dd-2, 78ff (a)(c) (1988 & Supp. IV 1992). For a review of the case law, see Pendergast (1995).

evidence indicates a wide range of viewpoints among American business people. In one study 30 percent of the American managers surveyed stated that it was never acceptable to pay a "consulting" fee of $350,000 to a foreign official in return for a contract worth $10 million in profits. At the other end of the scale, however, 6 percent found the payment always acceptable (Longenecker, McKinney, and Moore 1988). Of course, it is not just the managers of foreign firms who have such beliefs. Domestic companies often operate in the same fashion.

There are two difficulties with a policy of widespread tolerance. First, one cannot rely on investors to pay bribes only to avoid inefficient rules and taxes. They will, instead, want to reduce the impact of all state-imposed burdens, justified or not. Of course, one can construct models in which the laws on the books are all payoffs to politically powerful groups with no public legitimacy (Brennan and Buchanan 1980; Stigler 1971). Then avoiding the burdens imposed by such laws seems a worthy goal. Unless one is a strong libertarian who believes that all state action is illegitimate, however, such a criterion would be impossible to implement. Should firms or individuals be able to defend against a charge of corruption with a showing that the law was unjust or inefficient? Should they be able to justify the bribery of politicians by claiming that the law they favored will enhance competitiveness? This would put a policy analytic burden on the law enforcement system that it is ill-equipped to handle in practice and that it is illegitimate to impose on the courts in theory.

Second, it seems strange indeed to tolerate business firms' judgments that a well-placed payoff is justified because it increases their profits. Such an attitude can do serious harm in nations struggling to build a viable state. These states need to develop effective mechanisms that translate popular demands into law, that provide a credible commitment to the enforcement of these laws, and that provide legal recourse to those facing extortionary demands. If investors and ordinary citizens make individualized judgments about which laws are legitimate, the attempt to create state institutions will founder. Bribery will determine not only which laws are enforced but also what laws are enacted. All states, even those that have most successfully curbed the power of special interests, enact inefficient laws, but no state could operate effectively if individuals could take the law into their own hands and justify doing so by reference to cost–benefit criteria.

The discussion thus suggests that corruption may be more tolerable not when it increases the efficiency of individual deals, but when it is carried out in clearly illegitimate regimes that can make no claim to popular support. Then even bribes to avoid taxes seem less harmful than in other contexts because the fewer resources available to the state, the less powerful it is. Still, costs do remain. The beneficiaries of corrupt transactions will be a strong constituency against reform because they will fear the loss of their special advantages. Furthermore, when a reform regime does take power, its efforts will be made more difficult if corruption has become systemic. One of the regime's first tasks must be to change the behavior of corrupt officials, firms, and individuals. Tolerating individual efforts to circumvent even burdensome laws is not consistent with state legitimacy.

Organized Crime and Corruption

Illegal businesses seek to operate securely by paying off the police, politicians, and judges or by permitting them to share in the profits of the illegal businesses. But such businesses are also especially vulnerable to extortionary demands. Law enforcement authorities – from the police to prosecutors and judges – can demand payments to overlook criminal law violations or limit penalties. If the evidence of criminal behavior is clear, such businesses will be unable credibly to threaten to report corrupt demands.

Of course, illegal businesses are hardly innocent victims. They often actively try to corrupt the police. They seek not only immunity from prosecution for themselves but also assurance of monopoly power in the illegal market. In both the United States and Latin America, gamblers and drug dealers have paid officials to raid their competitors or to restrict entry.[15] In Thailand some local public authorities shelter criminal enterprises both from competition and from the law (Pasuk and Sungsidh 1994: 51–97). In Russia those engaged in illegal businesses sometimes engage in outright intimidation of potential rivals, often paying off the police not to intervene in their private attempts to dominate the market (Handelman 1995).

The danger for economic development arises when organized criminal groups begin to dominate otherwise legal business. Southern Italy and the countries in transition in Eastern Europe and the former Soviet Union are cases in point. Several Latin American and Asian countries face similar risks. Organized crime groups can use the profits of illegal enterprise not only to assure the complicity of public officials but also to infiltrate legal businesses. The profits generated by illegal businesses,

---

[15] Rose-Ackerman (1978: 163); "Bribes and Publicity Mark Fall of Mexican Drug Lord," *New York Times*, May 12, 1996; "Mexican Connection Grows as Cocaine Supplier to U.S." *New York Times*, July 30, 1996; "Popular Revulsion Is New Factor in Chronic Colombian Drug Scandal," *Washington Post*, January 28, 1996.

earned without paying taxes, can then be reinvested in legitimate business and in obtaining public contracts (Gambetta 1993; Varese 1994).

The stakes are especially high in Eastern Europe and the countries formed after the collapse of the Soviet Union. Nothing less than the entire wealth of the state is up for grabs. The value of sharing in the privatization of a socialist state dwarfs the benefits of sharing in the privatization of a public utility in Western Europe or a steel mill in a developing country. Both criminal groups and legitimate business concerns seek to share in the wealth. If criminals can create an atmosphere of uncertainty and the threat of violence, they will drive competitors away, especially Western firms, leaving the criminal groups with a free field (Shelley 1994). In fact, FDI from legitimate business has not been large in the countries of the former Soviet Union and varies widely across countries.[16] One explanation for these results is the weakness of state institutions and the corruption and organized crime influence this generates.

Even in developed countries some legitimate businesses are especially vulnerable to criminal infiltration. Organized crime is both wealthy and unscrupulous. It is willing to use not only bribery but also threats and violence to enforce its contracts and get its way. In the most successful examples the legitimate businesses which operate under Mafia protection earn sufficient monopoly rents to make them supporters of continued organized-crime influence. Diego Gambetta and Peter Reuter provide a list of the factors favoring the emergence of Mafia-controlled cartels (Gambetta and Reuter 1995: 128). In the most favorable cases product differentiation and barriers to entry are low; technology is unsophisticated and labor unskilled; demand is inelastic; and the industry consists of a large number of small firms. Private garbage collection provides a good example. Entry is inexpensive – one need only purchase a truck. However, because garbage trucks operate alone on the public streets, it is relatively easy to intimidate unwanted rivals by attacking their trucks without attracting police attention. To minimize the risks for organized crime, but at a cost, the Mafia can pay the police to look the other way (Reuter 1987).

Similarly, whenever a business needs to obtain a license to operate, the

---

[16] Alexander Pivovarsky (1997–1998) cites data from the World Investment Report showing that in 1996 three countries in Eastern Europe (the Czech Republic, Hungary, and Poland) accounted for 68 percent of inflows in the whole region of Central/Eastern Europe and the former Soviet Union and 73 percent of the region's accumulated capital stock from FDI. In 1996 FDI stock per capita ranged from $6 in Belarus, $25 in Ukraine, and $40 in Russia to $1471 in Hungary and $556 in Estonia.

ability to corrupt officials to gain approvals for yourself and deny them to your rivals yields an obvious competitive advantage. Labor unions, with or without organized crime connections, can use this tactic. For example, an official of the Roofers Union in Philadelphia was convicted of bribing an official of the Occupational Safety and Health Administration to harass nonunion roofing contractors [*United States v. Traitz*, 871 F.2d 368, 375 (1989)].

Legal businesses that benefit from prime urban locations are especially at risk in countries with weak or corrupted police forces. This includes restaurants and shops serving tourists and business travelers. Manufacturers can hide in out-of-the-way locations (Charap and Webster 1993), but service businesses cannot "go underground." If the police are unreliable, criminal groups may demand protection money where the funds are, in part, protecting the business from attacks by the group itself (De Melo, Ofer, and Sandler 1995; Webster 1993; Webster and Charap 1993).

Businesses, such as road repair and building construction, that do a heavy business with the state are also prime candidates for organized crime influence. If a government has been corrupted by organized crime in connection with its illegal businesses, it may be a relatively short step to make payoffs to obtain public contracts on favorable terms. In the extreme, organized crime groups manage cartels that share contracts and pay off public officials to buy their complicity or at least their silence. In southern Italy, for example, a survey reports that over half of the small- and medium-sized businesses reported that they withdrew from a public tender after pressure from criminal groups or their political allies.[17]

The wealth, unscrupulousness, and international connections of many organized criminal groups suggest the difficulty of control by any one country. The danger is that, rather than being a stage of development that will wither away over time, criminal activity becomes so intertwined with politics that it is difficult to tell them apart.

Conclusions

One defense of bribery focuses on the inefficiency and arbitrariness of many government rules and regulations. If administered by underpaid and unmotivated public officials, the incentives to pay bribes are high, and the benefits seem obvious – private firms and citizens can go about their business. Individual bribes sometimes not only benefit the payer and the recipient but also enhance overall efficiency or fairness. The existence of such cases, however, is not a valid argument for tolerating low-level official corruption.

---

[17] "Still Crooked," *The Economist*, February 5, 1994.

First, and most obvious, not all bribes have this result. Consider, for example, tax evasion, violation of environmental rules, certification of unqualified people for public benefits, and grants of immunity to organized crime. Second, if bribes do serve a valid resource allocation function, they should be legalized, and the fees made public. A market based on illegal payoffs is inefficient.

Third, the defense of bribery as a allocative tool is static. It assumes a given set of laws and public program requirements. Instead, corrupt officials, seeing the financial benefits of accepting bribes, frequently have the discretion to redesign their activities. They may create scarcity, delay, and red tape to encourage bribery. They may threaten the reluctant with arrest and criminal prosecution. In such cases individuals can justify payoffs as a way to avoid greater harms, but the systemic costs are serious. Furthermore, toleration of corruption in some areas of public life can facilitate a downward spiral in which the malfeasance of some encourages more and more people to engage in corruption over time.

Fourth, pervasive corruption undermines the legitimacy of government. Corruption in the provision of public goods and services and in the imposition of costs casts a cloud over governments seeking popular legitimacy. Bribery is not a stable, long-term substitute for law reform.

3

Corruption of High-Level Officials

"Grand corruption" occurs at the highest levels of government and involves major government projects and programs (Moody-Stewart 1997). Governments frequently transfer large financial benefits to private firms through procurement contracts and the award of concessions. Bribes transfer monopoly rents to private investors with a share to the corrupted officials. Privatization processes are vulnerable to corrupt insider deals.

Payments to Obtain Major Contracts and Concessions
Corrupt payments to win major contracts and concessions are generally the preserve of large businesses and high-level officials. The important cases represent a substantial expenditure of funds and have a major impact on the government budget and the country's growth prospects. These deals are by definition the preserve of top officials and frequently involve multinational corporations operating alone or jointly with local partners.

If the government is a buyer or a contractor, there are several reasons to pay off officials. First, a firm may pay to be included in the list of pre-qualified bidders and to restrict the length of the list. Second, it may pay for inside information.[1] Third, bribes may induce officials to structure the bidding specifications so that the corrupt firm is the only qualified supplier. Fourth, a firm may pay to be selected as the winning contractor.

---

[1] Many Italian corruption cases involve payoffs to obtain confidential information about minimum and maximum price thresholds, average-offer prices, and project evaluation criteria. Corruption in the divulgence of information is difficult to prove in court, but it is also difficult for a firm to be sure that it is the only buyer. "[T]he the value of 'confidential' information is inversely proportional to the number of people who possess it" (della Porta and Vannucci 1997b: 9).

Finally, once a firm wins the contract, it may pay to get inflated prices or to skimp on quality.

Corruption in contracting occurs in every country – even those at the high end of the honesty index such as the Scandinavian countries, Singapore, and New Zealand.[2] A few examples will suggest the range of possibilities.

In Paraguay corruption in the award of international construction contracts during the regime of President Alfredo Stroessner (1954–1989) typically ranged from 10 to 20 percent. Corruption helped inflate the cost of the Itaipú dam on the Brazilian border and led to the construction of projects that exceeded domestic needs (Nickson 1996: 244–245). In Indonesia in the 1970s two German companies reportedly paid bribes of 20 percent of the value of construction contracts for a steel mill to an official of the state-owned oil company (Schwarz 1994: 138).

In Zimbabwe collusion between senior ministers in Posts and Telecommunications and a Swedish telecommunications company may have circumvented local tender board procedures. Kickbacks were reported to be as high as $7.1 million.[3] In an airplane deal in South Korea several United States companies allegedly paid bribes to President Roh Tae Woo. Multinational suppliers were questioned, but denied involvement. In another arms deal Roh Tae Woo's national security advisor acknowledged receiving payments that may have been as high as $300,000.[4] A major scandal in Singapore involved several multinational firms and a senior official of the Public Utility Board. The official was paid to reveal confidential information about tenders. The case led to the blacklisting of five major multinationals implicated in the scandal. The official received a fourteen-year jail term.[5]

Grand corruption is not limited to developing nations dealing with multinational businesses. Similar procurement scandals are frequent in

---

[2] Transparency International prepares a cross-country index of corruption that is a compilation of others' rankings based on perceptions of the level of corruption. The Scandinavian countries are at the top of the list along with New Zealand, Canada, Singapore, and the Netherlands. The 1998 Transparency International Corruption Perception Index is available on its web page at: www.transparency.de/documents/cpi/index.html.

[3] Economist Intelligence Unit, *Zimbabwe Quarterly Report, 6/95.*

[4] In particular, the head of a Korean conglomerate was accused of giving $65,000 to the advisor. He admitted giving the money but said it was a gift. "Roh's Former Security Advisor Arrested on Graft Charges," *Agence France Presse,* December 13, 1995; "Seoul Shaken as Ex-Presidents Are Charged with Insurrection," *Jane's Defense Weekly,* January 10, 1996; "S. Korea's Daewoo Head Faces Bribe Charges," *Reuters North American Wire,* January 17, 1996.

[5] "Singapore Exposes Tip of Corruption Iceberg," *Financial Times,* February 15, 1996.

industrialized countries. In Germany bribes were apparently paid to win contracts worth DM 2.5 billion to build Terminal 2 at Frankfort Airport. According to the public prosecutor, corruption led to an increase in prices of about 20 to 30 percent.[6] In the French department of Seine-Maritime, fourteen people have been charged with corruption in connection with contracts for computers. Civil servants distorted normal procedures leading to a loss estimated at 50 million francs, according to the French Department of Interior.[7] In Belgium $1.9 million in bribes may have been paid to senior figures in the Socialist party in connection with a defense contract.[8] In Italy the cost of several major public construction projects reportedly fell dramatically after the anticorruption investigations of the early nineties. The construction cost of the Milan subway fell from $227 million per kilometer in 1991 to $97 million in 1995. The cost of a rail link fell from $54 million per kilometer to $26 million, and a new airport terminal is estimated to cost $1.3 billion instead of $3.2 billion (Wiehan 1997). Overall successful bids on public tenders were reported to be 40 to 50 percent lower in 1997 than five years before (della Porta and Vannucci 1997a: 524). The most recent large-scale scandal in the United States Defense Department was Operation Ill Wind, a sting operation of the Federal Bureau of Investigation that led to the conviction of fifty-four individuals and ten corporations for disclosing technical specifications on competing bids for contracts in return for money and jobs.[9]

Not all procurement and contracting scandals involve large-scale construction or capital goods projects. Goods that are used up in consumption are prime candidates for payoffs because it may be difficult ex post to discover whether or not they actually were delivered. In Malawi, for example, auditors found that millions of dollars of nonexistent stationary had been "purchased" by the Government Press Fund.[10] In Kenya, the government lost about $1.5 million through irregular drug procurement by the Ministry of Health.[11]

---

[6] "German Airport Corruption Probe Deepens: Five Jailed and 20 Companies Under Investigation," *Financial Times* July 2, 1996; "German Corruption Wave Prompts Action," *Reuter Business Report*, September 25, 1996.

[7] *Transparency International Newsletter,* June 1996, reporting on a story in *Le Monde*, March 19, 1996.

[8] "Tentacles of Defense Scandal Reach Out for Claes," *Financial Times,* October 19, 1995; "Belgians Seek to Arrest Dassault," *Financial Times,* May 10, 1996.

[9] Noelker, Shapiro, and Kellogg (1997).

[10] *Transparency International Newsletter*, December 1995, reporting on a story in *Saturday Nation*, October 14–20, 1995.

[11] *Transparency International Newsletter*, June 1996, reporting on a story in *Daily Nation,* May 3, 1996.

Is there anything distinctive about these cases other than the size of the deals? At one level, they appear analogous to cases in which government disburses a scarce benefit. As before, systemic corruption can introduce inefficiencies that reduce competitiveness. It may limit the number of bidders, favor those with inside connections over the most efficient candidates, limit the information available to participants, and introduce added transactions costs.[12] However, the scale of the corrupt deal and the involvement of high-level officials does introduce new concerns. First, if top officials, including the head of state, are concerned primarily with maximizing personal gain, they may favor an inefficient level, composition, and time path of investment. Second, investors' decisions may be affected by the fact that they are dealing with corrupt political leaders.

Officials

Consider the officials' decision calculus. The impact of high-level corruption goes beyond the mere scale of public investment and lost revenue for the public budget. Top officials may select projects and make purchases with little or no economic rationale. For example, if kickbacks are easier to obtain on capital investments and input purchases than on labor, rulers will favor capital-intensive projects irrespective of their economic justification. One empirical study demonstrates that high levels of corruption are associated with higher levels of public investment as a share of GDP (and lower levels of total investment and FDI). More corrupt countries spend relatively less on operations and maintenance and have lower quality infrastructure (Tanzi and Davoodi 1997). Corrupt rulers favor capital-intensive public projects over other types of public expenditures and favor public investment over private investment. They will frequently support "white elephant" projects with little value in promoting economic development.[13]

The demand for cement is one tipoff. In Nigeria in 1975 the military government ordered cement that totaled two-thirds of the estimated

---

[12] Da-Hsiang Donald Lien (1990a, 1990b) canvasses these difficulties and shows that a corrupt official who discriminates in favor of some bidders will frequently select an inefficient contractor. See also Susan Rose-Ackerman's (1978: 121–132) model of corruption in public contracting.

[13] A study of structural adjustment lending in seven African countries concluded that much investment spending was of dubious worth. "'White elephant' projects, inflated contracts, flight capital, and other associated ills became rampant before – and eventually contributed to – the [government fiscal] crisis in each case. A major aim of adjustment programs has been to weed out these undesirable investments (particularly in the public sector) and to improve overall efficiency" (Faruqee and Husain 1994: 6).

needs of all of Africa and which exceeded the productive capacity of Western Europe and the Soviet Union. The price exceeded the international market price by a wide margin, presumably to make room for kickbacks, and freight companies collected compensation for having to wait in the clogged Lagos harbor. The cost to Nigeria was $2 billion, or one-fourth of 1975 oil revenues (Lundahl 1997: 40). In Italy the annual per capita consumption of cement has been double that of the United States and triple that of Germany and Britain. A review of the Clean Hands corruption cases in Italy reveals that many construction projects were poorly conceived, overpriced, and had little or no justification beyond their ability to produce kickbacks (della Porta and Vannucci 1997a: 518–519, 523).

For large, capital-intensive projects the time path of net corrupt benefits may be quite different from the pattern of net social benefits. This will affect the choices of rulers. Suppose, as seems likely, that the benefits of bribery are relatively more concentrated in the present than those of the overall project. At least some of the bribes are paid up front before the project has begun. Then even if the rulers and the populace discount the future at the same rate, the rulers will support projects and policies that have an inefficient time path of net social benefits. For example, with major construction projects, a country's leaders will extract bribes in the present and may experience few of the future costs of shoddy workmanship or an excessive debt burden.

Furthermore, corrupt officials may well have a higher discount rate than the country's citizens. Even a ruler who has good short-term control over society may not have secure long-term tenure. The ruler's very venality may make him insecure and subject to overthrow. This insecurity induces him to steal more, making him even more insecure, and so forth. As a consequence, he or she will have a relatively high discount rate for government projects and will support projects with quick short-term payoffs and costs spread far into the future. Paradoxically, an active prodemocracy movement that destabilizes an incumbent autocrat can lead to an increase in corruption and inefficient rent-generating policies as the ruler reacts to his new insecure status. In short, corrupt rulers are likely to support an inefficient time path of social benefits and costs.

Corrupt gains can also be extracted from government concessions. Rulers may create fiscal crises not only by supporting too many capital projects but also by failing to obtain adequate returns from government concessions for natural resources such as hard rock minerals, petroleum, or timber. Returns that should enter the government budget are instead earned by corrupt officials and private contractors. For example, some countries allegedly have awarded timber concessions at prices far below market value. Guyana and Surinam in northern South America and Papua New Guinea and the Solomon Islands in the Pacific Ocean are all said to have signed very unfavorable contracts with international companies (Environmental Investigation Agency 1996: 5, 9).

Private Firms

Now consider the decision-making calculus of outside investors. The ruler's corruption introduces an additional element of uncertainty into the investment climate. Officials may find it difficult to make credible commitments to stay bought, and the state may be open to domination by criminal interests that can impose additional costs on legitimate business in the form of demands for protection money. Lacking credible commitment mechanisms, such as independent law enforcement institutions, corrupt autocrats may have difficulty convincing investors to make capital investments because they may fear expropriation or confiscatory tax and regulatory systems. Even if the ruler does not favor a distorted net benefit stream and does not discount the future differently from the nation's citizens, the very existence of such a person as head of state influences the calculations of investors. The only investors willing to commit funds may be those with a short-term, get-rich-quick attitude.

In short, the result is likely to be an inefficient time path of public benefits and costs. The ruler may favor projects with short-term benefits, and these may be the only type of project of interest to multinational investors. The exceptions are countries where an autocratic ruler has been able to make a credible commitment to stay bought, thus giving investors confidence. Such countries can experience high levels of investment and growth although the pattern of investments across sectors is likely to remain distorted. Indonesia under President Suharto is probably an example of this case where many investments, although inefficiently costly, did, at least, take place. In the later years of Suharto's regime, however, as the issue of succession arose, the rent-seeking behavior of Suharto's children and cronies increased, fueled by their worries about the future (Campos and Root 1996; Schwarz 1994: 133–161).

To illustrate the inefficient responses of private firms to high-level corruption consider a logging concession obtained corruptly by a company that out-bribes its competitors. Suppose, to begin, that the corruption "market" is efficient so that it operates just like an idealized competitive bidding process and that the corrupt ruler's rate of time preference is the same as society's. Suppose that as a result of corruption, the government obtains less than fair market value for the resources under its control.[14] If corruption does not restrict entry and if the official cannot affect the size of the concession, the high briber is the firm that values the benefit the most. It is the most efficient firm that would offer the highest price in a fair bidding procedure. Only the government budget suffers losses so that the state must either levy extra taxes or cut back public programs. Honest officials, however, receive distorted information about the value of the concession and may in the future support fewer of them.[15] In this simplified competitive case, the winner is indifferent to whether the concession is won through an honest or a dishonest auction. The bribes paid do not affect the time path of benefits and costs.

But this extreme case will seldom prevail. In practice, the bribe will be extracted partly from returns that would otherwise flow to government and partly from the profits of the winning firm. If a corrupt official has more leverage than an honest one, he or she will be able to extract a larger share of the profits. In addition, the corrupt official may often be able to structure the deal to maximize the profits available to share between officials and the bidding firm. In so doing, values may be sacrificed that an honestly negotiated contract would include. For example, in a timber contract, environmental damage or harm to indigenous people may be ignored (Environmental Investigation Agency 1996). In Indonesia, for example, inefficient and environmentally destructive practices are widespread.[16]

Now consider a firm that has obtained a secure long-term timber concession at a bargain price even if the bribe is added in. If it operates in

[14] Evidence that this frequently happens is presented in Environmental Investigation Agency (1996: 5, 8). A similar result could occur if suppliers form a cartel. For example, in Indonesia one source estimates that the government loses $500 million a year in royalty revenues on logging concessions because of the political power of the Indonesian Plywood Association (Schwarz 1994: 140).

[15] A similar situation can arise for government contracts. The most efficient firm will be selected under competitive bribery, but the benefits to the government are reduced. Part of the cost of the bribe is hidden in the value of the contract.

[16] A study of Indonesia concludes that "Indonesia's natural forests are approaching severe and permanent degradation on a very wide scale." One reason for this is that lumber plantations are being created by clearing existing forests instead of using already degraded land. Indirectly acknowledging the problem of corruption, the study concludes that Indonesia needs to establish "an independent forestry inspection service outside of the Ministry of Forestry with adequate resources and enforcement powers to police concession activities" (Hamilton 1997: 195).

the international market, its subsequent actions should depend upon the market for timber. The fact that it has underpaid for the concession should not affect its production decisions. It still seeks to maximize profits, and the concession payment is a sunk cost. The cost of corruption is felt by the public fisc, but no inefficiency has been introduced into the international timber market. Even if the total payment is above that expected in an honest system, there should be no impact.

The claim of no impact on firm behavior is, however, too simple to reflect reality. The operative terms are *secure* and *long-term*. The corrupt nature of the deal introduces uncertainties that can affect the way private firms do business. Difficulties may arise even if the most efficient firm wins. The corrupt nature of the deal may give the firm a short-run orientation.[17] There are two reasons for this. First, the concessionaire (or contractor) may fear that those in power are vulnerable to overthrow because of their corruption. A new regime may not honor the old one's commitments. Second, even if the current regime remains in power, the winner may fear the imposition of arbitrary rules and financial demands once investments are sunk. It may be concerned that the ruler will permit competitors to enter the market or worry that its contract will be voided for reasons of politics or greed.[18] Having paid a bribe in the past, the firm is vulnerable to extortionary demands in the future. For these reasons, the corrupt firm with a timber contract may cut down trees more quickly than it would in more honest countries. Like other investors in risky environments, it may also be reluctant to invest in immovable capital that would be difficult to take out of the country should conditions change. For example, one way to do this in the electric power area is to build a floating power station on a barge. Such stations have been put in place in several developing countries to make exit relatively

[17] For an example of the short-run orientation of corrupt timber concessionaires in Malaysia, see Vincent and Binkley (1992). A Malaysian company operating in Guyana was reported to be logging its concession twice as fast as planned (Environmental Investigation Agency 1996: 28). Robert Deacon (1994: 415) reports studies showing that security of tenure is negatively associated with deforestation rates. He points to case studies showing that if property rights are poorly enforced, deforestation is more rapid. Of course, corruption is only part of the reason why firms might have a short-run orientation. Deacon shows that deforestation rates are associated with political variables reflecting insecure ownership, but the explanatory power of his model is low.

[18] For example, in Malaysia firms involved in the privatization of both electricity and telecoms have complained that the government subsequently admitted numerous additional competitors with strong political links. See Kieran Cooke, "Malaysian Privatisation Loses Allure," *Financial Times*, October 13, 1995.

inexpensive.[19] In short, both the timing of production and the input mix may be chosen with a eye to the special risks introduced by the corrupt nature of the system.

Furthermore, corruption will seldom be limited to a one-time payment to top officials. Instead, the winner may be a firm more willing than others to engage in ongoing corrupt relationships up and down the hierarchy to protect its interests. For example, if the timber concession includes a royalty per log that is calibrated by the type of timber, the firm may pay inspectors to misgrade the logs. It may also pay to cut down more trees than the concession permits.[20] Under a construction contract, the high briber may anticipate bribing building inspectors to approve work that does not meet the nation's safety standards. In fact, the expectation of a long-term ongoing relationship may be part of the appeal of signing with a corrupt firm in the first place. Alternatively, the corrupt firm may itself hold back some promised bribes as a way to guarantee performance by the country's officials. Thus a firm might sign a contract to deliver cement to a road-building agency but pay bribes only as payments are received from the public authority. Frequently, such arrangements take the nominal form of consulting contracts with payments tied to the receipt of funds under the contract.

Privatization

Privatization can reduce corruption by removing certain assets from state control and converting discretionary official actions into private, market-driven choices. However, the process of transferring assets to private ownership is fraught with corrupt opportunities. Many corrupt incentives are comparable to those that arise in the award of contracts and concessions. Instead of bribing a state-owned firm to obtain contracts and favorable treatment, bidders for a public company can bribe officials in the privatization authority or at the top of government. Bribes may be solicited for inclusion on the list of prequalified bidders, and firms may pay to restrict the number of other bidders. However, other corrupt incentives are more specific to the privatization process. Three factors seem particularly important.

First, when large state enterprises are privatized, there may be no reliable way to value their assets, and the tax and regulatory regime that will

---

[19] See William M. Bulkeley, "Energy: More Power Plants Are Floating Off Developing Nations," *Wall Street Journal,* May 22, 1996.

[20] For numerous examples, see Environmental Investigation Agency (1996). In Indonesia environmentalists claim that the country's tree felling rules were routinely violated under President Suharto in part because of the influence of a close associate who headed the Plywood Association (Schwarz 1994: 140).

prevail ex post may be poorly specified. The uncertainties of the process create opportunities for favoring corrupt insiders by giving them information not available to the public, providing information early in return for payoffs, or giving corrupt firms special treatment in the bidding process. Even the assessment process can be corrupted by compliant insiders or by outside assessors with close ties to the multinationals seeking to bid on the assets.[21] In extreme cases no assessment is made, and no auction occurs. The firm is simply awarded to those with the best political connections: "Sales, at unstated prices, have sometimes been made to dubious purchasers, such as ruling party politicians and others lacking in business experience" (Nellis and Kikeri 1989: 668).

In Brazil when it became clear that an ally of President Fernando Collor de Mello was in line to receive a privatized firm, others withdrew their offers (Manzetti and Blake, 1996). Collor sought to use market reforms to create a financial empire of his own (Manzetti 1999). In Greece an Italian company was accused of bribing the Prime Minister for favorable treatment in the privatization of a Greek cement company (Savona and Mezanotte 1997: 107). Similar examples come from Argentina, Peru, Zaire, Ivory Coast, Thailand, and Slovakia, to name just a few (Manzetti 1999; Pasuk and Sungsidh 1994; Van de Walle 1989).

Weak conflict-of-interest laws make insider dealing easy. In Argentina several officials who designed the highway privatization bidding process were on the staff of companies that acquired the highways (Manzetti 1999). In Venezuela, an American consulting firm organized the privatization of the state airline in spite of its close ties to the Spanish airline Iberia (Manzetti and Blake 1996). Later, Iberia was involved in valuing the airline in spite of the fact that it also planned to bid on the company and did eventually end up purchasing the airline (Celarier 1996: 65). According to Russia's senior prosecutor, the privatization process in that country has been undermined by bid-rigging by banks that both arranged and won privatization auctions.[22]

Second, corrupt officials may present information to the public that makes the company look weak while revealing to favored insiders that it is actually doing well. The insiders then are the high bidders in what appears to be an open and above-board bidding process. Similarly, corrupt bidders may be assured of lenient regulatory oversight, something an outsider cannot rely upon. Ex post evaluations reveal that the

---

[21] See Antonia Sharpe, "CVRD Sale Shows Limits of World Bank Adviser Rules," *Financial Times*, December 18, 1995.

[22] "Russian Privatisations Face Crime Probe," *Financial Times*, February 6, 1996. See also Celarier (1996: 66).

privatization was a huge success with the newly private company earning high rates of return. Observers in both China and Ecuador have noted cases of this type. In Venezuela a major bank was undervalued by the minister of national investment amid payoff allegations (Manzetti and Blake 1996).

Third, a privatized firm is worth more if it retains whatever monopoly power was available to the public firm. To an economist the retention of monopoly rents undermines the justification for privatization. To an impecunious state and its bidders, assuring monopoly power is in the interest of both. Thus the conflict between revenue maximization and market competition arises for all privatization deals. If a state gives lip service to competitive principles, however, it may be unable to endorse monopolization openly. Corrupt back-channel deals can then accomplish that objective, but with some of the benefits transferred to individuals rather than the government. Luigi Manzetti argues that many Latin American privatizations increased, rather than decreased, market concentration (Manzetti 1999). He argues that the privatization of the telephone company in Argentina and the electrical utility in Chile were carried out in a way that generated monopoly rents for the winners. Subsequent regulatory oversight has been weak. Such deals are not inevitable. Apparently, the privatization of telecommunications in Chile and of electric power in Argentina did encourage competition and limit monopoly rents (Manzetti 1997).

Although they provide no direct evidence of corruption, John Nellis and Sunita Kikeri (1989: 668) list several examples of special benefits firms may obtain.

> In one African country ... the new private cigarette manu-
> facturer received heavy protection, with confiscatory taxes on
> competing production and a monopoly on imports. An 11 year
> monopoly on the sale of Coca Cola was obtained by a privatized
> distributing firm, and production limits on other soft drinks were
> imposed on competitors. High rates of protection have been
> granted to a leased (and thus partially privatized) steel mill in
> another country.

Even though corruption occurs during the privatization process, the end result can still be a competitive private firm subject to market discipline. But moving a firm into the private sector does not assure this outcome. First, the firm, especially if it retains some monopoly power, is likely to maintain a close relationship to the state. After all, outside the former socialist countries, most public enterprises are in industries with substantial economies of scale and in areas that are viewed as being closely associated with the national interest, such as public utilities or transportation (Yotopoulos 1989: 698). Bribery may simply be a substitute for the self-dealing that prevailed under state ownership.

Second, frequently the state sells off only a portion of the state firm, often retaining control, at least in the early years. Such hybrids may be especially subject to corrupt inside arrangements (Kaufmann and Siegelbaum 1997: 442). Private shareholders in a firm that is partially owned by the state may attempt to shift losses onto the state with the connivance of public officials. In Italy, for example, a joint public–private venture in the chemical industry seems to have involved just such a transfer. Bribes were apparently paid both to benefit the private firm when the venture was formed and to obtain a high price for the same assets when the venture broke down and the firm was renationalized (Colazingari and Rose-Ackerman 1998).

Corrupt incentives may mean that the most efficient bidder loses out to a corrupt insider. Even if the most efficient firm does win, corruption in the tendering process assures that the government receives too little from the sale. This implies higher taxes or lower public spending.

Conclusions

Corruption that involves top-level officials can produce serious distortions in the way government and society operate. The state pays too much for large-scale procurements and receives too little from privatizations and the award of concessions. Corrupt officials distort public sector choices to generate large rents for themselves and to produce inefficient and inequitable public policies. Government produces too many of the wrong kind of projects and overspends even on projects that are fundamentally sound. Corruption reduces the revenue-raising benefits of privatization and the award of concessions. Firms that retain monopoly power through bribery and favoritism undermine the efficiency benefits of turning over state firms to private owners.

4

Reducing Incentives and Increasing Costs

Corrupt incentives exist because state officials have the power to allocate scarce benefits and impose onerous costs. Because scarcity lies at the heart of corrupt deals, basic insights derived from microeconomics can help structure efforts to reduce corruption. This chapter and the next focus on incentive-based reforms that reduce the benefits or increase the costs of malfeasance. This chapter considers the following reform options:

- program elimination,
- privatization,
- reform of public programs,
- administrative reform,
- the deterrent effect of anticorruption laws, and
- procurement systems.

Program Elimination
The most straightforward way to limit corruption is to eliminate corruption-laden programs. If the state has no authority to restrict exports or license businesses, this eliminates a source of bribes. If a subsidy program is eliminated, the bribes that accompanied it will disappear as well. If price controls are lifted, market prices will express scarcity values. In general, reforms that increase the competitiveness of the economy will help reduce corrupt incentives (Ades and Di Tella 1995, 1997b: 514).

Some public programs work so poorly that they function principally as bribe-generating machines for officials. Structures that allow officials unfettered discretion are particularly likely sources of payoffs, especially if citizens and firms have no recourse. In such cases program elimination is sometimes better than more subtle reform strategies. For example, the

licenses and permissions needed to set up businesses and continue them
in operation may have no sound policy justification. Studies of Africa,
Latin America, and Eastern Europe suggest that this is the case in many
countries and that such programs are often very corrupt (Bigsten and
Moene 1996; Kaufmann 1997; Stone, Levy, and Paredes 1992). Eliminating some rules and streamlining and clarifying others seems a good policy
response.

Subsidy programs can also become permeated with corruption. If both
bribers and bribees are better off with a dishonest system, detection will
be difficult, and program elimination may be the only feasible option.
For example, an Argentine program to encourage the growth of underdeveloped regions through export subsidies was very ineffective because
of fraud and corruption. A given product could "be exported several
times through southern ports," and "close-to-fake" factories were set up
in favored regions that did little or no processing of products manu-
factured elsewhere. A World Bank-sponsored study concluded that the
program was ineffective with an estimated 25 percent of the subsidy lost
to fraud (Nogués 1989: 25–27). This seems to be an example of a program
that the government ought simply to eliminate.

One way to reduce corruption is to legalize formerly illegal activities.
Frequently, when a product is outlawed, production continues but with
illegal businesses paying off the police to stay in operation. Then policy-
makers need to ask if the benefits of illegality outweigh the costs. For
example, after a short experiment with Prohibition, the United States
repealed the Eighteenth Amendment to the Constitution outlawing the
manufacture and sale of "intoxicating liquors." Its time in force between
1919 and 1933 was a period of widespread illegal production and sale of
alcohol and pervasive corruption of law enforcement officers. The worldwide debate over legalizing drugs turns on the feasibility of controlling
the industry through the criminal law when law enforcement authorities
are vulnerable to corruption. Gambling, formerly outlawed in many
American jurisdictions, was also an important source of corrupt receipts
for the police. The response in many jurisdictions has been to turn gambling into a legal business – albeit under heavy state supervision and
even, at times, state ownership.

Sometimes removing one set of corrupt incentives may create new
opportunities elsewhere. Eliminating nine of the ten licenses needed to
open a business may just give the remaining official access to higher
bribes. Removing entry barriers for private firms may induce managers
to pay off the police to harass their competitors. Deregulating in one
area may increase corruption elsewhere. This will be especially true
if a profitable activity must go through a series of "checkpoints." For

example, a successful effort by the United States Agency for International Development to reduce corruption in the transport of agricultural products in one African country increased corruption in neighboring countries on the same transport route. The project reduced the number of bribe-extraction checkpoints established by police and customs officials along onion transport routes in Niger. Unfortunately, this led to an increase in payoffs and tax levels in Côte d'Ivoire as the onions neared their destination – the food markets of Abidjan (Rogers and Iddal 1996). Such examples highlight the importance of taking a systemic approach, which may mean tracing the impact across national boundaries.

Although eliminating corruption-prone programs can limit the incentives for payoffs, a general program to shrink the size of government will not necessarily reduce corruption (Rose-Ackerman 1996c). Recall that scarcity produces corrupt incentives, and notice that reductions in government spending can produce scarcity when spending programs are cut or when regulatory budgets fall with no change in the underlying statutes. Even worse, if a government under fiscal pressure cuts back spending, it may at the same time seek to maintain its influence by increasing regulations and mandates. The result can be increased corruption (Chhibber 1996: 127).

Program elimination removes the corrupt incentives that accompanied it, but budget cutbacks that leave the program intact may not. For example, suppose that subsidies for higher education had previously been available to all students who passed an entrance exam, but that they are now given only to the top 50 percent. The scarcity created by the cutbacks creates corrupt incentives where none existed before. So long as exam grading is free of taint, the corruption-reducing solution is to raise the passing grade so the shrunken program retains its entitlement character. Other ways of reducing demand – such as complex applications, long queues, cutoffs based on need – all generate corrupt incentives.

When government spending falls, the contractors who benefited in the past from public contracts may suffer – especially firms so specialized that they cannot change direction easily. Domestic military contractors are usually in this category. Multinationals are likely to be less affected both because of their diversified product mix and because they can sell in other countries. Firms that have trouble shifting direction may bribe to obtain a share of the shrinking pie of government business. The total quantity of bribes might fall, but the bribe per project can rise. Once the government is locked into dealing with a particular contractor, bribery can still be used to get inflated prices, to overcharge for materials, or to skimp on quality.

Similarly, suppose budget cutters halve the budget of a regulatory agency with no change in the underlying statute. First, consider a statute that permits firms to act unless the state finds a violation. In that case few business people will complain about budget cutbacks Inspections and other checks will be reduced – a benefit for firms. A firm's manager still has an incentive to bribe an inspector but will do so less often because inspectors come less often.

Second, suppose that a law requires firms to obtain a license. Then a budget cutback with no change in the underlying statute increases corrupt incentives. Firms and individuals will be encouraged to pay bribes to get the scarce attention of the regulatory authorities or to get to the head of a long queue. Bribes paid by some lead to more delays for others, a result that may induce more to pay bribes, and so on – producing a vicious cycle (Rose-Ackerman 1978: 85–108). Just as in the case of cutbacks in subsidy programs, shrinking government regulatory activity may increase, not decrease, corruption unless the statutes are changed to reflect the lower budget totals.

In short, the elimination of spending and regulatory programs can be a potent corruption-reducing strategy. However, policy makers must check to be sure that the payoffs do not just reappear elsewhere. Furthermore, an overall contraction in the size of the government budget may simply make government benefits scarcer. Corruption may then increase as potential beneficiaries compete for the increasingly scarce pool of benefits. Spending cuts accompanied by increases in regulations may simply shift the locus of corruption. It is not enough for a country to get its macroeconomic totals in line with IMF guidelines. Nations should be concerned with the underlying structure of public programs, not just the size of government.

Establishing a Credible Privatization Process

As the previous chapter made clear, privatization is both an anticorruption reform and a new potential source of corrupt gains. Although privatization is desirable in a wide range of cases, reformers ought to design the process to reduce the incentives for rent seeking that remain. The process should assure the widest level of participation rather than favoring consortia with strong ties to local elites and must be transparent and well publicized, especially in the evaluation of assets.[1] When an inside

---

[1] Kaufmann and Siegelbaum (1997), Manzetti (1999), Nellis and Kikeri (1989: 669). The costs to a country of lack of transparency are illustrated by the case of privatization in Brazil as described in a speech by a Chase Manhattan executive. He advises foreign investors to take on local partners because little public information is available. According to him, "Investors typically receive the bid package . . . 30 to 45 days and sometimes as little as 15 days before a company

deal appears inevitable, privatization is not likely to be worthwhile because a public firm is easier to monitor than a private one. However, sometimes even a transfer to an insider may be desirable if the new owner is insulated from some of the political pressures that interfere with efficient performance.

If privatized firms will retain monopoly power, new regulatory institutions must be created that are not themselves subject to improper influence. It is important to set up the regulatory framework in a credible way before tendering begins. Developing and transitional economies with newly private public utilities must set up strong apolitical regulatory agencies with transparent and open processes (Tenenbaum 1996). This will reduce both the uncertainty associated with tendering and the possibility that the winning bidder can manipulate the process by which regulatory institutions are created (Manzetti 1997; Nellis and Kikeri 1989: 670).

Regulatory models from developed countries may not be directly transferable to those with less bureaucratic capacity and more risk of corruption and capture by the regulated firms. New institutions must be designed with this crucial variable in mind. Discretion must be both limited and managed. New regulatory agencies need relatively clear, simple, and enforceable guidelines.

Case studies of telecommunications regulation in six diverse countries demonstrate the need for restraints on discretion, a stable legal environment, and credible enforcement institutions (Levy and Spiller 1996). The authors conclude that an independent judiciary is a necessary condition for effective regulation of privatized industries. Even if an independent judiciary exists, however, it will be ineffective unless the political process can establish binding legal constraints. If either of these conditions is missing, privatization may generate few benefits for the public. Only firms with corrupt inside relations to political leaders may be willing to bid when public firms are put on the auction block. The result will be low bids and excessively favorable treatment in the future.

Finally, if credible commitments are possible, the strength and quality of the bureaucracy determines whether a country ought to settle for simple regulatory rules. Jamaica, for example, has a respected independent judiciary, but its weak administrative capacity counsels the use of

is sold. The information is skimpy and not necessarily reliable. . . . Not much due diligence is allowed. Don't expect a company to open its books and allow your accountants to come in. Few representations and warranties are given. If surprises come up later, they are your problem." Quoted in Rosemary H. Werrett, "Brazil: Privatization Program Throws New Curves at Foreign Investors," *Development Business*, January 16, 1996.

simple rules (ibid.: 7–9). Some discretion will inevitably remain. Regulators must therefore be protected from improper influence through a transparent appointment process, limits on conflicts of interest, and security of tenure that insulates them from political pressure. Some recommend that a single agency should be given broad jurisdiction over several regulated industries – both to conserve on resources and expertise and to limit improper political interference. In a government with some degree of public accountability, a broad-based agency will benefit from a higher political profile so that the stakes of inappropriate political interference will be higher (Smith and Shin 1995: 7). The regulatory system could also be organized to give consumers a stake in an effective regulatory system. For example, telecommunications regulators in New Zealand and the United Kingdom are establishing systems to give consumers rebates if firms fail to meet clearly defined performance obligations (ibid.: 8). Such checks on bureaucracy are important because even simple regulatory tasks can be influenced by corruption.

The integrity of the privatization process is especially at issue in countries in transition in Eastern Europe and the former Soviet Union. In these states, large portions of the national patrimony have been privatized. To limit corruption both at the point of sale and in the present, greater care should have been taken to establish a transparent and reliable legal environment. This did not happen in most countries, with predictable results (Rose-Ackerman 1994; Shelley 1994). Although a recent study argues that privatization in Eastern Europe and the former Soviet Union has been, on balance, beneficial, the authors point to serious deficiencies in the legal system (Kaufmann and Siegelbaum 1997). They argue that voucher-based mass privatization and liquidation appear least susceptible to corruption, with management–employee buyouts and spontaneous privatization most conducive, because of their slow pace, high levels of discretion, and lack of transparency. Initial public offerings and tenders and trade sales are intermediate options whose slow speed is balanced against their transparency and independent administration. Countries in the midst of a large-scale privatization effort need to balance speed against the long-term value of clear legal rules and of a wealth-transfer process that is viewed as legitimate by the population.

Reform of Public Programs

Many regulatory and spending programs have strong justifications and ought to be reformed, not eliminated. Corruption in the collection of taxes cannot be solved by failing to collect revenue, and other programs are responses to market failures and citizen demands for public goods and social justice. One solution is to clarify and streamline the necessary laws to reduce official discretion and to make monitoring simpler and less arbitrary. Rules can be made clearer with publicly provided justifications. Government might favor simple nondiscretionary tax, spending, and regulatory laws.

Revenue Collection

Tax reform frequently involves simplifying taxes and levying them on bases that are difficult to hide or underestimate. Business taxes can be fixed independently of a firm's actual profitability. The reduction in corruption and tax evasion is traded off against the reduction in fairness. For example, Mexico introduced an alternative minimum tax of 2 percent on the real value of firm assets. A firm pays the maximum of the value of this tax and the corporate tax otherwise due. Small businesses pay a lump-sum tax per person employed, and medium-sized businesses are taxed on turnover. All these reforms raised additional revenue through reductions in tax evasion and in corruption. Some companies complained of unfair treatment, but the tax was upheld in the courts (Das-Gupta and Mookherjee 1998: 311–312). Such reforms are, however, unlikely to be sufficient if tax collectors have no incentive to work effectively and if the underpayment of tax is not punished. For example, tax simplification in the Philippines apparently provided few benefits because steps were not taken to improve the incentives facing tax collectors and taxpayers (ibid.: 410).

In the reform of the Mexican customs service, the number of steps in the customs process at the Mexico City airport was reduced from sixteen to three. The system was streamlined to reduce delays, and staff was significantly reduced. Officials who remained were paid higher salaries, and monitoring was made more credible and effective.[2] Although Mexico's past experience suggests the difficulty of sustaining initial gains (Morris 1991: 91), one government official claimed that these reforms have increased customs revenues significantly,[3] and businesses reported that waiting times and corruption and theft fell.

Successful reform of a country's system of revenue collection should permit a reduction in nominal rates of tariffs and taxation. This may permit an escape from the trap where high rates lead to evasion, and evasion leads to higher nominal rates and even more evasion. A study

---

[2] Dick (1992: 24–27); "Airport Customs Harnesses 3 Billion Mexican Pesos Per Year," *El Economista,* February 13, 1992.

[3] "Mexico Fine-Tuning Customs Area Ahead of NAFTA," *Reuters News Service,* February 24, 1993.

of India provides a classic case. Despite an increase in rates, total revenue declined because of both an increase in corruption and a shift into off-the-books activity. In such cases nothing short of a thoroughgoing reform of the structure and administration of the tax system will allow a break-through. Simply raising the wages of tax collectors and increasing surveillance are unlikely to be sufficient (Das-Gupta and Mookherjee 1998: 101–102).

Regulation and the Allocation of Government Services

Economists have long recommended regulatory reforms that limit the discretion of regulators. In environmental regulation, for example, they support market-based schemes such as effluent charges and tradeable permits. They also recommend user fees for scarce government services. These reforms often have the additional advantage of reducing corrupt incentives by replacing bribes with legal payments. The sale of water and grazing rights, tradeable pollution rights, and the sale of import and export licenses can improve the efficiency of government operations while limiting corruption. Queues can be managed through a set of differential fees based on the value of speed to the applicant (Lui 1985). The United States passport office, for example, provides expedited service for a fee.[4] Surveys of private individuals and firms in Pakistan and India indicate that, when corruption is widespread, domestic businesses and quite poor people would be willing to make legal payments for improved service (Paul 1995; Rose-Ackerman and Stone 1998). In all such schemes, the services go to those who value them the most, and payments are legal prices, not bribes.

Incentive schemes, if properly designed, represent not deregulation, but regulatory redesign that can permit the more cost-effective achievement of statutory goals. The use of more decentralized incentive mechanisms for regulation differs both from simple agency inaction and from a slavish devotion to business interests. In areas such as pollution of the air and water, market tests and efficiency imply regulation, not deregulation. The use of financial incentives may mean that higher levels of cleanup are possible than with command and control regulation. Such schemes could produce genuine reform, not a sellout to regulated firms. As a consequence, they may be opposed by the very firms that praise the virtues of the market in other contexts. Efficient regulation implies a concern for both costs and benefits; it does not imply less regulation (Ackerman and Stewart 1988; Lave 1981; Schultze 1977).

---

[4] See http://www.travel.state.gov/passport_expedite.html.

In corrupt systems, market-based reforms may substitute legal payments for bribes. Unfortunately, the regulated firms may object to reforms that in less corrupt countries would be viewed as cost-reducing. Thus in Mexico businesses have not generally endorsed proposals to substitute incentive-based schemes for command and control regulation of environmental pollution. According to one commentator, "widespread alleged corruption among environmental inspectors means, says one businessman, that 'usually it is cheaper to pay off the official than to make the improvements.'"[5] Furthermore, corruption may undermine reforms just as it can undermine more conventional command and control efforts. Firms may still bribe officials to misrepresent monitoring reports. Clearly, civil servants still need to be properly motivated and monitored. However, incentive systems simplify the job of those bureaucrats who interact with regulated firms. For example, in the environmental area, the government need not issue firm-specific compliance orders. The public agency monitors the pollution discharges and fee payments of firms. Private agencies might help administer the program. In the United States, for example, the Chicago Board of Trade provides a forum for the purchase and sale of federal government rights to discharge sulphur dioxide.[6]

Reforms that give firms a legal means of paying for scarce benefits or avoiding costs can limit corrupt incentives. Even if firms are harming others, as in the environmental area, market-based reforms can help both allocate the burden of cleanup more efficiently and limit corruption. However, corrupt dischargers will have no incentive to support such reforms if they are presently avoiding most liability through payoffs. Before such reforms are possible, the state must establish its credibility as a regulatory watchdog.

Reform of Social Benefit Programs

User fees are obviously an inappropriate way to allocate services designed to benefit the poor. But if the service is already being allocated via bribes, a legal system of charges may be a reasonable second-best response to scarcity. As an alternative, the public services could be given to the needy who could resell them if they wished. In contrast, if the goal is to assure that the poor actually use a public benefit, such as health care or education, more direct anticorruption techniques will be required.

[5] "Passage to Cleaner Air," *Financial Times,* April 10, 1996.
[6] "Pollution Auctioneer Chosen: Environmental Protection Agency Chooses Chicago Board of Trade to Conduct Auction of Permits Allowing Power Plants to Emit Sulphur Dioxide," *The New York Times,* September 28, 1992.

Once again, program simplification can be a potent anticorruption strategy. One type of simplification involves the determination of eligibility – every open-ended judgment risks corruption. At the limit, a service might be allocated via a lottery; although this may be unfair to those who lose, at least the lucky winners stand a good chance of actually gaining access to the benefit.

A second sort of simplification concerns the nature of the program itself. If an in-kind benefit program is riddled with corruption, conversion to a direct cash grant may remove a range of corrupt incentives. For example, in a review of programs to reduce the often-bloated civil service in developing countries, the World Bank recommends direct cash payments to those who lose their jobs. The Bank argues that such payments "bypass the rent-extracting bureaucracies sometimes encountered in more elaborate retraining and directed credit schemes" (World Bank 1991: 21).

Alternatively, if cash payments are not a viable option, the difficulty of monitoring suppliers may push the government toward simple, difficult to fake criteria. Although they may not be ideal in a bureaucracy with strong oversight, they may be the only feasible option. Sometimes, incentive systems that use market-like devices can be helpful. For example, if the government uses private providers to supply subsidized services, it could establish a proxy shopping system. A provider would receive capitation payments for subsidized clients only if it was also able to attract paying customers. The paying customers would thus act as "proxy shoppers" for the needy clients. This method of monitoring would be successful only if paying customers demand the same type of services as the needy and are not repelled by the prospect of consuming the service alongside the poor. It also must be hard for providers to discriminate between paying and nonpaying customers in the provision of services. Nor can they be allowed to pay people under the table to act as fake proxy shoppers. Nonetheless, it may well be possible to reproduce these conditions in a rather wide range of medical and educational contexts (Rose-Ackerman 1983). Even if it is feasible, however, proxy shopping is a response to only one kind of fraud. Suppliers will find it difficult to cut quality and still be eligible for subsidy payments. But the plan does nothing to limit fraudulent attempts to enroll for benefits – which must be dealt with by other means.

Obviously, the value of these reforms depends upon the costs of limiting the flexibility of public officials. Sometimes a certain risk of corruption must be tolerated because of the benefits of a case-by-case approach to program administration. But even in such cases transparency and publicity can help overcome corrupt incentives.

Competitive Pressures in Administration

Corruption is often embedded in the hierarchical structure of the bureaucracy. Low-level officials collect bribes and pass a share to those at higher levels – perhaps in the form of an up-front payment for the job itself. Conversely, higher-ups may organize and rationalize the corrupt system to avoid wasteful competition between low-level officials. The top officials may then share the gains with subordinates, perhaps using them to run errands, transfer funds, and do other risky jobs that expose them to arrest. Breaking such patterns requires a fundamental reorganization effort.

One technique involves the creative use of competitive pressures within government. The usual picture of a bureaucracy is a tree with each official responsible to his or her superiors for completing a unique task. For example, officials might all provide the same service, issuing building permits, for example, but be each assigned a different geographical area. So long as officials must exercise discretion, this form of organization gives every official some degree of monopoly power over clients. The organization chart is clear and well organized, but the result can be pervasive corruption. This pathology can be avoided if officials provide the same interchangeable service. They can be given overlapping jurisdictions that permit clients a choice of which bureaucrat to approach. Because clients can apply to any of a number of officials and can go to a second one if the first turns them down, no one official has much monopoly power. Thus, no one can extract a very large payoff.

Under what conditions is competitive bureaucracy a realistic reform strategy? The best case is a public benefit available to all comers. Consider something as mundane as the sale of postage stamps (Alam 1991). Anyone can purchase them without demonstrating his or her worth as a citizen. This means that official discretion is low. If a clerk demands a bribe, customers can simply go to another sales window or another post office. Of course, clerks could take tips in return for dispensing free stamps, but the nature of the product makes financial controls relatively easy to establish. This simple case illustrates the basic requirements for a successful introduction of competitive bureaucracy. People should be entitled to the benefits, and it should be difficult for officials to give away more than clients deserve. The possibility of reapplying to a new official will then limit the bribe potential of any single bureaucrat. If these conditions do *not* hold, clients and officials are in a collusive relationship that both prefer to continue. The size of the bribe will be reduced by the existence of other corrupt officials, but the loss to the state remains large. Thus, the feasibility of competitive bureaucracy depends importantly upon the ability of higher bureaucratic levels to monitor outcomes. They do not need to be able to observe the bribes themselves, but they must be able to monitor output. In the postage stamp example, higher authorities must be able to track the number of stamps sold and hold low-level officials accountable for the revenue collected. Hierarchy is still needed, but its function is shifted toward the monitoring of results, not behavior.

In cases where officials must decide whether an applicant is qualified to receive a benefit such as a license or a permit, competitive bureaucracy also has promise under some conditions. Suppose that the benefit, like a passport or a driver's license, is not scarce, but is restricted to qualified applicants. The criteria for receiving the benefit are clear and known to both clients and officials. Unqualified applicants cannot obtain the benefit without bribery; qualified applicants can report corrupt demands and reapply to another official if the first demands too high a bribe. Suppose that citizens do not know whether or not an official is corrupt until they are actually approached for a bribe. With a competitive bureaucracy, qualified applicants will pay no more than the cost of applying to another official, taking into account that the next official may also demand a bribe. Now the honesty of some officials increases the cost to unqualified applicants and may drive them away, reducing bribe revenues and inducing some formerly corrupt officials to switch, further increasing the risk of detection, and so forth. Bribery is a gamble both for citizens and for officials who must consider the possibility that the citizen will report the corrupt demand. If the stakes become too unfavorable, officials will no longer demand bribes and will not service unqualified applicants (Cadot 1987). An example of this case occurred in Indonesia in the 1970s among officials competing for the privilege of approving investment offers from foreign investors. Competition was so great that the benefits of paying "speed money" eroded, and corrupt demands could not be sustained.[7] Later President Suharto appeared to have solved this "problem" by consolidating such decisions in his own office.

Even if bribers are not qualified for the benefits they seek, competitive bureaucracy may still yield some benefits. Although the unqualified will still pay bribes, even they will not pay much so long as they too can try other officials (Rose-Ackerman 1978: 155–159). Unfortunately, a benevolent spiral will not occur in this case. Consider, for example, corruption in the award of drivers' licenses. The honesty of some officials in the Motor Vehicle Department increases the gains to the corrupt, induc-

---

[7] Theodore Smith, "Corruption, Tradition and Change," *Indonesia*, April 11, 1971, cited in Cariño (1986: 179).

ing more officials to become corrupt in the next period. As more become corrupt, the gain to accepting bribes falls so that a stable intermediate solution can result. The lower bribe levels produced by competition, however, induce more unqualified applicants to make payoffs. The social costs of such a system can be high, as the unqualified take to the roads with their new licenses.

Competitive bureaucracy has limited value in cases where officials, such as tax collectors and police officers, impose costs rather than benefits. Nevertheless, it can, at least, reduce the level of payoffs. Police officers seeking to control illegal businesses can be given overlapping enforcement areas. That way gamblers and drug dealers will not pay much to an individual policeman because a second one may come along later and also demand a payoff. No individual policeman is able to supply protection and so cannot credibly demand a large payoff. The low level of reward available to policemen may induce some to remain honest after balancing the risks and benefits of accepting payoffs (Rose-Ackerman 1978: 159–163).

Officials charged with enforcing regulatory laws or fairly administering benefit programs are a little like policemen. Regulators can be paid by businessmen to overlook violations, and program administrators can be paid to violate the rules of distribution. Thus overlapping enforcement areas can be a solution here as well. For example, in Brazil in the 1970s corruption was controlled in a land reform program in one town because of interagency rivalries. Those who complained of extortion by officials from one agency could go to officials from another agency to seek redress (Cohen and Bunker 1983: 109).

Of course, policemen, factory inspectors, and program administrators may respond by organizing themselves into collusive groups to extort payoffs from businesses and individuals. This has happened often enough to be a realistic concern. But it is sometimes possible to break up such cartels by involving law enforcement officers or inspectors from different political jurisdictions – local, state, and federal. Although collusion sometimes occurs even in this setting, it is generally more difficult to organize. In the Brazilian case described above collusion was limited because officials from the different agencies had little direct contact. In a second town, where this was not true, corruption was rife (Cohen and Bunker 1983).

Although competitive bureaucracy may drive down the level of bribes, and thereby discourage some potentially corrupt officials, the lower bribe prices will also encourage more individuals and businesses to enter the illegal market. The key question in this case is whether the social costs of bribery are inversely related to the size of the bribe. Consider, for example, the case of tax officials in India. Each tax office is organized so that officials have overlapping jurisdictions. Those offices with large numbers of support staff performed poorly compared with offices with fewer staff. Arindam Das-Gupta and Dilip Mookherjee (1998: 236) speculate that in larger offices more officials are competing for the bribes paid by taxpayers to reduce their liabilities. This keeps bribe levels low. Given the low chance of being punished, low payoffs do not induce many officials to behave honestly, but they do encourage more taxpayers to pay for special treatment. Assuming a fixed downward-sloping demand curve for corrupt services, a shift outward in the supply of potentially corrupt support staff leads to lower bribe levels and more corrupt transactions. A similar situation was reported in Nepal where sub-customs officers competed to provide reduced customs fees in return for payoffs. Traders flocked to the cheapest entry points where the sum of fees and bribes was lowest. Some officers tried to limit competition by hiring bandits to harass traders using routes favorable to other corrupt officers (Alfiler 1986: 48). Notice the important way in which these situations differ from the law enforcement case. A gambler or drug dealer can never feel secure because a new policeman may arrive at any time to arrest him or demand a payoff. In the tax case, officials may compete to provide tax breaks, but once a taxpayer has paid off a low-level official, no one at the same level has the authority to step in. Monitoring from above is necessary to increase the risks faced by corrupt civil servants.

The Deterrent Effect of Anticorruption Laws

All countries draw the line somewhere between illegal bribery and acceptable "gifts of good will." Countries differ in where the border is set, but in this section I take that judgment as given and seek an effective deterrence strategy. The sanctioning strategies I propose focus both on improving the deterrent effect of arrest and punishment and on rewarding those who come forward with documentation of corrupt deeds.

The optimal amount of corruption is not zero even if one gives no value to the benefits received by bribers. Once one takes the costs of prevention into account, the level of deterrence expenditures should be set where the marginal benefits equal the marginal costs (Anechiarico and Jacobs 1996; Becker and Stigler 1974; Rose-Ackerman 1978: 109–119). The deterrence of criminal behavior depends on the probability of detection and punishment and on the penalties imposed – both those imposed by the legal system and more subtle costs such as loss of reputation or shame (Becker 1968). Law enforcement authorities can vary either or both of these variables, but we lack strong empirical evidence on their relative importance.[8]

Successful detection of corruption depends on insiders to report wrongdoing. Often this requires officials to promise leniency to one of the participants. This creates an important paradox for law enforcement efforts. High expected punishments ought to deter corruption, but a high probability of detection can be accomplished only if some are promised low penalties. I begin by discussing deterrence based on expected punishment and then consider strategies that take account of the interaction between punishment and the probability of detection.

Because it takes two to enter into a corrupt deal, the crime will not occur if the law can deter at least one of the parties. In some countries, bribe payers are treated more leniently than recipients (Hepkema and Booysen 1997). Some countries do not even criminalize the payment of bribes.[9] In others the reverse is true – the criminal law distinguishes between "active" and "passive" corruption. The briber is viewed as the "active" party and the public official as "passive" (Vermeulen 1997). These distinctions do not capture the rich variety of cases. Often the public official can be described as the active party who extorts a payoff (Mény 1996: 311). In practice, the distinction between active and passive corruption and between extortion and bribery means little because both parties must agree before corruption can occur.

Instead, bribery can be more usefully distinguished on the basis of its social harm. Begin by considering whether the briber is entitled to the benefit received and whether or not scarcity exists.[10] This produces three categories: an illegal benefit, a legal but scarce benefit, and a legal benefit that is not scarce if allocated honestly. If the benefit provided is illegal,

---

[8] One study using United States data from 1970 to 1984 showed that both a greater probability of conviction and longer prison terms deter corruption (Goel and Rich 1989).

[9] In an interview in Taiwan in 1995 the Justice Minister Ma Ying-Jeou complained that Taiwanese law did not make it a crime for a citizen to offer a bribe. He claimed that the lack of such an offense "seems to encourage businessmen to give out all kinds of gifts" and has been "a major obstacle to rooting out the *hung bao* culture [of giving money in red envelopes to officials]." Quoted in "Ma Main Man," *Far Eastern Economic Review,* March 23, 1995. Conversely, in Chile payment of a bribe is a criminal offense, while accepting a bribe is not unless accompanied by other wrongdoing (Hepkema and Booysen 1997: 415).

[10] Shleifer and Vishny (1993). Law and economics scholars distinguish between bribery and extortion depending on whether the payer receives "better than fair treatment" or must pay to be treated fairly (Ayres 1997: 1234–1238; Lindgren 1988: 824). However, both are often combined in practice (Ayres 1997: 1236–1237).

the social harm of corruption is the distortion introduced by corrupt payoffs. If the benefit is legal but scarce, the corrupt official gives preference to bribers over other potential beneficiaries. The social harm is the net cost of allocating by willingness-to-bribe instead of by the stated criteria of the corrupted program. Finally, the benefit may be legal and appear scarce only because of corrupt public officials. The social cost is then the distortion created by the officials' efforts to generate payoffs. In deciding how to allocate law enforcement resources, the degree of social harm should be the most important variable. In general, highest priority should be given to corruption in the allocation of illegal benefits. In the abstract, it is difficult to rank corrupt transactions that affect the allocation of legal benefits. The social costs depend upon the damage done by using a willingness-to-pay criterion, on the one hand, versus the inefficiencies and inequities of officials' efforts to design in bottlenecks and scarcity, on the other.

Turn now to punishment strategies. A ranking of the social harm of different kinds of corruption can help set enforcement priorities. However, the penalties actually levied on the convicted should be tied not to these social harms, but to the benefits received by the corrupt. Assuming that society does not give positive weight to corrupt gains, the goal is to reduce corruption as far as possible given limited law enforcement resources. To deter bribery at least one side of the corrupt transaction must face penalties that reflect its own gains. Because the chance of detection and conviction is far less than one, those convicted should sacrifice a multiple of these gains. From a pure deterrence point of view, either side of the corrupt deal can be the focus of law enforcement efforts. From the point of view of public acceptability, however, bribers who seek legal benefits are likely to arouse public sympathies, not blame. Whatever the focus, actors should face expected penalties tied to their own benefits from corruption.

Officials' penalties should be tied to the size of the payoffs they receive and the probability of detection. If penalties are not a function of the size of the bribe, an anticorruption drive would quickly confront a paradox. A high fixed penalty will lower the incidence of corruption but increase the size of bribes paid. If the penalty is high, officials must receive a high return in order to be willing to engage in bribery. Thus the expected penalty should increase by more than a dollar for every dollar increase in the size of the bribe (Rose-Ackerman 1978: 109–135). This could be done either by tying the penalty levied upon conviction to the size of the bribe or by increasing the risk of catch as the size of the bribe increases. However, if the probability of catch is lower for small payoffs, the penalty for each detected offense must reflect the low incidence of detection. This could mean that those convicted of petty bribery could face severer penalties than those found to have taken larger bribes.

On the other side of the corrupt transaction, a fixed penalty levied on bribers will lower both the demand for corrupt services and the level of bribes. However, it will have no marginal impact once the briber passes the corruption threshold. To have a marginal effect, the penalties imposed on bribe payers should be tied to their gains (their excess profits, for example), not to the size of the bribe.[11] Bribes represent a cost to those who pay them; thus penalties should not be tied to these costs unless they are a good proxy for the briber's benefits.

American law does little to recognize this asymmetry between bribe payers and bribe recipients in its prescribed punishments. The criminal penalties are equivalent – both payers and recipients can be fined "not more than three times the monetary equivalent of the thing of value [i.e., the bribe] or imprisoned for not more than fifteen years, or both" [18 USC § 201 (a)]. This is appropriate for officials who receive bribes except that multiplying by three may be a poor measure of the risk of detection and punishment. The actual probability of catch is likely to be well below one-third. The law, however, does recognize the asymmetry of corrupt transactions by permitting the President to rescind any contract or other benefit if there has been a conviction under the statute governing bribery, graft, and conflicts of interest. The United States can also recover, in addition to any penalties, "the amount expended or the thing transferred or delivered on its behalf, or the reasonable value thereof" (18 USC § 218). This right of recovery is designed to avoid losses to the government. It is a weak deterrent to corrupt payoffs because the recovery is not multiplied by a factor that reflects the probability of detection.

If expected penalties do not increase along with the benefits of corruption for bribers and bribees, government may be caught in a trap where high corruption levels beget high corruption levels. A low corruption equilibrium may also exist but be unreachable in small steps from the status quo. High corruption equilibria occur when the net rewards of corruption *increase* as the incidence of corruption increases. This might occur, for example, if law enforcement officials discover a

---

[11] Alternatively, if potentially corrupt firms are repeat players, they can be deterred by debarment procedures that prohibit corrupt firms from contracting with the government for a period of years. To have a marginal effect, the debarment penalty should be tied to the seriousness of the corruption uncovered. For examples of debarment, see "Singapore Blacklists Scandal-Tinged Firms," *Nikkei Weekly*, February 19, 1996, and Thacher (1995), who describes the practices used by the New York City School Construction Authority.

smaller proportion of corrupt deals when the incidence of corruption is high and if penalties levied upon conviction are not adjusted to take account of that fact. Any multiple equilibria case, however, can be converted into a single equilibrium, low-corruption case with the appropriate choice of law enforcement strategy or a change in the information conditions. Strategies that tie expected penalties to marginal gains can remove a society from a high corruption trap. Doing so, however, may require a large increase in law enforcement resources to tip the system to a low corruption equilibrium. The good news is that the sharp increase in enforcement resources need not be permanent. It must simply be sufficient to tip the system to a lower corruption level (Lui 1986: 21–22). The idea is to change expectations. A concentrated cleanup campaign can change expectations about others' cooperation in the corrupt system. Once a new low corruption equilibrium has been established, it can be maintained with reduced enforcement resources so long as the honest are willing to report corrupt offers, and law enforcement officials follow up on reports of malfeasance (Cadot 1987; Rose-Ackerman 1978: 137–151).

Effective deterrence is impossible unless the police can obtain relevant evidence – a difficult task because often the participants are the only people who know of the corrupt deal. The probability of detection is a function of whether any of the participants has an incentive to report to the police. In this context, police promises of low penalties or even rewards are often essential. Suppose, first, that the benefit is legal and would be freely available in an honest world to those who now pay bribes. Because the bribers receive benefits to which they are legally entitled, they are likely to believe that they are extortion victims who would be better off in an honest world. Such bribe payers are potential allies in an anticorruption effort who will cooperate in efforts to eliminate payoffs. A promise of leniency will give them an incentive to report corrupt demands and will encourage beneficiaries of public programs to demand services that are free of payoff demands.

Consider next a scarce but legal benefit that is corruptly allocated to many individuals who would not qualify if payoffs were eliminated. Neither those who pay nor those who receive bribes will voluntarily report the corrupt transaction. Those shut out of the process, however, have a grievance. For example, disappointed bidders for public contracts can facilitate efforts to limit corruption (Alam 1995). They should be rewarded for coming forward with evidence even if the reason they lost the bid was not moral scruples, but their own unwillingness to make a large enough payoff. This can be done by permitting the firms to sue for damages. A survey of the antibribery laws in thirteen developed countries found that such suits are permitted in most jurisdictions (Hepkema and Booysen 1997: 416).

Bribes paid to obtain illegal services are likely to be the most difficult to control. Bribers are often also engaged in other illegal activities and those who fail in their corruption efforts can hardly come forward to claim that they should have been the ones obtaining the illegal benefit. Nevertheless, the very vulnerability of bribers can be used to uncover corruption. They may accept lenient treatment with respect to, say, a violation of the drug laws, in return for providing evidence in a corruption trial.

In the business world, most bribes are paid by employees and agents, not top management. If payoffs help a firm obtain business, managers and owners may hope to facilitate their subordinates' bribery while remaining ignorant of the details.[12] If corporations are held criminally liable for the corrupt acts of their employees and agents, top management may not support an effective monitoring system. Jennifer Arlen analyzes this problem for the general case of corporate crimes and concludes that a number of alternative rules are superior to present United States law that imposes pure strict liability on firms. One possibility is a negligence rule under which firms are liable only if they have neglected their internal enforcement responsibilities. For such a rule to be workable, however, courts must be able to evaluate internal firm behavior, a difficult task. One solution may be quite precise directives stating what type of internal monitoring is required (Arlen 1994).

Along these lines, the U.S. Foreign Corrupt Practices Act (FCPA) supplements its prohibitions against paying bribes with accounting provisions that apply to firms within the jurisdiction of the Securities and Exchange Commission. These firms must establish accounting systems that accurately reflect transactions involving the firm's assets, and they must have an effective system of internal accounting controls. Firms and their managers can be subject to both civil and criminal penalties for violating these accounting provisions.[13] There is no formal due diligence defense to the FCPA. But in practice, firms that establish and enforce effective internal control systems appear to experience more lenient

---

[12] Top managers hope to rely on their subordinates' ability to rationalize such payoffs. In one experimental study business students and managers expressed a strong commitment to honesty as a value, but over 70 percent were willing to pay a bribe to get business. The most frequently expressed justification was that "the first duty of a manager is to reach the company's goals. Therefore, it sometimes becomes necessary to forget about ethics" (Rosenberg 1987).

[13] Foreign Corrupt Practices Act, 15 U.S.C. §§ 78m(b) (1988 & Supp. IV 1992), section 102; Jadwin and Shilling (1994: 679–680); Nobles and Maistrellis (1994: 9, 19); Pickholz (1997: 237).

treatment. The Federal Sentencing Guidelines also reward internal firm efforts to detect and punish violations of the law (Nobles and Maistrellis 1994: 18–24). Thus American law attempts to counter management's incentive to insulate itself from the profit-maximizing malfeasance of employees and agents.

An alternative system rewards "whistleblowers" within firms and public agencies who come forward with evidence of wrongdoing. Reporting the peculations of others can be dangerous. If corruption is systemic, one risks being disciplined by corrupt superiors and attacked by coworkers. One study of corruption in China suggests that this is a serious problem (Manion 1996a). The whistleblower may even end up accused of corruption.[14] Thus governments should consider promulgating statutes that protect and reward those who report malfeasance (Pope 1996: 59–61). The United States, for example, has two statutes. The False Claims Act rewards those who report irregularities in government contracts and protects private sector whistleblowers from reprisals (31 U.S.C. §§ 3729–3731; Howse and Daniels 1995; Kovacic 1996). The second protects whistleblowers inside government agencies from retaliation [Whistleblower Protection Act, Pub. L. No. 101–12, 5 U.S.C. § 2302 (b) (8)].

The False Claims Act (31 U.S.C. § 3730) pays whistleblowers a share of the total penalties and other damages levied against firms for wrongdoing that has injured the federal government. The rewards are available to people both inside and outside the firm – although not to government officials with direct responsibility for detecting contract violations. If the whistlebower brings suit and is successful, he or she can recover from 25 to 30 percent of the penalty. If the Justice Department opts to join the action, the minimum recovery is reduced to 15 percent because the government will bear most of the legal costs. Unsuccessful private plaintiffs must bear their own legal costs but not those of the firm unless the court determines that the suit was clearly frivolous or vexatious [31 U.S.C. § 3730 (d) (4); Howse and Daniels 1995: 526]. The law also protects whistleblowers from retaliation by their employers.

A number of objections have been raised to this statute, but, on balance, the law appears to serve a valuable purpose and can complement efforts at internal monitoring. In particular, the idea that corporate whistleblowing will undermine internal control efforts seems misplaced. Robert Howse and Ronald Daniels argue that "the fear of being exposed to prosecution as a consequence of external whistleblowing may be an important incentive for some corporations to adopt *credible* internal disclosure policies and procedures" (ibid.: 537). The main problem in coun-

---

[14] See "Mexican Army Whistle-Blower on Trial," *New York Times*, March 6, 1998.

tries in the process of establishing a rule of law will be to clarify what practices are illegal and subject to criminal penalties. It will not make sense to protect or reward whistleblowers unless it is clear what they should be looking for.

Sometimes public officials claim that large firms virtually force bribes upon them. This seems a little disingenuous because the payoffs are a cost to the firms involved. Nevertheless, to the extent this claim is credible, public officials could come forward with evidence of corrupt offers and seek protection under the Whistleblower Protection Act. Firms would predictably defend themselves by arguing that the official demanded the payoff. The distinctions in American law may be useful here. Under the False Claims Act, the court can reduce the award for a whistleblower who was involved in wrongdoing, but only if he or she planned or initiated the wrongful conduct. The award need not be eliminated, however, unless the whistleblower is convicted of a crime [31 U.S.C. § 3730 (d) (3)]. Prosecutors with the authority to grant criminal immunity can thus set up a kind of a race in which the first to report the corrupt transaction will be rewarded while the others are punished.

Procurement Reform

Corruption scandals frequently involve government procurement of goods and services. Bribes can not only determine who obtains a contract, but also the size and specifications of government purchases. Anticorruption reforms should focus not just on reducing malfeasance but also on improving the efficiency of government purchasing decisions.

Procurement reform highlights the tradeoffs between avoiding corruption and giving officials the flexibility to make decisions in the light of their own knowledge. Discretion increases corrupt incentives, but critics of elaborate procurement codes point to their excessive rigidity. Nevertheless, even skeptics do not call for their complete abandonment. Many scandals involve situations where no codes exist or where tender boards are simply overruled by corrupt or self-seeking political leaders. Especially if impartial courts enforce the rules, codes protect the process against improper high-level influence.

How then should the balance be drawn? In recent years America has been especially active in procurement reform. Although the reforms are controversial and still in progress, they contain some lessons for developing and transitional countries facing similar problems.

Reform in the United States

We can divide the procurement problem into four stylized categories: purchases that require specialized research and development, such as newly designed military aircraft; purchases of complex, special purpose projects, such as dams or port facilities, that do not involve advances in technology but require managerial and organizational skills; purchases of standard products sold in private markets, such as motor vehicles or medical supplies; and customized versions of products sold privately, such as special purpose computer systems or fleets of police cars.

Traditional procurement doctrine recommends a different process for each of the first three categories. The first, of great concern to the United States Department of Defense, involves the difficult question of how to write a contract for a product that has not yet been developed and may require advances in the state of the art. I leave this category to one side because it is not very important in developing countries. For the second category, a sealed bidding process under International Competitive Bidding (ICB) principles is the accepted standard of fairness and economic efficiency. It is required by the World Bank under its infrastructure loans and has influenced the development of procurement codes worldwide.[15] The process is appropriate for a project, such as a dam, that is capital-intensive, self-contained, and uses known and tested technology.

Procurement advice in the third category is straightforward – purchase the goods at the lowest price available, taking into account discounts that may be available to large purchasers. The fourth category – customized products also sold privately – requires new approaches. The procurement problem is less difficult than the first category where research and development are required, but neither sealed bidding nor off-the-shelf purchase is appropriate. Procurement processes need to be rethought for government purchases of such goods and services.

The perceived disjunction between standard procurement techniques and the realities of public purchasing has been central to the Clinton administration's attempts to reform the federal system.[16] The effort is spearheaded by Steven Kelman, a professor at the Kennedy School at Harvard, who is serving as President Clinton's director of the Office of Federal Procurement Policy (OFPP). Kelman's preparation for the job

---

[15] See World Bank (1997a). The World Trade Organization's (WTO) Agreement on Government Procurement and related documents are available on the Internet at http://www.wto.org/wto/govt. The WTO agreement and the United Nations Model Code are discussed in Hoekman and Mavroidis (1997).

[16] Three acts have been passed: The 1993 Government Procurement and Results Act, the 1994 Federal Acquisition Streamlining Act [10 U.S.C. 2305(b) (5) (A), and 41 U.S.C. 2536(e) (1)], and the 1996 Clinger–Cohen Act (41 U.S.C. 423). The statutory reforms have been incorporated into the revised part 15 of the Federal Acquisitions Regulation.

was his in-depth study of federal government computer procurement (Kelman 1990, 1994). Computers are in the fourth category. They are widely available in the private market, but the technology is changing rapidly, and the government often has specialized needs that are not identical to those of private business. Neither simple off-the-shelf purchases nor a mechanical sealed bidding system will work well. Kelman's case study was very critical of government practices, arguing that existing rules were too cynical about bureaucrats – assuming that they will be lazy and corrupt if given a chance. Procurement processes then in use resembled the sealed-bid system. Kelman argued that negotiated sole source contracts would be better and that reforms were needed to encourage discretion and improve incentives for good performance. Fundamental to the old system was a rigid reliance on contractors' written responses to specifications. In a complex area like computer procurement, Kelman concluded that this system failed to look at the bidders' records on previous government contracts and so gave firms no incentive to point out problems in the government's specifications. Computer firms may have experience in installing systems similar to the one the government wants. They should be rewarded for helping the government avoid mistakes. Furthermore, if suppliers know that a strong performance on one contract will help them obtain others, they will make investments and innovations that are specific to their government work.

As a member of the Clinton administration, Kelman has attempted to put his recommendations into practice. He developed a system to prequalify a subset of potential contractors who would then form the pool from which actual sellers are chosen for particular projects. One of Kelman's first experiments as head of the OFPP was new regulations for the purchase of computers by the Department of Transportation. Sixty teams applied, and twenty were selected to compete for specific orders over four to seven years. The orders come from many federal agencies, not just Transportation. He also supported experiments with performance-based contracts, and a number are in use for services from grass cutting to restoration of nuclear production sites.

Kelman argues that procurement officers should be given very specific instructions about the goals of procurement and be held accountable for the contractor's ability to fulfill them. They should, however, have considerable flexibility to determine the means. Agencies would still be required to justify their decisions in writing, and multimember evaluation panels would still be used to make procurement decisions. Contractors would be evaluated in terms of outcomes, not inputs. Agencies must define outcomes carefully and reward contractors on the basis of performance. The government would favor top performers when new contracting opportunities arise.

The use of past performance as a factor in awarding new contracts has proved difficult to implement because there is no generally accepted technique for evaluating performance. Kelman's office is working to develop a system to record quality, timeliness, cost control, business relations, and customer satisfaction (Laurent 1997), but the process has been controversial, and early agency efforts have been successfully challenged in the United States federal courts (Miller 1997a). Opposition to experience rating is centered in the small business community. Many small businesses are startup firms with no track records, and if they are growing, their capacity may improve over time, making past experience a poor guide to the future (Behr 1997). The federal government has proposed ways to counter these objections, but worries persist.

Also difficult to implement is Kelman's idea of letting contractors help determine the specifications. This is a controversial part of the revised part 15 of the Federal Acquisition Regulation that governs all negotiated government procurements. The revised rules encourage prebid communication between vendors and agencies for negotiated procurements, a practice that was not previously permitted. Restrictions remain in force for competitive procurements (Noelker, Shapiro, and Kellogg 1997). The controversy surrounds the potential for favoritism under this practice. Critics worry that the revisions will encourage cronyism and other types of abuse, especially because certain forms of bid protests have been eliminated or restricted (Miller 1997a, 1997b).

As the controversy over prebid communications indicates, Kelman has not fully confronted the corruption implications of his proposals. Kelman treats malfeasance as a problem for the criminal law, not procurement regulations. He argues that the current American record-keeping system for procurement is almost useless against miscreants with any degree of subtlety and skill. He has a "rotten apple" view of the problem – some bad people exist, and the criminal law should deal with them. The penalties for corruption should be increased and more resources should be put into public investigations (Kelman 1994: 121–122). Of course, increasing the expected costs of paying and receiving payoffs is one line of defense against corruption, and Kelman may well be correct about the ineffectiveness of record-keeping requirements. However, it does not follow that the best solution is to detach anticorruption strategies from procurement practice.

Instead of delinking the control of malfeasance from other procurement practices, government purchasing specifications should take account of the risk of corruption. This can be done without too much sacrifice of the flexibility that Kelman favors. Goods sold in international markets where benchmark prices exist should be favored over custom-made or state-of-the-art products for that reason. In fact, Kelman himself recommends just such a shift, arguing that it is closer to the practices of private firms. For example, the United States General Services Administration now has a list of computer products and technology services that can be purchased without competitive bidding (Behr 1997). Recent statutory reforms encourage purchasing officers to do market research and favor commercial items. The state can look to private market prices as benchmarks and state their specifications in terms of standard off-the-shelf items to lower the cost of submitting a bid (Laurent 1997). Kelman does not stress the anticorruption benefits of such off-the-shelf purchases, but they are clearly one reason why the use of standardized products can be cheaper for government (Rose-Ackerman 1978: 132–135; Ruzindana 1995). The basic idea is to replace competitive bidding with negotiation and haggling on the basis of background market conditions (Behr 1997). Competitive pressures are introduced by the private market, not the bidding process itself.

Performance evaluations that influence future prospects are also consistent with anticorruption goals. Debarment processes based on corruption and organized crime connections are a widely used form of performance evaluation. Kelman focuses not on crimes committed but on the quality of work done. This can also be an indirect anticorruption device because it prevents public officials from favoring weak but well-connected firms that have performed poorly in the past. However, performance measures must be objective and must make provision for new entrants. Otherwise they can cement the position of entrenched contractors (Gray 1996).

Worries about prebid communications are not easily resolved. The open-ended communication that Kelman favors as a way to exchange information can also be a way of exerting illegal influence. Of course, if illicit contacts are already common, legalizing contacts may favor competent and honest firms that previously lacked a legal means of access. Kelman convincingly argues that such communications will improve contracting performance in a range of public procurement areas, but the balance in an individual case will depend upon the relative risks and benefits. Nevertheless, in the United States a move in the direction that he recommends seems worth trying if it is combined with stronger efforts to reward firms on the basis of their ultimate performance.

Lessons for Developing Countries
The relative strengths and weaknesses of the American reforms should be watched closely by other countries for the lessons they can provide. Some of Kelman's proposals can be adopted by developing countries,

but others are not suitable for export to countries with less well-developed legal systems and weak private markets.

Kelman's proposal to use past experience with contractors could be adopted by countries where corruption of the procurement process is believed to be serious. It could both reduce malfeasance and improve efficiency. In contrast, under ICB principles, the lowest "responsible" bidder must be accepted. If followed mechanically, this rule can lead to low-quality work and collusive bid rigging. For small, aid-dependent countries, the reputation of bidders could be drawn from the international arena. An international organization might keep a roster of contractors with information on their past performance.[17] The controversy surrounding the use of performance ratings in the United States, however, suggests that such a system should focus on a few key variables that can be measured and compared across countries. Relevant indicators might include evidence of fraud, corruption, cost overruns, and time delays. Such a roster could be integrated into the World Bank's revised Procurement Guidelines which state that the Bank will declare firms ineligible for Bank contracts "either indefinitely or for a stated period of time" if it determines that the firm has engaged in corrupt or fraudulent practices in connection with Bank-financed projects [Section 1.15(d)].

The controversy over prebid communications in the United States echoes similar problems in developing countries. A common abuse involves procurement orders written so that only one firm can qualify. For example, an African country reportedly once set its telephone specifications to require equipment that could survive in a frigid climate. Only one telephone manufacturer from Scandinavia could satisfy this obviously worthless specification. In a system where government is publicly accountable, such favoritism would not be possible if the specifications were made public. Too great an intertwining of contractors and public officials invites corruption. Systems that are more transparent and accountable can afford to give procurement officers more discretion than others with less accountability. The problem is most serious when the choice of a contractor depends on the technical characteristics of the product. In contrast, if the government sets an output- or goal-

---

[17] Terry Miller (1997a), generally a critic of Kelman's reforms, supports performance rating but argues that it should be centralized with a grading system based on companies' entire contractual workloads worldwide. He also recommends giving government contracting officers access to commercial databases on financial fraud that would tell the government if the contractor owed back taxes. He would give vendors access to data on their own company and give them an opportunity to challenge the data.

oriented set of specifications, this could minimize the problem of insider influence. At the very least, goal distortion would be clearer.

As Kelman suggests, procurement reform can complement civil service reforms that provide incentives to officials to perform effectively. Bonuses earned by officials who achieve procurement goals could substitute for illegal payoffs. But civil service reforms are only necessary, not sufficient, for success in routine procurement. Scandals frequently have implicated top government leaders who profited from their inside knowledge and connections. Kelman's proposals are not much help in dealing with such "grand corruption." They focus instead on middle-level procurement decisions under the control of professional civil servants. They are, however, consistent with reforms that shift procurement decisions to career officials and tender boards. If rulers wish to insulate themselves from the demands of political supporters, they should create impartial bodies with independent procurement authority.

The basic reorientation of American reforms away from perfecting the bidding process toward making the overall purchasing environment more efficient and effective is a fundamental shift in perspective. It seems an especially valuable innovation for developing countries with limited capacity to carry out complex bidding procedures. Although competitive bidding sounds like a good idea, notice that bidding does not play a role in a truly competitive market. Instead, the market price is set through the multiple interactions of many buyers and sellers. Of course, frequently governments do need to make special purpose deals using a well-organized bidding process to minimize costs. But the United States experiments indicate that the benefits of competition can often be achieved if the government becomes a market participant. Decisions about *what* to procure are as important as decisions about *how* to carry out the procurement. Corrupt systems not only use bad processes; they also frequently procure the wrong things. For example, if a fair and transparent bidding system is not possible, this should push procurement choices toward goods and services where benchmark prices exist or that can be purchased in the private market. A government that demands customized products risks creating room for corrupt payoffs.

Bench marking may be relatively easy for those countries and subnational governments that are small relative to the markets in which they operate. If they purchase standard products in the international market, market prices are excellent standards because the small government's own demand is unlikely to affect prices. One way to obtain rough benchmarks is through data on United States trade. Two studies have calculated average prices and variances for goods using United States trade statistics (Pak and Zdanowicz 1994; Paul, Pak, Zdanowicz, and Curwen

1994). Because of product differentiation even within quite detailed categories, these price estimates are guesses, but they could give developing countries a starting point for negotiating with suppliers.

Of course, not all procurement can be redirected toward standardized products in international commerce. Developing countries will be making large investments in special purpose infrastructure for years to come. These projects are unlikely to require sophisticated new technology, but they are one of a kind. Thus the effectiveness of competitive bidding procedures will remain a central concern. Accepting the validity of the basic principles of ICB procedures for such projects, countries still need to assure robust competition among bidders. The same is true for competitive systems that make use of the prescreening processes that Kelman favors. There are two problems: the possibility of collusion and the difficulty of attracting bidders.

Consider collusion first. Robert Klitgaard (1988: 134–155) describes a case where repeat players used the openness and transparency of competitive bidding processes to maintain a cartel to fix prices and share markets. The case involved the supply of goods and services for the American army in South Korea in the 1960s and 1970s. The Korean contractors were highly organized and held meetings to decide who would be the low bidder and how profits would be divided. Intimidation was used to enforce decisions and discourage entry. The U.S. Army could not prosecute the Korean businessmen themselves, and its own practice of publicizing the bids after they were opened helped maintain the cartel by informing everyone of the results.

In Japan a prequalification process that seems close to Kelman's ideal helped maintain a similar cartel. Procurement officers selected a qualified pool of bidders based in part on past performance. In practice, the process limited the number of bidders to a small group and excluded new firms, especially foreign ones. A legal requirement that new tenders be issued each year, even for capital-intensive projects, produced pressures to collude on multiyear projects to assure continuity. A small number of repeat bidders divided up the contracts in a cartel-like arrangement (Gray 1996; Mamiya 1995).

In the Korean case benchmarking by the U.S. Army helped reveal overcharges of 10 to 30 percent that occurred as a result of the cartel. Because the army was unsuccessful in introducing competition in contracting, it instead began to rely on negotiation with a sole source. Similar to Kelman's preferred reforms, the aim was to use the army's bargaining power to secure a favorable price. Information about prices in the private market or for similar goods and services in other countries helped set the stage for negotiation. The situation of the U.S. Army in

Korea, however, may be a special case where an organization representing a foreign government is directly involved in procurement.

Collusion in the Japanese case may be harder to avoid since public officials as well as firms help maintain the collusive arrangements (Mamiya 1995). The only solution may be a more open and competitive process combined with credible law enforcement. In fact, Japan has tried both strategies. In 1995 prosecutors, in an unprecedented move, charged nine companies with bid rigging in connection with an electrical project. In a criminal case brought under Japanese antimonopoly law, the firms were convicted and fined. At the same time the government introduced an open-bidding system for federal public-works contracts in an attempt to make collusion more difficult. Major company bids fell 20 percent below the Construction Ministry's estimates, but part of the drop may have been due to the recession, not a decline in collusion. However, at least one firm reported a large drop in the funds set aside for payoffs.[18]

The second problem concerns the fear that too few firms will bid on major projects. However, information on the actual number of bidders may be a misleading signal of competitive conditions. Submitting a bid is costly. Firms compare the fixed costs of a bid with the expected benefit, that is, the profit multiplied by the chance of winning the bid. If the profit on a contract falls too low, the number of bidders may fall. For example, according to an experienced observer, when the profits on international construction contracts fell to 4 percent, many multinationals found bidding too costly if they had to compete against five or more equally qualified competitors (Strassmann 1989: 789). If low expected profit margins *cause* the number of bidders to be small, then it will be difficult to infer anything about the strength of competitive pressures by looking at the number of bidders on individual projects. A small number of bidders may just mean that the developing country is viewed as especially likely to assure a competitive bidding process. If a large number of bids is submitted, this may indicate that excess profits are anticipated perhaps through corrupt arrangements with officials. However, a contract with a very high rate of return and a small number of bidders should be especially suspect because it may indicate a deal based on patronage or corruption. Firms argue for subsidies for bid preparation or insurance for bidding costs. This seems unwise. The goal should be to prevent collusion and to increase the state's bargaining power, not simply multiply

---

[18] "Bid Rigours," *Far Eastern Economic Review*, March 23, 1995. In November 1996 the newly established Special Investigation Department of the Federal Trade Commission brought a second case against manufacturers and retailers of water meters (*The Daily Yomiuri*, November 17, 1996).

the number of bids. If specifications can be reasonably well determined beforehand and if collusion can be avoided, a process with three or four bidders does not seem obviously worse than one with seven or eight. The real problem is a state that is too weak or too venal to bargain successfully with outside contractors. Kickbacks then assure monopoly profits for successful bidders with a share of the gains going to corrupt officials.

Conclusions

Structural reform should be the first line of attack in an anticorruption campaign. If a public program is not serving a legitimate public goal, the bottlenecks and constraints it imposes do nothing more than create corrupt opportunities. The remedy here is elimination, not reform. Many other programs serve important goals and should be redesigned to limit official discretion. In some others, the administrative system should be reoriented to reduce the private gains available to officials.

The criminal law is the second basic part of a comprehensive strategy. Finding the right mix of penalties, rewards, and undercover law enforcement is not easy. Nevertheless, one important lesson of the economic analysis of crime is unproblematic: Anticorruption policy should never aim to achieve complete rectitude. Those who take an absolutist position are likely to impose rigid and cumbersome constraints that increase, rather than decrease, corrupt incentives. The goals of law enforcement should be to isolate those corrupt systems that are doing the most damage to society and then to organize the deterrence effort to make corruption costly on the margin and to give participants an incentive to report a corrupt deal.

Procurement reform serves as a third basic component of an anticorruption strategy. It should be viewed as an opportunity to rethink what the government buys as well as how it goes about making purchases. Although reforms in the United States should not be mindlessly transferred to other institutional contexts, they can provide a framework for thinking about the redesign of procurement processes. Developing countries could experiment with experience-rating for contractors, the adoption of more transparent processes, and more reliance on bargaining. In developing countries with a scarcity of skilled procurement experts and weak public accountability the case for benchmarking and the purchase of standard items is even stronger than in the United States.

In the next chapter I turn to the final, and perhaps most basic, economically based reform. A corrupt and incompetent civil service can defeat all other efforts. How then should a state structure its bureaucracy so that honest government service is a plausible career choice for educated citizens?

5

Reform of the Civil Service

A personnel system based on patronage and political loyalty undermines the efficient delivery of services and leads to the unfair administration of tax and regulatory laws.[1] If corruption and self-dealing are imbedded in a government that is otherwise democratizing and downsizing, this can delegitimize political and economic reform. The goal is not to isolate public administration completely from politics – an impossible task in any event – but to find ways to mediate the relationship. Traditionally, a professional civil service is politically neutral, has security of tenure, is paid a decent salary, is recruited and promoted on merit, and does not have property or business interests that conflict with the fair performance of its duties (Adamolekun 1993). Some present-day reformers question aspects of this traditional model, but even they support the principle that civil servants should not be hired and fired for political reasons (Reid and Scott 1994; Scott 1996).

Countries emerging from a period of one-party or authoritarian rule face the challenge of creating a professional civil service. The executive branch needs to be politically accountable, but it also must perform day-to-day tasks with a minimum of corruption and favoritism. In Mexico, for example, as the long history of one-party dominance weakens, the national government is considering the establishment of a professional civil service (Guerro Amparán 1998). A democracy where parties alternate in power does not appear compatible with a public employment system based on political patronage. With no civil service protection,

---

[1] As the British Treasury noted in 1723, "officers who themselves or whose kinsmen or political friends were canvassing for votes for parliamentary elections were hardly likely to be conspicuous in prosecuting defaulting maltsters and inn-keepers" (quoted in Parris 1969: 25).

officers who expect to lose their jobs after the next election may simply put money away for the future.[2]

Of course, there may be a self-interested motive for incumbents' sudden interest in an apolitical civil service. It may be the only way that middle-level officials can retain their jobs in the face of political turnover. Although skepticism about the motivations of existing job-holders may be warranted, this should not diminish the underlying value of reform. If political pluralism becomes well established, an apolitical civil service can smooth leadership changes (Adamolekun 1993: 41–43). In very stable political environments more top officials can serve at the pleasure of politicians than in countries with unstable, short-lived governments (Reid and Scott 1994: 67).

But even stable polities can benefit from a professional and apolitical officialdom. History provides many cases in which autocratic countries have recognized the value of a professional civil service to assure that services are delivered efficiently and fairly; the German and Chinese empires are obvious examples (Derlien 1991; Raadschelders and Rutgers 1996: 76–77). Similarly, modern China is instituting civil service reform based on merit recruitment, market wage rates, and retraining. This reform, however, lacks some key features of most developed systems. It continues to be managed by the Communist party, and no distinction is made between political appointees and civil servants (Burns 1993: 354–356). Nevertheless, these reforms may help increase the legitimacy of government in the eyes of its citizens and make it easier to attract outside investment.

Civil service reform is a pressing issue in many parts of the world. For example, the newly democratizing African states must develop a career civil service in order to modernize and develop. They must allocate tasks between the civil service and other types of organizations and groups outside the formal government structure. The government structures inherited from the former colonizers departed from the ideal Weberian bureaucracy in numerous ways. Not only were the top officials often representatives of the colonizers, but they violated Weberian principles by involving themselves too deeply in political struggles, favoring expatriate commercial interests, and treating local people unfairly. Ladipo Adamolekun, a longtime student of African bureaucracies, recommends a small career civil service with many functions removed from central

---

[2] In Britain as early as 1684 observers saw the value of secure tenure for those who handled money: "If it come to be a practice to put by the old clerk on admitting a new Teller [of the Exchequer], it will tempt the old clerk, who hath soe many opportunities, to provide for himself by sinister ways in the Teller's Lifetime" (quoted in Parris 1969: 26).

government responsibility. He also stresses the importance of political accountability for high-level officials. To him, the British Westminster model – in which civil servants provide confidential advice to ministers – does not work in the African context. Secrecy in dealings between bureaucrats and political appointees facilitates corruption and self-seeking. Thus the civil service in Africa ought to operate in an open environment where ordinary citizens and interested groups can monitor their behavior (Adamolekun 1993: 43–44).

Building from a very different history, the post-Communist economies must create new governments on a base of socialist institutions that are poorly adapted to present-day responsibilities. Like the post-colonial countries, the boundary between government administration and the private economy is blurred. In spite of a past structure based on hierarchical control, the public sector of today is not well organized. Decisions are often inconsistent, lack a legal basis, and are inordinately delayed. Implementation of reforms is frequently poor (Collins 1993: 325–329). Although the transitional countries in Eastern Europe and Asia face difficult tasks in creating a professional and honest civil service system, they have one advantage over many developing countries: They have a well-educated population capable of performing the tasks of modern government. However, many people need retraining to be able to take on the new responsibilities required of civil servants in a market economy (ibid.: 335).

There are two basic ways to reduce corrupt incentives in the public sector. First, the government can reform the system of public employment. Second, it can distance itself from the actual provision of services by contracting with private firms. Each has advantages and disadvantages. I begin with the basics of civil service restructuring including pay reform, conflicts of interest, incentive systems, and the control of corruption in hierarchies. The chapter concludes with a discussion of contracting out.

Pay Reform

Some developing countries have very poorly paid civil servants. At independence, most former colonies inherited civil service pay scales that exceeded private sector wages, but this advantage often has eroded over time. A similar pattern prevails in Eastern Europe, the former Soviet Union, and Latin America (Haque and Sahay 1996: 11; Reid and Scott 1994: 52). Pay has fallen in many countries relative not only to private sector wages but also to civil service pay in the past. In a sample of twenty-one countries in the late eighties and early nineties real wages fell at an annual average rate of 1.4 percent. The countries varied from a fall of 17.7 percent per year in Bulgaria during 1989–1992 to an increase of 4.4 percent in Ghana between 1986 and 1989 (Haque and Sahay 1996: 4).[3]

Wage scales have also become compressed. For example, in all but one of thirteen African countries, high-skill wages declined more than low-skill wages between 1975 and 1985 (Haque and Sahay 1996: 6). By the mid-1980s, the salary of top civil servants was less than ten times the lowest-paid rank in many African countries (Nunberg and Nellis 1995: 28). In such cases highly skilled employees will be difficult to attract, and there may be excess demand for low-skilled jobs. Reform programs have frequently sought to decompress salaries. Thus in Ghana the ratio moved from 2.5 to 1 in 1984 to 10 to 1 in 1991 – short of the reformers' goal of 13 to 1, but substantial progress nevertheless (ibid.: 27). At the same time, low-skilled workers may earn a premium over the comparable private sector wage. For example, public managers, engineers, and accountants in Trinidad and Tobago earned less than their private sector counterparts, and low-skilled workers earned more than twice the minimum wage in the private sector (Reid and Scott 1994: 48).

If public sector pay is very low, corruption is a survival strategy. One should be careful, however, not to exaggerate the public/private disparity. In most cases total remuneration includes not just formal wages but also perks such as housing or health care. These in-kind benefits become especially valuable during periods of high inflation. World Bank figures show that benefits as a percent of total compensation ranged from 20 to over 80 percent in the countries studied (Nunberg and Nellis 1995: 26; Reid and Scott 1994: 50).

But even a generous estimate of the value of perks would not close the pay gap in all countries (Reid and Scott 1994). In these cases, officials are likely to take second jobs or accept payoffs as salary supplements. Some may even operate businesses that can profit from their government positions. The problem is an old one. In Great Britain in the late eighteenth century a government commission worried that reducing the salary of officials will "recoil upon the public, by creating new claims for consideration, which must in justice be satisfied" (quoted in Chester 1981: 144). A recent cross-country study finds a negative association between civil service wages (relative to private sector wages in manufacturing) and the level of corruption (Van Rijckeghem and Weder

---

[3] Consider two other well-documented examples. In Peru in 1987 salaries in the tax administration had fallen to 33 percent of their 1971 level. During the same period the number of employees more than doubled (Das-Gupta and Mookherjee 1998: 265). In North Yemen salaries declined in real terms by up to 56 percent between 1971 and 1986 (Sultan 1993).

1997). Another piece of indirect evidence is the disparity between civil service pay and income. For example, salaries made up only 33 percent of the income of officials in Zaire in 1986, down from almost 100 percent in 1969 (MacGaffey 1991: 14). In Tanzania wages and benefits averaged 40 percent of household expenses, and the government encouraged officials to seek outside employment (Mans 1994: 378–380).

Sometimes low-paid, high-skill jobs in the civil service simply go unfilled, as revealed in a recent study of Guyana and Jamaica (Kitchen 1994: 121). But things may be even worse when these jobs are filled – because payoffs may be making up the wage gap. This helps explain why people will pay to obtain jobs that on the surface seem quite undesirable. In some developing countries there is a lively market for positions in the bureaucracy that generate large bribes (Wade 1982, 1984). Positions in corrupt police departments are likely to be especially valuable (Alfiler 1986: 39; Pasuk and Sungsidh 1994: 99–129). Jobs in departments with few such opportunities, such as foreign service, may attract few qualified applicants.

If government pay scales do not reward those with specialized skills, a selection bias will operate. Some people, qualified for public sector work, seek jobs in the private sector at home or abroad. Skilled workers, even those trained by the government itself, exit, leaving the less qualified behind. In the absence of corruption and moonlighting, a labor market equilibrium arises with those of low skill concentrated in low-paid government jobs they are unqualified to perform. Of course, some applicants may be especially committed to government service, but there may not be enough of them to staff the bureaucracy, and the public-spirited may not be well qualified on other grounds. If the system is in equilibrium, the marginal worker will be one who finds a government job at least as good a private sector job, but there may be many inframarginal workers who are not employable at the private sector wage.[4] After many years have passed, the civil service will be disproportionately

---

[4] One caveat is in order here. In some very poor countries estimates of the wages of skilled workers in the urban sector may not be meaningful because the sector is very small with wage levels affected by multinationals' pay scales determined outside the country. Such jobs are rationed, and their wages do not represent the opportunity wage of public employees. Information on earnings in the informal sector may provide a more accurate measure of private opportunities. This is indicated by successful efforts to reduce civil service employment levels in some African countries. Furthermore, the state may have a policy of guaranteeing jobs to all high school or college graduates or use public employment as a way to soak up excess labor that would otherwise be unemployed. The problem in such cases is not low pay, but excess employment (Nunberg and Nellis 1995: 15–16).

staffed with two kinds of workers: low-productivity workers who are not employable in seemingly "comparable" jobs in the private sector and those willing to accept bribes (Besley and McLaren 1993).

Given this distribution of talent, production processes and service delivery systems may be designed both to require few skills and to produce corrupt opportunities. Under such conditions, civil service reform must be thoroughgoing if there is to be any hope of success. Increasing pay and improving working conditions may have little impact on performance. In addition, new hires must replace much of the existing work force. A careful redesign of public programs will also be needed to reduce incentives for corruption and create incentives for productive activity. This conclusion is consistent with Van Rijckeghem and Weder's (1997) attempt to explain changes in the corruption index within countries over time. As in the cross-country regressions, the quality of the bureaucracy was negatively associated with the level of corruption, but wage levels were unimportant.

Civil service reform is part of many reform projects supported by international organizations, but they are often poorly designed (Nunberg and Nellis 1995; United Nations Development Programme 1997b). To succeed, reformers need to know the value of perks and their distribution, the relationship between public sector wages and family income for civil servants, the importance of corruption and conflicts of interest in affecting public decisions, the productivity of comparable public and private workers, macroeconomic conditions, and the size and role of the informal economy. The government needs to know whether a modest offer of severance pay will be taken up by a significant number of government workers. If so, wages can be raised and employment cut without undue strain. In some past reform programs, absorption of dismissed workers into the agricultural and informal sectors has been less difficult than some anticipated, especially in Africa (World Bank 1991: 16).

The strain of reform can be reduced by complementary policies to create jobs in the private sector and to encourage businesses to come out from underground. A good start might focus on the creation of an honest tax collection system. This would both assure revenue for the state and encourage firms to join the formal economy. One might then follow by cutting the civil service as private sector growth permits. Unfortunately, growth itself will cause its own problems – because existing corrupt officials will seek a share of the new wealth by imposing new restrictions on private firms. This problem may require unorthodox solutions. Reformers may need to take away work from already underutilized officials in order to reduce their access to bribes. As underemployed officials spend less time on public sector work, they are likely to get second jobs in the private sector. Once this happens, it may be easier to ease them out entirely. Structural changes in the operation of government should be combined with more conventional proposals to raise pay and improve working conditions. The goal is not only to deter corruption among existing officials but also to attract more qualified applicants for public sector jobs.

Conflicts of Interest

Conventional civil service systems attempt to insulate career officials from politics and to pay them adequate salaries. These are important goals, but they are only part of the task of creating a professional civil service. Even if pay is at a parity with private sector earnings and political involvement is forbidden, officials may face incentives to use their positions for private economic gain. Some countries, even though they outlaw bribery, have done little to control economic conflicts of interest.

Conflicts of interest were rife in the early days of the American republic. Postmasters published newspapers, treating themselves to free postage; whiskey tax collectors owned taverns and waived taxes on their suppliers; and some customs officials were prominent merchants (Prince 1977). Similarly, in post-colonial Africa, many countries encouraged public officials to engage in business activities that overlapped with their official duties. The resulting conflicts of interest and corruption seriously undermined state efficiency (Adamolekun 1993: 39–40, 42). Widespread conflicts presently exist in Russia, Eastern Europe, and China (Chow 1997; Collins 1993: 326). In China, where many joint ventures involve government partnerships with private business, the government has urged cadres to "drop into the sea of commerce" (Burns 1993: 358). The problem of divided loyalties is obvious. Officials may unduly favor the businesses in which they have an interest at the expense of other firms that could perform public tasks more inexpensively or competently. Similar favoritism is possible in the regulatory and privatization contexts. No bribery is necessary. Officials simply follow their own economic self-interest.

Because of these concerns, most developed countries forbid civil servants from involvement in decisions in which they have a financial interest. In many cases, both civil servants and top political appointees must disclose their financial assets at least to a public agency, and top officials may be required to place their assets in a blind trust. Acceptance of gifts or honoraria is also regulated.

Ethics-in-government rules and legal constraints developed gradually in the United States but are today pervasive (Gilman 1995; Roberts and

Doss 1992). The first code of ethics in the United States was promulgated by the postmaster general in 1829 (Gilman 1995: 64–66). Today a mixture of ethical codes and statutory requirements constrains public officials. Principles of Ethical Conduct for Government Officers and Employees are contained in a fourteen-point executive order (Executive Order 12674, as amended October 17, 1990; Gilman 1995: 65). Many of its provisions were given teeth by the Ethics in Government Reform Act of 1989 and regulations issued by the Office of Government Ethics in 1992 (5 CFR 2635). The Executive Order deals with both the acceptance of benefits and the discharge of duties. Officials are not permitted to "use public office for private gain" and are not to hold financial interests that conflict with their duties, use inside information for personal profit, or accept gifts. Other provisions deal with the responsible performance of duties. Both the payment and receipt of bribes are criminal offenses. The receipt of a salary from sources outside government is against the law, as are payments to officials for representing a private party in a "particular matter" in which the United States has an interest. The law applies both to public officials and to those who pay them (18 U.S.C. §§ 201, 203, 207, 208; Chakrabarti, Dausses, and Olson 1997: 597–605). Finally, officials must avoid the appearance of violating the law even if their conduct technically complies with it.

By way of comparison, French and Canadian conflict-of-interest restrictions have similar goals, but use different methods. French law focuses more on administrative than criminal remedies compared with the United States, but shares the fundamental goal of avoiding "an unwholesome alliance between personal financial interest and the exercise of the power of the state" (Rohr 1991:284). Nevertheless, French restrictions seem, in practice, less stringent. Financial disclosure of assets is not required as a routine matter, and post-employment restrictions are poorly enforced (ibid.: 284–286). Canadian and British rules are also less restrictive. Parliamentary government puts the Prime Minister in charge of the legislative agenda. This means that, unlike in the United States, conflict-of-interest laws are unlikely to impose more stringent controls on executive branch personnel than on members of parliament. Civil servants are regulated by administrative rules, not statutes (Stark 1992: 429).

The United States restricts the political activities of civil servants to avoid making public servants dependent on political party connections. In contrast, in France a common career path is to move from the civil service into electoral politics. Civil servants can run for office without losing their civil service status and can hold local office. If they win election to the French parliament, they must take a leave of absence but can return with no loss in rank. Between 1958 and 1986, 33 percent of the members of the National Assembly came from the civil service (Rohr 1991: 287). The value of such a system depends upon the existence of a respected civil service. In developing countries with such a tradition, the French model may have merit. In others, where the civil service is corrupt and patronage-ridden, a stricter separation of administration and politics along American lines seems preferable.

In practice, the most difficult enforcement problems concern job seeking. Although in the United States federal government outright quid pro quos seem fairly well controlled by the code of conduct and the legal sanctions behind it, officials are often hired after they leave government by firms that have business with their previous governmental employer. The code of conduct states that "employees shall not engage in outside employment or activities, including seeking or negotiating for employment, that conflict with official Government duties and responsibilities." Subject to several conditions, former officials cannot represent others before their former employer within two years of termination. The ban is not absolute, however, but applies only to issues on which the person worked within a year of leaving government [18 U.S.C. § 207 (a)–(d); Chakrabarti, Dausses, and Olson 1997: 608–612]. President Clinton tightened these requirements for senior officials, asking them to pledge to avoid dealings with government for five years after leaving his administration (Executive Order 12834 of January 20, 1993; Gilman 1995: 75).

The American mix of codes of conduct and criminal, administrative, and civil sanctions is complex and not always easy to understand and interpret. Some critics argue that American conflict-of-interest laws are intrusive and counterproductive (Anechiarico and Jacobs 1997; Roberts and Doss 1992). According to these critics, the rules introduce too much red tape, stifle creativity, and discourage qualified people from joining the public service. Even if the United States model is too complex to be readily exported, however, it can still provide guidelines for countries beginning to develop norms of professional bureaucratic behavior. The harshest critics of the American system do not seriously argue that procurement officers ought to allowed to own shares in their contractors or accept salaries or large gifts from firms with which they do business. Yet in many developing countries such practices have only recently been recognized as troublesome. To prevent government service from becoming a cynical route to easy wealth, all countries need a basic conflict-of-interest program that stresses ethical conduct backed up by legal sanctions. But simple and basic rules of behavior are the best place to start – especially if one wishes to avoid turning the oversight process itself into a locus of corruption.

Carrots and Sticks

Pay reform, merit recruitment, and controls on outside interests and political involvement are necessary first steps. Sometimes reformers can change the nature of the service to reduce corrupt incentives, but this is not always possible. Tax collectors, policemen, procurement specialists, and regulatory officials will always face corrupt incentives. Thus effective corruption control also requires a credible system of rewards and punishments. Formal legal sanctions provide an important backup, but incentives within the bureaucracy can also be used to reduce the incidence of corruption. Both carrots and sticks are needed to encourage efficiency and limit payoffs. Incentives can stress individual performance or provide rewards and punishments tied to group performance.

The most obvious deterrent to corruption is a credible, apolitical monitoring system that searches out corrupt officials. If civil service employment is well paid, corrupt officials suffer real pain if they are caught and forced out. One form of sanction is a pension that will be received only if the worker retires under honorable conditions (Becker and Stigler 1974). But such oversight is not enough. Loss of a job is a one-time penalty that is not tied to the marginal benefits of individual corrupt deals. Improved pay reduces the value of accepting bribes but may not reduce the value to zero. High pay may simply increase the bribe an official demands in order to overcome the risks of losing what is now a desirable job. Officials may go from being "lean and mean" to being "fat and mean."[5] The incidence of bribery may fall as fewer officials solicit or accept payoffs, but the size of each bribe increases. Thus some rewards and punishments should be tied to the bureaucrat's level of performance. In the previous chapter I discussed the way punishments could be tied to officials' behavior. Here I focus on positive incentives for good performance.

Civil service systems are often managed in a way that undervalues performance. For example, in many Latin America countries rigid rule-bound systems set wages using technical criteria unrelated to market realities. Nonwage allowances, distributed with little concern for productivity, exacerbate the problem. Because of worries about corruption and favoritism, centralized systems control expenditure, employment, and performance reviews. Managers have little discretion. With no reward for good performance, however, if managers were granted greater discretion, they might abuse it by hiring "unqualified personnel simply to keep politically important clients satisfied . . . [and] dispense

---

[5] "India: Belt Loosening," *The Economist,* August 2, 1997. See also "India: Taxing Again," *The Economist,* September 29, 1997.

wages, promotions and other perquisites on the basis of favoritism rather than employee performance . . ." (Reid and Scott 1994: 45). The answer is not ever more rigid and overreaching input controls but reforms that stress performance and reward managers who achieve public sector goals (ibid.: 46–47).

Sometimes bonuses can be tied to the value of the public service provided. Recall that bribery sometimes acts as an incentive fee for bureaucrats. In cases where corruption's only efficiency cost stems from its illegality, the payments could be legalized. The effectiveness of such a strategy depends upon the extent to which the servers "own" a portion of the payments so that they have an incentive to speed up service. For example, an agency might establish dual tracks – expensive fast tracks for those who value speed and a slower track for the rest. A share of the "speed" payment could then be used to reward officials for good performance (Paul 1995: 163).

Many public and private agents are responsible for making decisions with financial consequences that far exceed their pay levels. In such cases it is unrealistic to suppose that incentive bonuses can equal a high proportion of the value of the benefit dispensed. The evidence presented above on overall pay levels and corruption suggests, however, that it is sufficient to make officials' wages comparable to the earnings of those with similar skills in the private sector. Officials would earn both a base pay and an incentive bonus tied to performance so that their overall earnings would equal their expected pay in the private sector. If there is some uncertainty about the connection between effort and measurable outcomes, the division of earnings into base wage and performance pay would depend upon employees' willingness to accept uncertainty (Weitzman and Kruse 1990: 100–102).

Incentive systems can be effective, but they must be designed with care to avoid giving bureaucrats monopoly power that they can use to extract increased levels of rents (Rose-Ackerman 1978: 85–108). Officials must be unable to create onerous new conditions that they can then waive in return for payments. Thus British reformers in the 1830s urged that salaries be substituted for fees as a means of remunerating public officials. A parliamentary committee worried that accepting fees exposed a high official "to the suspicion of occasioning impediments to the exercise of [official] functions" (quoted by Chester 1981: 135).

As an alternative to individualized incentive pay systems, rewards can be given to work groups or public agencies based on their overall performance. For many public services this may be the best solution. If joint efforts are decomposed into individual rewards, the result can be a hostile, adversarial work environment (Mitchell, Lewin, and Lawler

1990: 64–67). This concern has led some students of the private labor market to argue in favor of rewarding workers for the achievement of group goals. Such incentive systems work best if employees participate in setting working conditions (Blinder 1990). But sometimes teamwork is the problem to which individualized incentive pay is the solution. Public officials can work together to provide high-quality services or to maximize bribery revenues. Teamwork among officials is the hallmark of many cases of police corruption. If performance can be measured, individualized incentive pay systems can be a tool to break up circles of corruption.

Public enterprises ought to be obvious candidates for institutional rewards based on performance. Although some might argue for outright privatization, this option is not always available. If such enterprises are selling goods and services to private customers, outcome measures will usually be available. Both New Zealand and Korea have tied rewards to performance with positive results (Scott 1996: 21–29; World Bank 1991: 28). In Korea the annual incentive bonuses earned by the firm are distributed to all staff, but the firms themselves have also introduced internal evaluation systems. Thus the state rewards the enterprise as a whole, and the firm's managers establish internal reward structures. Such techniques look promising but require comprehensive and reliable data on the performance of public enterprises. This information condition must be satisfied before rewards for good performance can be instituted in developing countries.

Both individual and group-based incentive payments will frequently be more difficult to administer in the public sector compared with the private sector. Outside of public enterprises selling commercial products, good performance is often hard to judge. As a consequence, government agencies may develop measurable output indicators that are not the ultimate goals of policy (Scott 1996: 30–43). If pay is tied to these output measures, officials may try to game the system to earn high bonuses. The experience of developed countries with performance pay in government has been mixed at best. New Zealand is usually seen as a success story although implementation problems persist. There are tradeoffs between allocative efficiency and technical efficiency. Individuals may spend too much time negotiating over what outputs to measure and how performance will be rewarded (Campos and Pradhan 1997: 443; Scott 1996). Performance evaluation and incentive pay in Britain have apparently not been successful (Madron 1995). Evaluations of recent reforms in the United States are not very encouraging, but it is difficult to know whether the problem is the system itself or the weakness of its implementation (Ingraham 1993, 1996: 260; Perry 1988–1989).

As for group incentives, empirical evidence from the private sector suggests that a participatory workplace will succeed best under certain conditions: stable aggregate demand, low unemployment, wage and salary compression, and long investor time horizons (Levine and Tyson 1990: 214). In short, the conditions for successful worker participation may not be met in public employment systems. Furthermore, stable employment and wage compression are in conflict with the need for many public sector agencies to reduce employment and provide pay parity with the private sector.

Clearly, designing an effective incentive system can be difficult and is not always the best solution. Nevertheless, there are a range of cases in which it will be a valuable anticorruption tool. There have been some success stories, particularly in the revenue area. Most of the tax collection reform efforts studied by Arindam Das-Gupta and Dilip Mookherjee (1998: 257) combined the creation of a relatively autonomous bureaucracy with a budget linked in part to its success at collecting revenue. Reforms of revenue collection services in several African countries had similar features (Dia 1996). For example, Ghana in the eighties tried an enclave approach to tax and customs reform by creating a new National Revenue Service (NRS). Corruption, moonlighting, and other inefficiencies were common. Salaries were low, and accountability was poor. Under the reform, the most corrupt existing officials were dismissed or retired. Pay and working conditions were improved. Increased salaries were accompanied by incentive systems to reward strong performance by individuals and by the agency as a whole. Revenue targets were established, and the NRS was given a bonus of 3.5 percent of tax revenue and 2.5 percent of customs revenue. Between 1984 and 1988 tax and customs revenue rose from 6.6 to 12.3 percent of GDP. The reforms illustrate the importance of combining improved base pay with incentives for good performance. The program was a relative success, but it was not without problems. The rest of the civil service chafed at the special treatment afforded tax collectors. After all, the bonuses received by the NRS increased not only if effort increased but also if taxes rose because of an exogenous increase in GDP.[6] Furthermore, the Ministry of Finance objected to its loss of authority. In 1991 revenue collection was again placed under the authority of the Ministry of Finance although it retained some of its independence (Dia 1996: 86–90; Terkper 1994).

[6] In Britain in the eighteenth century chief clerks shared between them one-third of the fees received. Their income from that source rose from £330 a year in 1711 to £700 in the 1750s to £1278 at the height of the American War of Independence. Fees were often unrelated to the amount of work involved (Chester 1981: 134).

In general, incentive payments based on performance will be more likely to be successful if additional effort actually does produce substantial gains, if employees are not too risk averse, if effort and results can be measured, and if officials have sufficient discretion to respond to incentives (Klitgaard 1997: 19). Widespread corruption is evidence that monetary payments can buy something valuable from officials. Thus incentive-based plans might begin with those systems now permeated with corruption. A successful reform would both limit illegal payoffs and improve performance.

Corruption in Hierarchies

Another crucial variable in reform efforts is the relationship between high- and low-level corruption. There are two variants. In the first, "bottom-up," variety low-level officials collect bribes and share them with superiors either directly or indirectly through the purchase of their offices. Initially, payoffs to superiors may be a means of buying their silence, but if payments are institutionalized, they become a condition of employment, organized by superiors for their own gain.[7] In some cases, a pyramid operates – each tier purchases its positions from the one above it. If "street-level bureaucrats" have the most discretionary interactions with the public, the bottom-up pattern holds. Police corruption frequently originates with the power that officers on the beat exercise over businesses – both legal and illegal. For example, in Nepal policemen involved in the transport of hashish and the enforcement of highway regulations collected illegal fees that were shared with district officers (Alfiler 1986: 46). In tax and customs agencies lower-level officials dealing with taxpayers frequently must share their payoffs with superiors. In one Korean case officials explained the size of their bribe requests by claiming that the payoff must be shared with their director, division chief, and section chief (ibid.: 41).

Second, a "top-down" pattern may operate where corrupt superior officials buy the silence of subordinates by sharing the gains through high pay and perks or under-the-table benefits. In Korea, where top officials view their subordinates as "family," it used to be considered appropriate for heads of government offices to raise illicit funds and openly give a share to subordinates (Lee 1986: 86). Higher-ups may also tolerate the petty corruption of subordinates to assure their complicity in a corrupt

---

[7] Cadot (1987). Dey (1989) and Rose-Ackerman (1978: 170–179) note that interactions may also occur between officials with no formal hierarchical connections. For example, a person trying to build a house may need to obtain the permission of several different government offices. Dey suggests that networks of corrupt officials can develop under such conditions.

system. If most major decisions are made at the top, but low-level officials provide essential inputs, the top-down pattern should prevail. For example, the award of major contracts is likely to be the preserve of top officials, but they will need help in assessing bids and overseeing implementation. Thus in Nepal higher-level officials arrange "commissions" on public contracts which are collected by field representatives who take their cut and pass up the rest (Ostrom 1996: 212). Alternatively, top officials may collect most of the illicit income but assure that low-level officials earn high legal salaries to buy docility and peace. This is apparently the case in Gabon where top politicians benefit from oil industry payoffs while the civil service earns high salaries (Rose-Ackerman and Stone 1998).

Several recent theoretical efforts have tried to capture aspects of this phenomenon. In one model of bottom-up corruption, high-level officials can cover up corruption of subordinates in return for a share of their gains (Cadot 1987). The superiors are not active in organizing the system, but simply wait for denunciation letters to arrive and then decide whether to accept the proffered payoff. "As high-ranking officials cover up lower-level corruption in exchange for bribes, corruption at high levels of an administration feeds on lower-level corruption, while at the same time shielding it, and each level is encouraged by the other" (ibid.: 224). The model has two possible equilibria. In the first, only low-level bribery occurs. Subordinates are not willing to pay enough to eliminate the risk of being detected and fired. They simply accept the risk as part of the cost of obtaining payoffs. In the second, the rewards of corruption are higher, and corruption permeates the hierarchy. Low-level bribes are high enough to be used, in part, to pay superiors who receive information about corrupt deals.

In another bottom-up model, low-level corrupt officials calculate the chance that superiors will hear of their corruption and demand a bribe (Basu, Bhattacharya, and Mishra 1992). If they do not satisfy this payoff demand, they must also figure in the risk of criminal penalties. This problem can be modeled as either an infinite chain or a finite hierarchy with an honest official at the top. The model is structured so that officials always make deals, and the penalty is never paid. Nevertheless, higher levels of the penalty increase the threat point of higher-ups, thus reducing the benefits to the official at the bottom and thereby deterring bribery. Because expected penalties imposed on bribe-takers are not a function of the size of the bribe, they will deter corruption and simultaneously raise the level of individual bribes that are paid. The high bribes that are occasionally paid are evidence of the success, not the failure, of the strategy.

If corruption pervades a hierarchy, solutions that appear reasonable in other contexts can be counterproductive. Reformers have frequently recommended rotating officials so that they are unable to develop the close, trusting relations needed to reduce the risks of accepting payoffs. But the rotation of officials may not be desirable if it makes other types of incentives ineffective and gives corrupt superiors undue power. Thus rotation of Indian tax audit officials makes it impossible to follow up on assessments that are appealed by taxpayers. This makes it difficult to reward these officials on the basis of their success in ferreting out tax evasion (Das-Gupta and Mookherjee 1998: 178). If an entire agency is corrupt, superiors can use their ability to reassign officials as a punishment for honesty. A study of corruption in an irrigation system in India found that such practices were common (Wade 1982, 1984), and they have been observed in corrupt police forces in the United States and Thailand (Pasuk and Sungsidh 1994: 99–120; Sherman 1974). The basic problem is that lower-level officials are at the mercy of their superiors and have no way to appeal transfers linked to their failure to join a corrupt system.

Halfway measures are unlikely to be successful in such cases. If reformers cannot simply start over with a new collection of public officials and a new set of rewards and punishments, the best medium-term solutions are those outlined in the previous chapter that change the nature of public service provision and reduce the number of civil servants. Officials who remain need to have avenues for lodging complaints and some assurance that the state will follow up. If corruption has pervaded the bureaucratic hierarchy, ordinary civil service reform measures are too limited. Instead, solutions that improve the public accountability of government are necessary. I discuss these later when considering the political sources of corruption. Another option is to turn over certain government tasks to private firms. As I argue below, however, this is unlikely to be a valuable tool unless state agencies are reformed as well.

The Rediscovery of Contract

In the late twentieth century reformers have rediscovered the virtues of contract as a means of separating administration from politics. In the United States, Great Britain, and elsewhere in the British Commonwealth, efforts to deregulate and downsize government have led to a rethinking of public officials' role. The aim is to keep the civil service as small as possible, eliminate many government activities, and contract out the remaining tasks to private firms, both for-profit and nonprofit.

In Great Britain local governments are required to open core government services to competitive tender – with the government department permitted to be one of the bidders. Both Australia and New Zealand also invite bids from private sector providers for some government services (Campos and Pradhan 1997: 441). In Great Britain although existing government departments win the bulk of the bids, the process does seem to improve performance (Boyard, Gregory, and Martin 1991; Painter 1991, 1994; Rhodes 1994; Shaw, Fenwick, and Foreman 1994). A similar development is proceeding apace in the United States (Maranto and Schultz 1991: 173–174). Private firms provide not only such mundane services as trash collection and street maintenance but also prisons, security services, and check writing (DiIulio 1994). Some federal agencies employ more contract employees than civil servants (Ingraham 1996: 257).

Although this movement has been greeted with praise, the historical record suggests the need for caution. Nineteenth-century New York, for example, used private firms to clean the streets and collect the trash, but private contractors failed to provide even minimally acceptable service. Patronage and payoffs dominated the award of contracts, and the city did not hold private firms to the terms of their contracts. The system was no better than a public bureaucracy dominated by patronage employment. Service improved only when the system was taken over by a strong, independent public official (Darrough 1998). Of course, this case does not demonstrate that contracting out can never work, but it does caution against trading one form of corruption and self-dealing for another.

Contracting out to private firms does not necessarily mean that the state obtains the benefits that flow from competitive markets. Clearly, the government will obtain none of the benefits of competition if only a single provider is available. For example, some studies of the performance of public and private utilities suggest that public firms are more efficient (Ross 1988: 24–36). The private firms are monopolies that must be regulated to prevent the accumulation of excess profits. The appropriate contrast is between public production and regulated private production. Nevertheless, studies of a wide range of public services, particularly those provided by local governments, demonstrate that in many situations private provision can improve cost-efficiency without a decline in quality (Borcherding, Pommerehne, and Schneider 1982: 130–133). But careful monitoring is required. In many instances the difficulty of writing enforceable contracts will counsel against a wholesale turnover of service provision to private firms. A city can contract out towing services but not the arrest of criminal suspects. It can contract for food service in prisons, but should be more cautious about contracting for the operation of entire prisons (Rose-Ackerman 1992: 177–178).

One of the most controversial forms of contracting out is "tax farming" where private firms or individuals purchase the right to collect taxes by paying the state a fixed fee. In spite of the risks involved, some positive examples exist. However, absent stringent monitoring, systems of "tax farming" are unlikely to function well because tax collectors have an incentive to extract excess revenue from taxpayers (Azabou and Nugent 1988; Das-Gupta and Mookherjee 1998: 256; Stella 1992). For example, the Ottoman Empire relied heavily on tax farming, auctioning off the rights to the high bidders. As the power of the state weakened, the system was subject to abuse (Azabou and Nugent 1988: 686–689). In contrast, a study of tax farming in Tunisian municipalities demonstrates that it can function well by shifting the risks of fluctuating revenues from the government to the tax farmers. Abuses were limited by several factors: Tax rates were uniform and well publicized, abused taxpayers could appeal to the courts or complain to municipal authorities, and tax-farming franchises were of limited duration so tax collectors needed to protect their reputations (ibid.: 700). An ongoing experiment in Pakistan may also produce positive results. Pakistan imposes license fees on televisions, VCRs, and satellite dishes, but few people paid the fees. A fixed price contract with a private firm has increased collections but has been accompanied by some allegations of intimidation.[8]

As these examples demonstrate, incentive schemes can be used only if the level of performance can be measured by external monitors. Incentive payments do not eliminate the need for oversight, but they redirect it to the review of outputs, not inputs. Monitoring and sanctions for corruption must remain as a backup.

In some cases the current push to deregulate, privatize, and contract out has been combined with improvements in the provision of core government functions. In others, downsizing has had the unfortunate consequence of furthering corrupt relationships, establishing private monopolies, and undermining the legitimate functions of government. Poorer countries, especially those with very unequal income and wealth distributions, need to create an effective civil service system at the same time as they decentralize and downsize (Adamolekun 1993: 43). They should not rush to downsize government if the result will be to concentrate wealth further while maintaining corrupt relationships. Instead, for core government services such as street repair, sewage treatment, or trash collection, they should work first to reform the operation of the public agency. Privatization might come later if the government has the

---

[8] "Tax Collection: On the Farm," *The Economist*, August 22, 1998.

capacity to provide effective oversight of public contracts. Otherwise the result will simply be the creation of new sources of private gain at the expense of the general public. More generally, the development of a vibrant private sector requires a well-functioning government to protect property rights and regulate market failures (Collins 1993: 329).

Conclusions

Civil service reform is expensive and politically difficult, and it may appear beyond the capacity of many poor countries. Yet it cannot be avoided. In some countries government pay has fallen rapidly in recent years as fiscal pressures have led governments to cut spending. Sometimes World Bank and IMF insistence on reductions in the wage bill as a condition for assistance has unwittingly contributed to corruption. Under pressure from international institutions, borrower countries carry out across-the-board pay cuts or wage freezes because they are politically easier to manage than the selective firing of workers (World Bank 1991: 16). The newly impoverished public employees turn to bribery as a way of regaining some of their lost wages. Obviously, the World Bank and the IMF should stop these counterproductive policies. But many difficulties are internal to the politics of developing countries. Nations making good progress in achieving fiscal balance may jeopardize their success by bowing to pressure from civil servants for broad-based pay hikes. This is what happened, for example, in Ghana in 1992 when civil servants' wages were increased across the board by 80 percent (World Bank, 1995: 20). Pay increases may indeed be necessary for good performance, but only if the increases are tied to productivity and are accompanied by a reduction in the overall level of public sector employment. Reductions in the number of officials, however, are likely to be feasible only if jobs are available in the private sector. Policies that encourage the development of a well-functioning private sector can make civil service reform feasible.

The reforms discussed here and in the preceding chapter will work best if combined. Entrenched corruption needs to be fought both by the reform of the civil service and by changes in the nature of government work. If the underlying legal framework remains unchanged, a fall in corruption may yield few benefits. Some observers of the Italian situation, for example, claim that corruption has fallen but that the bureaucracy is performing poorly by mechanically enforcing restrictive rules. If the fundamental cause of corruption is the type and level of public intervention, reforms will be needed there as well. A reforming state should reduce the underlying incentives for payoffs by eliminating or restructuring programs and by simplifying tax laws and procurement requirements. It should also improve both positive and negative incentives in the form of civil service, procurement, and law enforcement reform.

Because everything cannot be done at once, the best place to start is with the demand for, and supply of, corrupt services. This means restructuring programs that generate corrupt incentives and reorganizing the civil service to allow professionals to make an honest living. Reform could begin with one or two key agencies – such as tax administration – or with a credible effort to carry out a key privatization in an open and transparent manner. Beginning with a narrow focus is pointless, however, unless it is eventually broadened. Otherwise, officials outside the reformed agency will resent the special treatment accorded one small group, and the reform itself will likely be overwhelmed by the background level of corruption.

A large task is to change public attitudes and to convince ordinary people that the government is serious about tackling corruption. This suggests an emphasis on reducing corruption where it is most obvious to citizens. It should begin with services that people are entitled to obtain for free. If the service is not a basic necessity, people may accept the introduction of a user fee to substitute for bribes. A next step is the reform of corrupt systems that permit people to avoid taxes or violate laws with impunity. In those cases credible reform must start at the top. A crackdown should reach the rich and powerful. If large taxpayers are required to pay their taxes, others may be more willing to go along. Focusing only on ordinary citizens generates resentment that can undermine the entire effort.

PART II

Corruption as a Cultural Problem

6

Bribes, Patronage, and Gift Giving

Corruption is the misuse of public power for private gain.[1] Agency–principal relationships in the public sector give rise to corrupt opportunities. This definition, however, simply assumes that a distinction exists between one's public and private roles. In many societies no such clear distinction exists. In the private sector, gift giving is pervasive and highly valued, and it seems natural to provide jobs and contracts to one's friends and relations. No one sees any reason not to carry over such practices into the public realm. In fact, the very idea of a sharp distinction between public and private life seems alien to many people.

Nevertheless, people in developing countries do make distinctions between appropriate and inappropriate behavior in terms of their own cultural norms. Formal surveys and informal discussions indicate frustration with corruption and suggest that expressions of toleration sometimes reflect both resignation and fear of reprisals against those who complain.[2] Furthermore, even if gift giving and patronage are well

---

[1] This chapter is a revised version of Rose-Ackerman (1998a).

[2] Tanzania's Commission on Corruption reported in 1996 that people were irritated with corruption but feared bodily harm if they reported incidents (Tanzania, Presidential Commission of Inquiry Against Corruption, 1996: 65–67). Field research in Kenya in the early 1990s demonstrated that most people believed that corruption was rife, with 80 percent having personally come across corruption at least twice in the past two years. About 83 percent believed that corruption was very damaging to the country, but the populace was resigned. Over 55 percent reported that they had paid bribes, and only 1 percent reported such demands to the police (Kibwana, Wanjala, and Okech-Owiti 1996: 110–113).

In Thailand gift giving is highly valued, and people believe that if an official provides good service, they should show their appreciation with a gift. These gifts are part of the patron–client relationship between ruler and ruled. In a recent

accepted, they may impose hidden costs that are not well appreciated by ordinary citizens. Economics cannot answer cultural questions, but it can help one understand the implications of a society's choices. Societies can ask whether they have ended up with cultural habits that impose costs on the ability of the economy to grow and the government to function efficiently.

This chapter distinguishes between bribes, prices, tips, and gifts. The difficulty of distinguishing gifts from bribes has its roots in their fundamental similarity. In neither case will the legal system enforce a quid pro quo. Thus the recipient of a bribe or a gift must use other informal methods. The final section outlines the benefits and costs that such informal transfers can have for developing countries and for those in transition from state socialism to a market economy.

Bribes, Gifts, Prices, and Tips

Payments, whether in money or in kind, can be characterized along two dimensions. First, does an explicit quid pro quo exist? If so, the transaction can be labeled a sale even if there is a long time lag between payment and receipt of the benefit. Both market sales and bribes involve reciprocal obligations. Gifts to charities or loved ones often do not explicitly involve reciprocity, although many do generate implicit obligations. The second dimension is the institutional positions of payers and payees. Are they agents or principals? A restaurant bill is paid to the owner; a tip, to the waiter. A speeding ticket is paid to the state; a bribe, to the police officer. Employers, sales agents, and customers can pay agents. Bosses give Christmas gifts to their employees, sales representatives give gifts to purchasing agents, and customers tip sales people for favorable service.

Some people, however, have duties to the public, or to some other amorphous group that lacks well-specified, sharp-eyed principals. Politicians, for example, can be described as the representatives of the public interest or of the citizens who elected them. Under either view, they have considerable discretion. The desire for reelection is a constraint, but one that does not always prevent lucrative side deals. Because the quid pro

study, people differentiated between gifts and bribes in terms of value. Small gifts were tokens of appreciation; large ones were illicit bribes. In the survey "corruption" was a form of behavior that "seeks to reap large profits with serious impacts on society" (Pasuk and Sungsidh 1994: 154). But value is relative. A businessman may view an automobile as a gift. A person observing the transfer may view it as a bribe. If the "normal" commission is 10 percent, anyone asking for 20 percent will be viewed as corrupt.

Table 1. Payments by clients or customers

	Quid pro quo	No explicit quid pro quo
Payment to principal	Price	Gift
Payment to agent	Bribe	Tip

quo is often vague, contributors commonly say they are giving gifts. Others disagree.

Concentrating only on these two dimensions – the existence of a quid pro quo and the presence or absence of agents – produces the four categories in Table 1 called bribes, tips, gifts, and market prices. Although the categories include the morally loaded terms "bribes" and "gifts," the table identifies payments only in terms of the agency relation and the existence of a quid pro quo. Even if no explicit trade is involved, there may be an implicit expectation of reciprocal behavior.

Gifts differ from prices by the lack of an explicit quid pro quo. But there may be more subtle links between gifts and beneficiaries' behavior. A university may start a new professional school in the hope of attracting donations, and a child may work hard in the hope of attracting parental gifts. Nevertheless, many gifts are purely altruistic transfers with no expectation of a material reward. They may provide psychological benefits such as the "warm glow" of sympathy, or the satisfaction of living up to a moral commitment (Andreoni 1988; Rose-Ackerman 1996a; Sen 1977) but no tangible gains. Some self-sacrificing gifts harm the giver, as when a person imposes sacrifices on family members or gives up his or her life for another person or for a cause.[3]

If individual gifts are large enough to have a marginal impact on the recipient's behavior, a quid pro quo is implicit. This will be true of many gifts to family members and some large donations to charities. In that case there is little functional difference between gifts given to further announced goals and those given under the condition that such goals be established. If conditional gifts create enforceable obligations, they are like sales except that the benefit given in return must be something that accords with the charity's purpose (Gordley 1995). Such gifts belong in the "price" box.

[3] See Monroe (1996), who interviewed people concerning their altruistic behavior and distinguishes between entrepreneurs, philanthropists, heros, and rescuers. Those in the last category included rescuers of Jews in Nazi Europe whose personal and familial sacrifices were extreme.

In terms of standard economic analysis, gifts come closer and closer to being prices as they move down the scale from gifts to charitable organizations and causes, to gifts to needy but unknown individuals, to gifts to friends and relatives, to gifts to people and institutions in a position to benefit you. But simple economics is only part of the story. Personal relations between giver and receiver or buyer and seller are an important dimension of many transactions that have intrinsic value independent of their role in regulating the transaction.[4]

Now consider the two agency relationships displayed in the table. Agents are generally paid by their principals, not outsiders, such as customers or sales agents. The principal needs to develop a system of remuneration and monitoring that gives agents an incentive to perform well. Most discussions of the relative merits of alternative remuneration schemes assume that laziness and shirking are the problem, not payoffs offered by a third party. There is a two-sided relationship between principal and agent operating with given background conditions.[5] Some scholars have brought in a third party and use their models to analyze the problem of corruption (Rose-Ackerman 1978; Tirole 1986, 1992). For some economists the fact that bribes are payments for services argues in their favor (Bayley 1966; Leff 1964). They look like prices. But, as I demonstrated in the previous chapters, this is a very limited analogy – payoffs to agents can have a range of distortionary effects on government and private sector activity.

Pervasive bribery may indicate that society has structured the agency relationship inefficiently. If customers commonly bribe agents, perhaps it would be more efficient to have the customers *hire* the agents to deal with their old principals. For example, suppose an automobile company provides free repair service to those who purchase its cars. In practice, customers eager for good service bribe repairmen to provide speedy, high-quality work. The fact that the customer is better at monitoring the repairman than the automobile company suggests that the service can be more efficiently provided by a contract between the customer and the repairman than by a contract between the repairman and the automobile company. In spite of this incentive for commercial bribery, the automobile company might continue to provide repairs as part of the warranty provided ex ante to buyers. Warranties improve a firm's competitive position by reducing the risk faced by customers, but like all

---

[4] In sociological analyses, personal connections are the key to gift giving. Donations to charitable organizations are not labeled gifts because they do not involve a personal connection (Zelizer 1994: 77–85).

[5] For citations to this work, see Laffont (1990), Rasmusen (1990: 133–222), Rose-Ackerman (1986), and Tirole (1986).

insurance policies, they create monitoring costs ex post (Cramton and Dees 1993: 366–367).

Similar issues arise in many professional service industries where customers buy the expertise of others. They can judge output – good health, a large damage award in a lawsuit – but cannot directly observe the quality of inputs. Is it more efficient to hire the professional directly or to pay a lump sum to a large organization (say an insurance company) that then monitors and reimburses the professionals? Should the outright sale of lawsuits to attorneys be permitted, thus avoiding the agency–principal problem altogether? Should the state subsidize legal services across the board?

To see the difficulties of the last possibility, suppose that the state provides free lawyers to anyone who brings a lawsuit and pays the lawyers a fixed fee. Suppose further that many clients make secret payments to their lawyers to induce greater work. If this type of commercial bribery is common, it implies that the sale of legal services should be privatized with a residual subsidized program for the indigent. In contrast, evidence that the parties to a lawsuit are paying judges to get favorable rulings does not imply that one should legalize such payments. They undermine the very idea of the rule of law. The judge is not the agent of the parties but has swore to uphold general legal principles. This is in the long-run interest of those who use the courts.

In the private sector a franchise arrangement is an intermediate solution to the problem of motivating agents. The ultimate sellers are independent businesses whose behavior is constrained by a franchise contract. If the principal – in this case the franchiser – benefits when "sales people" – in this case the franchisees – take a personal interest in selling the product, such arrangements may make sense. Franchisees earn profits for providing good service, rather than taking bribes for the same thing. This option is not always be available to the government. The National Parks Service can sign franchise arrangements with companies that provide food and lodging. A public authority that supplies housing units cannot do the same unless it writes a complex contract to assure that the goal of providing shelter to the needy is met.

The state's lack of organizational flexibility limits its ability to reorganize the agency relationship. A government uses agents where private businesses would simply sell their services directly. Conversely, the public sector uses contracts where private firms would vertically integrate because of monitoring difficulties. Sometimes deregulation and privatization can correct these difficulties, but some constraints are inherent in the special nature of government services. Legitimate public functions cannot by their nature be organized like private markets. This fact implies that all incentives for corruption in public programs cannot be eliminated.

With tips, the quid pro quo is vague, and service is usually delivered before the tip is paid. They are "legally optional, informally bestowed, the amount unspecified, variable, and arbitrary" (Zelizer 1994: 91). Tips permit customers to pass judgment on the quality of service in situations where business owners may have difficulty evaluating quality. If customers are better monitors than managers, tips make sense. In contrast, if management can infer good service from high levels of individual sales, it can give out the rewards itself. A restaurant might, for example, reward its waiters on the basis of the number of meals served, much as tips do. But such a scheme would be less effective than tipping. By basing rewards only on volume, managers could induce waiters to create bad feelings by rushing people out the door. Tying rewards to a mixture of volume and quality is more efficient, and allowing customers to pay agents directly for good service is one way to accomplish this. Tips would not be desirable for owners, however, if they caused agents to discriminate between customers in a way that undercut the revenues flowing to the principal. Imagine, for example, that waiters, like corrupt customs agents, gave diners discounts on their meals or served extra dishes in return for payoffs.

The Similarity of Bribes and Gifts

Gifts and bribes have one important similarity. In neither case can a disappointed individual go to court to demand payment or to insist on performance of the implicit contract. Alternative methods of assuring compliance must be designed if one wishes to induce others to act. In some cases, these extralegal mechanisms may be more effective and perhaps cheaper than those available to market traders.[6]

Several familiar informal enforcement mechanisms seem most relevant: trust, reputation, hostage taking, and reciprocal obligations (Cramton and Dees 1993; Williamson 1975, 1979). In many ordinary contracting contexts, these mechanisms are highly desirable. But they can facilitate corrupt deals as well as altruistic transfers. There may be a conflict between traits that seem virtuous in and of themselves, like trustworthiness, and the undesirable consequences they produce. An examination of bribery and gift giving helps one to see that otherwise

---

[6] Even gifts and bribes can sometimes give rise to legally enforceable obligations. In the case of gifts, both Anglo-American and Continental law make it quite easy to convert a gift into a legally binding transfer that also imposes obligations on the recipient (Gordley 1995).

admirable norms of behavior can, under some conditions, undermine efficiency and economic development.

Trust

In discussing the Sicilian Mafia, Diego Gambetta (1993) emphasizes the pervasive lack of trust in the Italian state. An increase in private property transactions occurred at a time when the state lacked the capacity to handle such transactions. The state failed to provide a reliable method of resolving disputes and managing private property transfers. The Mafia arose as a substitute. Other observers view the rise of "mafias" in Russia as due to a similar weakness of the state (Varese 1994).

Gambetta uses the word "trust" in two senses best kept separate. First, he points to the state's lack of competence and legitimacy. People do not trust the state to resolve disputes fairly and efficiently, so they look to alternatives. This meaning of trust has nothing to do with close personal ties. The relationship may be entirely at arm's length. In fact, one's trust in the state may be higher if officials are dispassionate and objective.[7] Second, people may trust each other because of close personal ties that depend on kinship, business links, or friendship. A person may trust his powerful friend to help him, not because the friend will apply the law fairly, but because he plays favorites.[8] Gambetta emphasizes how the failure of trust in either sense produces a demand for private protective services such as the Mafia.

In contrast, I stress how the second type of trust, based on personal ties, facilitates both corrupt and donative transfers.[9] This analysis complements Gambetta's discussion of the internal organization of Mafia "families" which demand unswerving loyalty from members. My concern is not with organized crime per se, but with the way trusting, personalized relations facilitate corrupt deals.

For example, a study of land reform in two towns in Brazil illustrates the way trust can maintain a corrupt system. In one town a corrupt program administration became entrenched because of personal rela-

---

[7] Empirical work has found that in the workplace trust can be created only by "procedural justice." Decisions must be fair and must be seen to be fair with opportunities for appeal (Kim and Mauborgne 1995).

[8] Consider the following Latin American quip: "A los amigos todo, a los enimigos nada, al extrano la ley" (For my friends everything, for my enemies nothing, for strangers the law).

[9] Barney and Hansen (1994: 184–186) call this "strong form trustworthiness" and discuss how it can give firms a competitive advantage. Hood (1996: 211–214) discusses how "contrived randomness" in the form of staff rotation and division of authority can help break up systematic cooperation that produces corruption and other "anti-system 'networking' activity."

tionships between agents from different agencies who all lived close to each other and established friendships outside the work environment. In the second town the program was generally honestly administered because officials had few interpersonal links so that officials of one agency were willing to respond to citizen complaints about those in other agencies. In some cases they helped the local people organize formal protests (Bunker and Cohen 1983).

Gift giving and bribery will be more common if legal dispute resolution mechanisms are costly and time consuming. If legal guarantees are not possible, trust is correspondingly more important. But the lack of a legal backup means that some transactions are less likely. Deals in which the bribe must be paid before the bribee performs may be too risky. The corrupted official who fails to deliver can claim that the payment he received was just a gift from a friend or admirer. Similarly, the recipient of a gift with implicit strings can characterize it as a bribe if the relationship sours. Both sides to the deal have an interest in blurring the meaning of the payment in the eyes of the outside world while keeping it quite explicit between themselves. Bribes will frequently be disguised as gifts to limit criminal liability.[10] But duplicity may make it difficult to insist that the official follow through.

Gifts that involve an unenforceable quid pro quo will be more likely if a trusting relationship between the parties already exists by reason of family ties or friendship. Thus gifts are often given to family members not only because the giver feels special affection, but also because the *recipient* has emotional bonds with the donor and may be more willing to perform his or her side of the implicit bargain.

By the same token, trust is important in corrupt deals. According to Gambetta, the lack of trust in government leads to the demand for private protective services. Conversely, the ability to establish trust based on close personal relationships helps reduce the risks of disclosure. It provides a guarantee of performance when payment and quid pro quo are separated in time. A public official may favor his own relatives in allocating concessions and other public benefits in return for a share of the benefits. He may do this not only because he cares about *them*, but also because they care about *him* and will be less likely than strangers to reveal the corrupt deal or to renege on the agreement. The interdependency of utilities reduces the risks to both participants (Schmid and Robison 1995).

---

[10] In Japan great care is taken to differentiate "gifted" monies by using only new bills and special envelopes. As a result, "bribes are often disguised as gifts by placing clean bills in a money envelope or by using properly wrapped gift certificates sold by department stores" (Zelizer 1994: 117).

The risk, of course, is that disgruntled family members may be especially dangerous. The interdependency of utility can mean that a bitter relative gets special pleasure in exposing the corrupt kinsman.[11] A corrupt ruler may end up wishing he had dealt with a cool-headed, opportunistic business leader who is unlikely to upset a lucrative arrangement. However, in a corrupt environment, where the law cannot be used to enforce contracts, there may be no alternative to dealing with friends and family members. The risk of trust turning to anger is part of the uncertainty of extralegal deals.

Reputation

As in legal markets, reputations developed from repeat play can substitute for both the law and trusting personal relationships.[12] A reputation for generously rewarding anyone who helps you will induce others to do you favors (Barney and Hansen 1994: 178–179). A reputation for maiming defaulters will help assure performance of corrupt deals. It will also discourage people from contracting with you in the first place.

Reputation acts on both sides of gift and bribe transactions. The reputation of the person who responds second is important to the one who makes the first move. For example, donors are more likely to give to a university with a reputation for awarding honorary degrees to generous graduates. A child is more likely to behave obediently if his or her parents have a reputation for rewarding their well-behaved children. Bribery can be more easily institutionalized if bribers can observe the past performance of corrupted officials and these officials have stable, long-term employment prospects. Sometimes the reputation of the first mover is important. Extortionary demands for payment may be more readily accepted if the extortioner has a reputation for carrying out vengeful acts. For example, police can maximize bribes by credibly threatening to beat up nonpayers or falsely to arrest honest people for crimes such as making illegal payoffs.

The illegality of bribes and the legality of gifts make reputations more difficult to establish in the former case than in the later. Gift giving can

---

[11] In Brazil the corruption of President Fernando Collor de Mello was revealed by a disgruntled brother angry at Collor's attempt to create a newspaper to rival the one that he owned (Fleischer 1997: 302–303; Manzetti and Blake 1996).

[12] Experimental work shows that reputations among traders are more likely to arise if product quality is difficult for buyers to judge before purchase (Kollock 1994). In the experiments subjects did not meet face to face, and there was no outside source of appeal. Thus the conditions were similar to corrupt or donative exchanges that lack the element of personal trust.

be public knowledge unless the implicit favors look too much like an illegal quid pro quo. Donors can announce their gifts in the hope of obtaining reputations for generosity. Charitable organizations may publish lists of donors as a way of persuading others to give as well. The ability to attract gifts from prominent people helps establish the respectability of the organization. In short, both donors and charities have a reputational interest in announcing gifts, and the two can feed off each other. A well-respected charity attracts gifts because it gives donors an aura of virtue, and past donors' reputation for virtue is then a fund-raising tool to attract more gifts.

Gifts or tips to service providers may have a different reputational dynamic. Suppose that the official price is uniform, but that agents can provide special favors or benefits to some customers. If they do this, others may experience declines in service. Then gifts from some customers may induce others to give as well. This seems to be the aim of parking garage attendants who publicly list gifts from monthly parkers (Tierney 1995). The spiral in gift giving will be especially powerful if there is a scarcity of desirable parking spots. Parkers are engaged in what game theorists call a "war of attrition."[13] They are induced to give not only to avoid a stingy reputation, but also to assure good service. Parking lot owners may try to capture some of these gains by charging different prices for different quality spaces. The inevitable discretion exercised by the attendants, however, means that owners will not be able to extract all of the gains.

Some corrupt "markets" operate the same way, but are less effective because bribes cannot usually be posted. This is an advantage of gifts over bribes. Campaign contributions frequently skirt the narrow line between gifts and bribes and fall on one side or the other depending upon the vagaries of campaign finance laws.[14] Potential contributors may be more likely to donate if they are informed about the donations of others. The possibility of an escalating spiral of donations suggests that a politician may publish a list of her contributors even if the law does not require it. The effectiveness of such a list, however, depends on the motivations of contributors. If they are concerned only with the election of a particular person, information on the generosity of others could discourage further gifts. In contrast, if contributors seek an advantage

---

[13] War-of-attrition games are analyzed in Bishop, Cannings, and Smith (1978), Krishna and Morgan (1997), and Rasmusen (1990: 74–76). I am grateful to Peter Cramton for pointing out this connection.

[14] See Jane Fritsch, "A Bribe's Not a Bribe When It's a Donation," *New York Times*, January 28, 1996.

over their rivals, news of their rivals' gifts could spur them to give more.

The stricter the laws governing private contributions and defining bribery, the more difficult it will be to establish a reputation. Bribers and bribees can develop a word-of-mouth reputation for strong-arm tactics, but they also want to be viewed as people who will carry out deals and not report corrupt offers. Because legal advertising and official certification are out, corrupt officials need to communicate by other means. The difficulty of establishing a reputation may lead crooks to deal only with known partners. Limiting the range of people who can pay bribes also reduces the risk of being exposed by newcomers. Establishing a corrupt relationship between strangers is risky because the first one who is explicit about wanting to make or accept a payoff is at the mercy of the others who can threaten to report the illegal act. Introductions by third parties are important, and in some cases the language of bargaining is veiled and ambiguous except to the initiates (Gambetta 1993).

Stable corrupt systems will be easier to maintain in small, local markets than in large national or international ones. The need for secrecy favors systems where a limited number of actors communicate easily. Thus corruption is more likely to be endemic in industries where producers are locally based, must deal with government on an ongoing basis, and have no choice about where to operate. In many cities construction firms, trash haulers, and vendors in city-owned markets are required to pay off city officials to obtain contracts and licenses to operate. In some areas of the world, local politicians are in league with criminal gangs who enforce payoff schemes with threats of violence (Gambetta 1993). These businesses cannot easily exit the market and move to a less corrupt community elsewhere.

Corrupt relationships may also be easier if the same small group deals with each other in different contexts. Reputations for honesty, reliability, or violence will be inexpensive to establish, making gift giving and bribery relatively advantageous. Trust is not necessary because everyone is always checking up on everyone else. Although such networks are common in local governments everywhere, small elites may control even quite large polities. Reputations can be firmly established within such a group for better or for worse.

The costs of establishing a reputation are less severe if bribery is widely accepted and credible law enforcement does not exist. Bribes may be a relatively efficient way to transfer rents from private individuals and organizations to public officials. Corruption is then a symptom of the underlying rent-generating character of the state. In an honest world, private actors seek publicly provided rents through wasteful spending programs and regulations that create monopoly rents. In a fully corrupt world they would not bother seeking legal benefits because the monopoly gains would be extracted by public officials at the implementation stage. There is an intimate connection between the incentive to create rents and the distribution of those rents. In less corrupt countries, private actors seek to use the state to get benefits for themselves. In more corrupt ones, public officials use the state to extract rents from private individuals and firms. They may do this by creating monopolies or by imposing restrictions. Alternatively, they may collude with private interests to extract benefits from foreign and domestic sources that are then shared between the corrupt public officials and their private sector allies.

Reputational Hostage Taking

Hostage taking is a familiar device for guaranteeing performance. The reality is generally less dramatic than the princess kept in the tower, but the principle is the same. Given a time inconsistency in a deal, the first mover demands that the second mover place something of value in trust. Hostage taking works best as a commitment device if the parties can appeal to a fair and honest tribunal to decide uncertain cases (Cramton and Dees 1993).

Such tribunals are hard to create for corrupt deals. But bribe payments create the possibility of a special kind of hostage taking. The "hostage" is the reputation of the other person. The first mover may keep secret records of the other person's actions.[15] If, for example, officials are punished more severely than business people, entrepreneurs can pay bribes for future favors and threaten to expose the payoff unless the official delivers. If bribes are paid for routine legal benefits, holding the official's reputation hostage is more difficult than if he provides an illegal benefit. In general, the greater the symmetry between the losses suffered by briber and bribee from exposure, the less credible is the threat to destroy the other's reputation. If, however, the briber's reputation has already been destroyed, then he may reveal his corrupt payoffs as well. For example, a member of a Colombian drug cartel turned himself in to the police to save his own life and helped U.S. authorities decipher records of payoffs to Colombian officials.[16]

[15] For example, in India a businessman accused of corruption had kept careful records of those he paid off. "Indian Premier Shrugs Off Scandal," *New York Times,* February 25, 1996.

[16] "Informant's Revelations on Cali Cartel Implicate Colombian officials," *Washington Post,* January 28, 1996.

Reputational hostage taking can also occur in charitable giving. A donor may seek to hold a university to its promised use of his money by threatening a campaign of negative publicity if the terms of the gift are violated. But a university might be reluctant to threaten negative publicity about a deadbeat donor for fear of discouraging others' gifts. Nevertheless, it can take steps to reduce the time inconsistency of the deal, for example, by not naming a building after a donor until all of her gift has been legally transferred.

Reciprocal Obligations

Many business people develop long-term reciprocal obligations. Each person has an incentive to act responsibly when he is an agent so that he can employ his current principal as an agent in the future. For example, Karen Clay (1997) studied the merchants in California between 1830 and 1848 when it was nominally under Mexican control but lacked a functioning system of contract enforcement. There were few traders, and an individual located in one city was likely to need the help of people in other cities. Instead of sending out his own agents, each used merchants in other cities to perform tasks. Direct bilateral deals were not necessary. Merchant A might act as an agent for merchant B, and B might be an agent for C, who acted as an agent for A. These arrangements were sustained by an active correspondence communicating information about the reputation of traders along with news about arrivals and departures of ships and the prices and qualities of goods.

How might such systems operate in a corrupt world? To function, the favors must not all go in one direction. Politician A votes for a project that will line the pocket of politician B and relies on B to support him in a similar project later on. The Minister of Planning favors a company partially owned by the Minister of Highways, and later, the Minister of Highways grants a contract to construct a new road to a firm in which the Minister of Planning has an interest. In Italy firms that engage in bribery "*invest specifically* in the creation of hidden channels of communication and exchange with the most influential public decision makers. This 'capital' of information, personal connections and trust is, at least in part, a 'patrimony' shared by the corrupt and their corruptors and limits the transactions costs involved in new contracts" (della Porta and Vannucci 1997a: 530). As in the cases described by Clay, the obligations need not be either bilateral or legally enforceable so long as the relevant group can easily identify defaulters and exclude them from future favors.

In these cases, the distinction between gifts and bribes is particularly difficult to draw. The quid pro quo is often paid in the same "currency" as the initial benefit – votes on bills, favoritism on contracts. Taken in isolation the behavior looks like favoritism, not corruption. A gift has been given or a favor done that some may view as inappropriate. The gain to the person who does the favor is not easy to identify. Only the reputation for doing well by people who have helped you in the past sustains the system.

The California system described by Clay broke down during the gold rush when the number of merchants increased dramatically. This can be a cure for any type of mutual back scratching. As the number of players increases, the accurate communication of reputation becomes more difficult. For example, some suggest that the elaborate set of connections characteristic of the overseas Chinese business community in Asia may break down as the market expands.[17] Another, quite different, solution is a centralized system of bureaucratic oversight that reduces the opportunities for reciprocal deals spread out over time. Of course, this option will not succeed if it just consolidates all deals in a single corrupt package. The hope is that centralized control will reveal more clearly any quid pro quos that remain.

Both market enlargement and improved oversight are moves in the direction of a more impersonal economic and political system. These changes can undermine corrupt networks, but they can also undermine whatever desirable functions such networks served as well.

Patronage, Gift Giving, and Economic Development

Developed market economies draw many formal and informal lines between impersonal market trades and official functions, on the one hand, and personal ties, on the other. Conflict-of-interest and campaign finance laws regulate the links between money and politics. Norms of behavior limit the intrusion of the market into family relationships and friendship. Journalism standards prevent reporters from accepting money to write particular stories. Yet even so, the distinctions between prices, bribes, gifts, and tips are difficult both to draw and to evaluate normatively. In developing countries the problem is much more vexing. The line between market and family and between the public and the private sectors is often blurred and in flux.

Standard neoclassical economics assumes away personal ties between buyers and sellers and argues that the impersonality of the market is one of its advantages. Trade is efficiently carried out by individuals who base their trading decisions on the characteristics of products and the prices

---

[17] "Inheriting the Bamboo Network," *The Economist*, December 23, 1995, to January 6, 1996: 79–80.

charged. Markets conserve on information, and their impersonality assures that sales are made to those who value the goods the most. One does not need to like or respect a person in order to trade with him. The process of trading is not itself a source of utility.

Nevertheless, in the real world the identity of buyers and sellers is often an important piece of information that establishes reputation and trust. Personal relationships between buyers and sellers can be functional in complex contracting situations. The connection may be based on affection and respect or fear and intimidation. If personal relations are relatively easy to establish, problems of fraud and shoddy merchandise may be reduced by efforts to create a reputation for quality and fair dealing. Free rider problems can be overcome by cooperation among interrelated groups (Bardhan 1993; Ostrom and Gardiner 1993).

Personalized ties are not always compatible with efficiency, however. Trust, reputation, and reciprocal obligations can facilitate corruption and undermine attempts to improve the operation of the state. If people deal only with their friends, this will limit entry into the market to insiders and lead sales and purchasing agents to favor relatives and friends. The monitoring and quality control provided by personalized links comes at the cost of increased entry costs for those not "in the loop." If private economic interests have personal links to public officials, patrimonial or clientelistic systems can develop where favors and payoffs are exchanged that undermine the transparency and effectiveness of public and private institutions. In patrimonial systems public officials are the patrons and private interests the clients. In clientelistic states, in contrast, private interests are dominant and control the state (Kahn 1996).

Bangladesh at independence is an example of a patrimonial state. After its separation from Pakistan, no locally powerful business leaders existed, and the business class was very dependent on state patronage.[18] The Philippines appears to fit the definition of a weak, clientelistic state dominated by private business interests (Hutchcroft 1998). Although many of the "cronies" are pure rent seekers, others are genuinely interested in developing productive business enterprises (Pinches 1996). In practice, it will often be unclear whether the government or the private sector is dominant because they work together for mutual gain. A study of recent Italian corruption cases demonstrates this interdependence and shows how it can be maintained by threats on

---

[18] According to Stephen Kochanek (1993), the level of patronage and corruption in Bangladesh has held down growth. The specific example of the jute industry in Bangladesh illustrates these general points (Bhaskar and Kahn 1995).

each side to reveal the corruption of the other (della Porta and Vannucci 1997a).[19]

In societies with embedded interpersonal networks, citizens may care little about market and public sector efficiency. They may view impersonal markets as illegitimate and morally bankrupt. In the extreme, the idea of an explicit quid pro quo may be questionable. People may believe they should give freely to others in their family or group and expect that "gifts" will be made in return. Although an observer may observe what appears to be an active trading culture, those within the system may not see it that way. Trade, for them, is legitimate only with particular partners on the other side of the transaction. A society based on such highly personalized relations will have difficulty developing large-scale capitalist enterprise or supporting active cross-border trade, but may produce a viable, if quite poor, autarky.

Societies based on strong interpersonal relations may have little notion of formal agency–principal relations and the obligations they impose on agents. The idea that one has distinct responsibilities to a superior – separate from ties of loyalty, friendship, and kinship – may seem strange and unnatural. Such societies will have difficulty establishing modern bureaucracies, with civil servants hired on the basis of skills who are expected to separate their roles as officials from their roles as friends or relatives. Citizens expect that personal ties with officials are needed to get anything done and think it quite appropriate to reward helpful officials with gifts and tips. Higher-ups in government seek to assure the support of the lower ranks by appointing loyal subordinates who will refuse "gifts" unless the superior approves. The patronage group will then set up systems for sharing payoffs up and down the hierarchy. Payments made at the top will be shared down the line and those collected at the bottom will be divided up with superiors. Loyalty to family, friends, and coworkers dominates loyalty to the state.[20]

---

[19] Other examples of states where strong patron–client connections exist are easy to find. Merilee Grindle's (1996) comparison of Mexico and Kenya in the 1980s and 1990s emphasizes the importance of patron–client links in both countries and the negative impact of corrupt networks on growth. See also Robison (1996) and Schwarz (1994) on Indonesia.

[20] See, for example, Kochanek's (1993) discussion of Bangladesh. Robert Scalapino (1989: 4) argues that Western colonizers in Asia faced a daunting task in creating a new civilian elite "in the image of the Western civil servant" because such concepts "as considering office holding to be a public trust, applying rules without fear or favor, and abiding by the verdict of the people as expressed through their elected representatives" were foreign to traditional Asian officials. This task was made more difficult by the inconsistency of Western efforts as colonizers whose legitimacy was dependent on military power.

Strong networks based on trust and reputation can be invaluable during periods when formal state institutions are weak and ineffective. In the early post-revolutionary period in the Soviet Union, for example, informal social networks substituted for formal organizational structure. Cadres who had been members of tight-knit underground organizations carried their loyalties and connections over into the new Soviet state. Over time, these networks became sources of corruption and favoritism. Stalin complained that informal social structures undermined formal ones, and Gorbachev's efforts at reform in the 1980s were hampered by informal networks that reduced the center's capacity to implement policies (Easter 1996: 574, 576–577).

Similarly, in the recent period of flux and change in Eastern Europe, corruption facilitated by personal ties expanded as the formal structures disintegrated. The lack of understanding of public administration principles has hindered bureaucratic development in post-Soviet societies in Eastern Europe. Loyalty to other members of the organization is as important or more important than good administration. According to a study of Bulgaria, "civil servants from the core ministry of finance in Bulgaria still feel that they have to protect their colleagues at the customs offices, rather than launch a serious inquiry into what seem to be corrupt practices by customs officials" (Verheijen and Dimitrova 1996: 205–206). The long-run consequences of this situation are profound, making creation of effective state structures difficult.

Suppose a country's leaders decide to introduce free market institutions and governance structures adapted from those of developed states. What impact will these new institutions have on underlying public attitudes?[21] The transition from a situation where personal ties are the norm to a more impersonal society with strong market and public sector institutions may be a painful one, and both vicious and virtuous cycles are possible.

The introduction of new institutions that fit poorly with underlying norms can produce pathologies that make gradual changes in attitudes

[21] Studies suggest that attitudes are subject to change as circumstances change. According to Scalapino (1989: 107), "Rapid cultural change is an inextricable aspect of the era in which we live, especially within the avant-garde societies." A study of Costa Rica and Nicaragua concluded that "political culture is far more contingent, utilitarian, and malleable than has previously been assumed" (Seligson and Booth 1993: 790). As Larry Diamond writes, in summarizing recent work by Gabriel Almond, "the cognitive, attitudinal, and evaluational dimensions of political culture are fairly 'plastic' and change quite dramatically in response to regime performance, historical experience, and political socialization. Deeper value and normative commitments have been shown to be more enduring and change only slowly" (Diamond 1993a: 9).

less likely as people observe the costs of markets and bureaucracies. Unlike established market economies, complex and subtle boundaries between market and nonmarket activities do not exist in countries that have relied little on the impersonal free market in the past. If such countries dramatically increase the role of the market and at the same time try to establish a modern bureaucracy and a democratic polity, the resulting system may include a number of pathologies. Payoffs to state officials may be common; many market trades may be based on personal connections; and state purchases and personnel appointments may continue to be part of a web of patronage.[22] On the one hand, the market may lose its fragile legitimacy by intruding into areas where it is viewed as illegitimate even in developed market economies. On the other hand, the market may have difficulty becoming established even in those areas where it produces clear efficiency gains elsewhere.

Virtuous cycles are also possible. If those operating in the modern, differentiated sector benefit, others may be induced to try it out, however reluctantly. In China, for example, the success of regions that liberalized their economies encouraged other more conservative regions to copy them (Shirk 1994). A successful small- and medium-sized business sector operating free of excessive controls can encourage others to try their luck as entrepreneurs. Robert Scalapino (1989: 77) worries that entrepreneurs drawn from the ranks of Chinese officialdom will continue long-established habits and depend "extensively upon political contacts and an exchange of favors." However, he points to an underlying spirit of pragmatism and of "creativity and independent entrepreneurship" that had been suppressed by the over layer of the socialist state. China is developing quickly. It is too soon to tell whether the trend is toward virtuous cycles that will produce a competitive market economy or toward vicious cycles where the treachery and corruption of some breeds more of the same in others.[23]

Do efforts to limit personalized dealings by public officials and market

---

[22] An article on China argues that the reallocation of resources from the state to private hands has increased efficiency and improved productivity. However, "the line between corruption and the more acceptable transfer of resources has not been clearly defined" (Goodman 1996: 241). An important task for government is to redraw "the distinctions between legitimacy and corruption in the private sphere . . . in a new atmosphere, and as a new entrepreneurial class emerges" (Scalapino 1989: 114–115).

[23] See "China's Paragon of Corruption," *New York Times*, March 6, 1998. According to the article, "virtually any multi-million-dollar company, striving to become modern in a system that remains stubbornly old-fashioned, is wide open to so much corruption that success almost inevitably leads to financial shenanigans that can spoil any chance of efficiency or genuine profitability."

actors undermine the desirable features of interpersonal links based on trust and respect? Richard Titmuss (1970) argued with respect to the supply of blood for transfusions that a greater role for the market may be accompanied by a lower sense of obligation to help relatives and friends. Cooperation to solve common problems may fall, and those in need may suffer. However, if a tradeoff exists, the experience of the United States suggests that it need not be a stark one.[24] In spite of the jeremiads of some writers, the United States has a remarkably dense network of nonprofit organizations and a strong tradition of volunteer work and of private gift giving both to charities and to relatives.[25] Many private business relations rely on trust and reputation to assure high-quality performance. Regulation of political campaigns and bureaucratic behavior limits self-dealing, although private wealth, of course, still remains an important influence on political life.

In Africa some observers, frustrated with past development failures, are urging a more careful study of indigenous institutions. Mamadou Dia argues that Africa faces a crisis of institutions. The crisis is "mainly due to a structural and functional disconnect, or lack of convergence, between formal institutions that are mostly transplanted from outside and informal institutions that are rooted in African history, tradition, and culture and that generally characterize the governance of civil society" (Dia 1996: 29). Dia provides a number of case studies of successful efforts to integrate local cultural values and practices into modern development efforts. For example, the public electric company in Côte d'Ivoire has made a systematic effort to reconcile corporate and societal culture without an unquestioning devotion to either (ibid.: 222–227). In Dia's view the aim is to ask how new and old institutional forms and practices might be blended, drawing on the best of both traditions to promote economic growth.

As one example, consider credit and banking services. In many developing countries they are a common source of corruption and patronage.[26]

---

[24] Zelizer (1994: 71–118) stresses the coexistence of different forms of exchange in modern societies.

[25] For a summary of the facts, see Rose-Ackerman (1996a) and Hodgkinson and Weitzman (1994).

[26] In Bangladesh, Kochanek (1993: 264) claims that under General Zia industrial loan funds provided by the World Bank and the Asian Development Bank were handed out as a form of patronage: "Of 3718 units financed under Zia from 1976 to 1981–82, fewer than half became operational. There exists no trace of some 898 or 24 percent of the units financed, and another 495 or 13 percent failed." In Africa development finance institutions founded on external loans have experienced problems of illiquidity and insolvency with nonperforming portfolios and high default rates (Nissanke 1991: 143).

Elites who control the allocation of credit are unlikely to want to give up their favored position based on their own close links with government. Reformers must find a way to provide credit outside existing patronage networks. Several recent experiments hold promise. The goal is not to recreate the institutional forms common in developed countries that stress arm's-length evaluations of risk and return. Instead, these experiments accept the importance of personal ties but provide an alternative to credit allocation based on membership in elite groups. Close ties between neighbors in poor communities complement efforts to establish a banking system. Social pressure encourages people to repay, but the initial loans are made to those outside the previously existing circle of borrowers. In practice some of these experiments have succeeded only in providing locally influential farmers with credit (Robinson 1992: 22–23, 27, 57). However, in other experiments social pressure has been successfully mobilized to encourage repayment. Nevertheless, it remains to be seen whether such programs can be organized without underlying subsidies.[27]

Conclusions

The definition of bribes and gifts is a cultural matter, but "culture" is dynamic and constantly changing. If behavior labeled "corrupt" by some observers is, nevertheless, viewed as acceptable gift giving or tipping within a country, it should simply be legalized and reported. If, however, these practices are imposing hidden or indirect costs on the populace, analysts can clarify and document these costs. Definitions of acceptable behavior may change once people are informed of the costs of tolerating payoffs to politicians and civil servants. Conversely, experts may learn something new about the organization of economic and social activity by studying systems where "implicit contracting" is the only form of contracting that exists and interpersonal relationships are central to economic life.

---

[27] A number of experiments are in progress in Africa and Asia (Dia 1996: 194–219; Robinson 1992). The most well known is the Grameen Bank developed in Bangladesh for lending to people lacking ordinary sorts of collateral (Robinson 1992: 59–63). The benefits of mutual surveillance by peers in bureaucratic settings is discussed by Hood (1996: 214–216).

PART III

Corruption as a Political Problem

7

Corruption and Politics

Corruption describes a relationship between the state and the private sector. Sometimes state officials are the dominant actors; in other cases private actors are the most powerful forces. The relative bargaining power of these groups determines both the overall impact of corruption on society and the distribution of the gains between bribers and bribees.

Analysis of corruption is part of the ongoing and inconclusive debate about which form of government is most conducive to economic growth. Although wealthy countries do tend to be democracies, there is no simple statistical relationship between growth and democratic government (Huber, Rueschemeyer, and Stephens 1993; Przeworski and Limongi 1993). The reason for this is not difficult to fathom: "Democracy" is simply too general a term to capture the range of government forms that come under that rubric. Furthermore, a government structure that works well in one country may be dysfunctional in another context. Widespread, entrenched corruption is one form of dysfunction.

Is the establishment of democracy an anticorruption strategy? The desire for reelection constrains the greed of politicians. The protection of civil liberties and free speech, which generally accompanies democratic electoral processes, makes open and transparent government possible. In contrast, nondemocratic states are especially susceptible to corrupt incentives because their rulers have the potential to organize government with few checks and balances. But this contrast is too sharp. One need look no further than Newark and Chicago in the United States to find well-established corrupt systems that compare quite well with autocratic systems. Recent payoff scandals have implicated elected politicians in Mexico, Italy, Korea, and Japan. Corruption is common at the local government level in France and Germany. Clearly, democratic forms do not always succeed in checking corruption. Thus it is worthwhile asking which features of democratic government help limit self-dealing and which contribute to corruption.

Before moving to a deeper consideration of this issue in the next chapter, I begin with a more general analysis of the bargaining power of government officials versus corrupt private actors.[1] This discussion abstracts from the details of political systems, stressing instead the "industrial organization" of corruption. The nature of corruption depends not just on the organization of government but also on the organization and power of private actors. The critical issue is whether either the government or the private sector has monopoly power in dealing with the other. One basic conclusion can be stated at the outset. To the extent that a democratic government disperses power among officials, it may give each one little bargaining power vis-à-vis powerful private interests. A successful democracy may need to encourage the creation of competitive private markets as well as establish a competitive system of politics.

I distinguish between kleptocracies where corruption is organized at the top of government and other states where bribery is the province of a large number of low-level officials.[2] The other side of the bribery "market" must be specified as well. Are there a small number of major corrupt private actors or is the payment of bribes decentralized across a large number of people and firms? Table 2 illustrates the four polar cases: kleptocracy, bilateral monopoly, mafia-dominated states, and competitive bribery. I begin with kleptocracy and then discuss the two cases where the bribers have monopoly power. The final case, where bribes play the role of prices in a decentralized market, requires separate treatment. A corrupt "marketplace" can be costly even if no one exercises any monopoly power over its operation.

Kleptocracy

Consider first the case where a kleptocratic ruler faces a large number of unorganized potential bribe payers. In the extreme, a powerful head of government can organize the political system to maximize its rent-extraction possibilities. Such a "stationary bandit" (in Mancur Olson's phrase) can act like a private monopolist, striving for productive efficiency, but restricting the output of the economy to maximize profits (Olson 1993). A private monopoly underproduces output because it

---

[1] This chapter is derived, in part, from Coolidge and Rose-Ackerman (1997) and Rose-Ackerman (1998b).

[2] The term "kleptocrat" appears to have originated with Andreski (1968). It refers to a ruler or top official whose primary goal is personal enrichment and who possesses the power to further this aim while holding public office.

Table 2.   Types of corrupt governments

	Multiple bribers	Few bribers
Bribe recipients concentrated at top of government	Kleptocracy (a) extortionary state or (b) weak state	Bilateral Monopoly
Multiple bribe recipients at low levels of government	Competitive bribery with a possibility of spirals	Mafia-dominated state

earns profits from the difference between selling prices and costs. If a kleptocrat, like a private monopolist, sold private goods to individuals and firms, it too would restrict output (Findlay 1991; Przeworski and Limongi 1993: 58–59; Shleifer and Vishny 1993). For example, if the state runs the railroads and the telephone system it may set monopoly prices, restricting supply to maximize rents. Similarly, a kleptocratic ruler of a country that dominates the world supply of some raw material or agricultural product would restrict production to keep world prices high and extract the profits. At the same time, he would seek to isolate this business from everyday politics. The ruler will sacrifice the benefits of patronage and petty favoritism to obtain the profits generated by a well-run monopoly business. Thus if the key export sector is in state hands, the ruler will favor a meritocratic system of recruitment and promotion that rewards high productivity and good business practices. The kleptocrat will favor policies that transfer the most resources into his pocket while maintaining the economy's productivity. The kleptocrat will oppose policies that distribute benefits widely throughout society with little opportunity to extract payoffs at the center. Corrupt rulers will support policies that produce personalized gains even if they result in lower overall social wealth.

Most kleptocrats, however, are not as all powerful as Olson's stationary bandit. Their goal is personal wealth maximization, but the tools at their disposal are imperfect. They control the state but not the entire economy. They may have a weak and disloyal civil service, a poor resource base, and a vague and confusing legal framework. The ruler must work with the levers at hand, and these may be quite inefficient rent-generation devices. He supports some interventions that do not increase overall national income because they provide personal benefits to himself as head of state. Even the kleptocrat, however, eventually reaches the point where the inefficiencies of additional government intervention become so large that marginal bribe revenues fall. The weak kleptocrat is likely to favor a bloated and inefficient state to maximize corrupt possibilities. Citizens in a weak kleptocracy prefer a smaller than optimal government when the government is corrupt, but they get one that is too large.[3]

Examples that fit this model quite well were the long-running dictatorships of President Alfredo Stroessner of Paraguay (1954–1989) and Mobutu Sese Seko of Zaire (1965–1997), and the rule of François and Jean-Claude Duvalier in Haiti (1957–1986).

In Paraguay, according to one scholar:

> The public sector was viewed as Stroessner's personal fiefdom. The administration of state assets revealed a lack of differentiation between the "economic" and the "political" sphere and the absence of any clearly defined boundary between public and private property. The result was that Stroessner and his retinue of military and civilian acolytes disposed of public sector resources as if they were their own (Nickson 1996: 239).

The key point here is not Stroessner's kleptocratic aims per se, but his "retinue" that insisted on accumulating wealth for itself. Instead of running an efficient monopoly state, Stroessner ensured military support by allowing the top brass to engage in contraband, narcotics trafficking, and trade in arms (ibid.). Projects such as a dam and an unneeded cement plant and airport produced corrupt gains for Stroessner and his associates but were not wealth-maximizing choices for the country as a whole (ibid.: 245–246).

Similarly in Zaire, President Mobutu and his associates can be described as "looting" the state. Mobutu placed a third of the state budget under his control and reportedly siphoned off a quarter of gross receipts from copper exports. But Mobutu too had to share his corrupt gains with both high-level cronies and low-level customs inspectors and other officials. Corruption and predation undermined the formal private sector, and grandiose infrastructure projects were used as sources of payoffs for the President and his associates (Wedeman 1997: 462–465). Clearly Zaire, with its kleptocratic ruler, was not run like a productively efficient profit-maximizing monopoly.

---

[3] These points are developed in Jacqueline Coolidge and Susan Rose-Ackerman (1997). See also Oskar Kurer (1993: 270). John Mukum Mbaku (1994: 31–37) argues that when autocrats or narrow interest groups win control of the state in Africa, many have expanded the role of government in an effort to enrich themselves. He argues that military coups are often motivated by rent seeking.

In Haiti the dictatorship benefited "just a few thousand people connected by marriage, family ties or friendship to those in power." Political instability arose "not so much from popular movements . . . but from fellow members of the elite seeking a larger share of the spoils of power" (Grafton and Rowlands 1996: 267). According to the United States Department of Commerce, in 1977–1978 government misappropriation of funds was 63 percent of government revenue (cited in ibid.: 267). The kleptocratic aims of the top rulers produced an inefficient scramble for gains. Institutions were created that impeded development; state monopolies were used as "cash cows"; and the state discriminated against people of motivation and ability (ibid.: 268–269).

As the cases of Stroessner, Mobutu, and the Duvaliers demonstrate, a corrupt ruler influences not only the size of government but also the mixture of taxes and spending priorities. Taxes, regulations, subsidies, price fixing, and privatizations are examples of public-sector activities that kleptocrats can manipulate for their own benefit. Because tax breaks can be awarded to corrupt individuals and firms in return for bribes, kleptocrats may set high nominal tax rates to encourage payoffs. They may set heavy duties on necessities used by the poor and exempt luxuries. In Haiti between the 1910s and the 1970s, for example, goods such as expensive liquor were almost untaxed, and duties were high on cotton, textiles, soap, and kerosene (Lundahl 1997: 35).

Kleptocrats view the regulatory system as a source of personal profits. Thus regulations and licensing requirements may be imposed that have no justification other than to create a bottleneck that firms will pay to avoid. Efficient regulatory reforms will be opposed by the kleptocrat if the reforms would convert illegal into legal pricing systems. The kleptocrat will focus subsidies on individuals and business firms willing to pay for them. Of course, even corrupt autocrats may need to satisfy the mass of the population in order maintain power, but they will also promulgate programs that induce the wealthy to pay for benefits. The ruler, for example, might institute a system of investment subsidies with discretion to distribute these benefits. No one can obtain these benefits as a matter of right. Everyone must bid to obtain them from the ruler. The allocation of scarce foreign exchange and access to credit are additional sources of rents for rulers.

A kleptocratic ruler can affect the benefits of privatization. A corrupt ruler is likely to be especially eager to privatize monopolies that earn excess profits so long as he can extract a share of the gains. But it is one thing for a kleptocrat to want to privatize a state firm, and quite another for private investors to make bids. A private firm will have little value to investors if it can be taxed on all its profits, renationalized at will without adequate compensation, or excessively and arbitrarily regulated. Only if the state can credibly commit to a reasonable future policy will the firm be worth more as a private entity. But a corrupt ruler faces special difficulties because he is committed only to personal enrichment. Furthermore, even if he can somehow write binding contracts with investors, they may worry that a corrupt ruler risks overthrow. A change in regime can lead to the cancellation of previous understandings.

A kleptocrat may oppose some privatizations that an honest regime would view as efficient and support others that are inefficient but produce corrupt payoffs up front. The ruler's inability to make credible commitments lowers the value of the firm to private investors, tipping the scales toward continued state ownership. In addition, state ownership is associated with opportunities for rent seeking over and above the profits of the enterprise itself. If the state enterprise can be used to generate rents through such devices as the sale of jobs, favorable contracting deals, and special treatment for customers, then the stream of benefits is higher for the kleptocrat than for the honest ruler. Sometimes the distinction between the public fisc and the private funds of the ruler is erased. In Haiti under the Duvaliers checks were simply written out to members of the presidential family and other private citizens from various state monopolies (Lundahl 1997: 39–40). Public control of large enterprises can itself be a way of increasing one's chance of remaining in power in spite of one's corruption. Such rulers create a web of obligations and can threaten to expose their corrupt counterparts if they are overthrown.

However, under other conditions, the kleptocrat may become an overenthusiastic privatizer. He may, for example, be able to engineer the privatization so that it involves a forced sale to himself or his family at a below-market price. In Indonesia, for example, Suharto supported a number of privatizations that involved the transfer of assets to firms controlled by his children and cronies (Schwarz 1994: 148–149). Even if the sale is to an outsider, a kleptocrat may support some privatizations that a benevolent social wealth maximizer would oppose. By accepting present gains, he gives up a future stream of revenue. This may be rational if the ruler has a higher discount rate than private investors because he fears being overthrown. The kleptocrat may value the up-front benefits of selling the public firm more highly than the private market.

In some ways, a kleptocrat is like a stockbroker or a real estate agent who makes money from turnover. Corrupt gains can be earned not just from the ongoing level of government intervention but also from one-shot changes. The ruler can extract a share of the gains from any type of transaction involving the state and thus may support the privatization of some firms while supporting the nationalization of others.

The ruler can be bribed either to privatize efficient state firms at low prices or to nationalize inefficient private firms at high prices. Without credible commitments to refrain from one-shot changes, private investors will be reluctant to enter into deals that risk being reversed in the future.

In short, the strong kleptocrat runs a brutal but efficient state limited only by his own inability to make credible commitments. The weak kleptocrat runs an intrusive and inefficient state organized to extract bribes from the population and the business community. Some analysts, however, are relatively sanguine about the corruption of high-level officials, arguing that the most serious problem is low-level corruption under which officials "overfish" a "commons" in their search for private gain (Olson 1993; Rodrik 1994; Shleifer and Vishny 1993). If no one owns the common pool, an inefficient amount of effort will be spent fishing (Hardin 1968). One way to extract rents is to create extra rules and regulations. Especially destructive, according to Shleifer and Vishny (1993: 606), is the possibility that new bureaucratic entrants will try to obtain a share in the rents. If a ruler has relatively little day-to-day control over state ministers, their freelance behavior can indeed be costly. If he has more control, he may be interested in limited "liberalization" and perhaps accompanying civil service reform to strengthen his control. He will back reform so long as it is consistent with his own income maximization.

Just because a ruler favors some types of reform, however, it does not follow that higher-level corruption is less destructive than low-level peculation. A ruler seldom literally controls all the resources of the state. The size of the common pool under state control is not fixed by external forces. Instead, officials may have the power to expand the resources under their control, and higher-up officials will generally have more power to increase the reach of the state than lower-level ones. Furthermore, corrupt rulers generally must work with imperfect tools. Instead of simply expropriating all private property and organizing it to produce efficiently, those at the top have options that are themselves inefficient. They can increase the level of taxes and regulatory authority, grant exemptions in return for payoffs, and nationalize industries. They can introduce general protectionist policies that are beyond the reach of lower-level officials. They can propose expensive, complex, capital-intensive projects that can be used to generate bribes.[4] In Haiti, for

---

[4] Vito Tanzi and Hamid Davoodi (1997) show empirically that high levels of corruption are associated with high levels of public investment. However, their data, based on surveys of foreign business firms and outside observers, do not permit them to distinguish between countries where corruption is relatively more pervasive at the top of government.

example, dictatorial governments favored institutions that impeded development since they were the most effective way to siphon off rents. Furthermore, the assets of the wealthy were invested either overseas or in secure, but unproductive, investments. State policies that impeded development encouraged talented Haitians to emigrate (Grafton and Rowlands 1996). No ruler can be absolutely confident of remaining in power for ever. Those who became rich from the ruler's favor will not wish to expose all their assets to the risk of regime change.

Of course, some powerful rulers manage to avoid such inefficient policies. They enrich themselves and their families, but do not push rent-generating programs so far as seriously to undermine growth. Countries with a high degree of corruption that are politically secure and tightly controlled from the top may suffer from fewer static inefficiencies than those with an uncoordinated struggle for private gain.[5] Their rulers have a long-run viewpoint and hence seek ways to constrain uncoordinated rent seeking so that long-term gains are maximized. This type of regime seems a rough approximation to some East Asian countries that have institutional mechanisms to cut back uncoordinated rent seeking by both officials and private businesses (Campos and Root 1996). Even in that region, however, countries with less corruption are better able to attract foreign direct investment than their more corrupt neighbors (Wei 1997). Furthermore, as the above discussion indicated, many corrupt rulers are not so secure, and their very venality increases their insecurity.

Kleptocrats may face additional problems of bureaucratic control not faced by benevolent rulers. Corruption at the top creates expectations among bureaucrats that they should share in the wealth and reduces the moral and psychological constraints on lower-level officials. Low-level malfeasance that can be kept under control by an honest ruler may become endemic with a dishonest ruler. Kleptocratic rulers may be unable to create the conditions needed for an honest bureaucracy to flourish (Lundahl 1997: 43). Yet many rent-generating possibilities cannot be achieved without staff to enforce the obstacles and collect the bribes. Thus the presence of venal civil servants makes the corrupt ruler less enthusiastic about increasing the size of the state because he obtains a smaller share of the gains than with honest subordinates. The efficiency with which the ruler can extract private benefits from society is reduced by a corrupt bureaucracy not completely under his control (Coolidge and

[5] Lundahl (1997). See, for example, "Indonesia: When Trouble Brewed," *The Economist,* February 10, 1996, p. 37, for an example of how such conflicts were handled in Indonesia in a controversy involving Suharto family members with interests in the beer and hotel industries.

Rose-Ackerman 1997). If the ruler can develop an honest civil service and share the gains with only a small number of trusted subordinates, he will be better off, but this will often be impossible.[6]

Corrupt low-level officials introduce inefficiencies in the form of additional delays and red tape and cross-agency interference. As a result, national income net of the ruler's rake-off will be lower than with an efficient bureaucracy at any level of state intervention. At least some of the efficiency losses of having a corrupt civil service are shifted to citizens. Would citizens prefer a kleptocrat able to insure an honest bureaucracy or one who must contend with a corrupt one? No clear answer is possible. In the former case, the ruler can select the level of state intervention that maximizes his gains given a well-working state apparatus. In the latter, he chooses a lower level of intervention, but services are provided inefficiently by corrupt officials (Coolidge and Rose-Ackerman 1997).

Bilateral Monopolies and Mafia-Dominated States

I now turn to the two cases where powerful private interests can resist corrupt demands and exert power over the state. The cases differ depending on whether or not the state is centrally organized to collect bribes.

In the first of these cases a corrupt ruler faces a single major opponent across the table. In this situation, similar to a bilateral monopoly, the rent-extraction possibilities are shared between briber and ruler. Their relative strength will determine the way gains are shared (Kahn 1996). It will also determine the overall size of the pie. If some rents can be created only with state help, and if the ruler fears losing all the gains to his adversary, he will not act. Each side may seek to improve its own situation by making the other's condition worse through expropriating property, on the one hand, or engaging in violence, on the other.

Diego Gambetta (1993) defines a mafia as an organized crime group that provides protective services that substitute for those provided by the state in ordinary societies. In some bilateral cases the state and the mafia share the protection business and perhaps even have overlapping membership. A powerful corrupt ruler in this context extorts a share of the mafia's gains and has little interest in controlling criminal influence. Because criminals are as interested in getting rich as anyone, optimists

---

[6] See Ozay Mehmet's (1994) discussion of the Indonesian system in which a small cadre of top officials divided the rents of government operation with a small group of outsiders and family members.

might contend that if criminals actually control the government they will modify their ways. But this seems utopian. One would expect that if criminals controlled the state, they would seek to limit entry through threats of violence and the elimination of rivals as they have done in the drug business. Furthermore, organized crime bosses may be more interested in quick profits through the export of a country's assets and raw materials than in the difficult task of building up a modern industrial base. The end result is the delegitimation of government and the undermining of capitalist institutions.

Alternatively, some states are economically dependent on the export of one or two minerals or agricultural products. These countries may establish long-term relationships with a few multinational firms. Both rulers and firms favor productive efficiency, but the business–government alliance that results may permit managers and rulers to share the nation's wealth at the expense of ordinary people. The division of gains will depend upon the relative bargaining power of the parties. If the firm has invested in fixed capital or if the product it produces is a raw material available in only a few places on earth, the country's rulers are in a strong position to extract a large proportion of the benefits. In contrast, if the firm produces an agricultural product, such as bananas, and can easily go elsewhere, or if the raw material is available to the firm in many different locations, it has a bargaining advantage and can require the country to provide useful infrastructure, guarantees of labor peace, and low taxes. One may not see much overt corruption in such regimes, but the harm to ordinary citizens may, nevertheless, be severe. The country becomes an appendage of the large investor.

Bilateral monopoly conditions can arise for particular contracting deals. In fact, a kleptocrat has an incentive to create such conditions through decisions about which projects to support and which firms to favor. Contracts with firms in competitive markets are undesirable because there are no excess profits to appropriate. The ruler distorts contracting priorities by favoring projects that can be produced only by firms in industries earning monopoly profits. Of course, a strong kleptocrat operating with impunity would not have to worry about such a "cover story." He can just take public funds or aid monies, send them to his offshore bank account, and earn international rates of return. This contrast between weak and strong kleptocrats recalls a familiar joke, repeated in various versions in the development community. Ruler A shows off his new mansion to ruler B. Pointing out a new highway, A explains his new house by saying, "Thirty percent." Later A visits B at his even more lavish mansion. Asked how it was financed, B says, "See that highway out there?" A looks puzzled because no highway can be seen. "That's just the point," says B, "one hundred percent."

This story is usually used to demonstrate that corruption is less harmful if the road is actually built. But that conclusion is not always justified. If the ruler supports projects designed to hide his kickbacks easily, the distortionary effect of such decisions may be large. A new highway seems like a valuable piece of infrastructure, but if it just improves access to the ruler's country house, there is not much to be said for it. If no road is built, fraud has been committed and development goals undermined, but the country is not littered with costly "white elephants." Taxpayers and foreign aid institutions have financed an increase in the ruler's wealth and seen their funds diverted from legal purposes. This is unfair and provides a justification for a coup or for cutting off aid. Under prevailing economic conditions, however, it is not as inefficient as actually constructing such projects so long as the ruler has access to a foreign bank account.

If a kleptocrat faces a single bribe payer across the table, they negotiate a deal to share the economic gains. Corrupt payments may be lower in a bilateral monopoly situation than in a one-sided kleptocracy. The briber has bargaining power and uses it to extract profits. However, the end result is not necessarily superior. The size of the bribes is not the key variable. Instead, the economic distortions and the high costs of public projects measure the harm to citizens. Private monopoly profits and bribes enrich the parties to the deal, with ordinary people still the losers.

Now consider the case where officials of a weak and disorganized state engage in freelance bribery but face a monopoly of power in the private sector. The state might be a poorly functioning democracy or an autocracy with a weak head of state. As in the case of bilateral monopoly, the monopolist could be a domestic mafia, a single large corporation, or a close-knit oligarchy. In each case, the private power dominates the state, buying the cooperation of officials. The private actor is not, however, powerful enough to take over the state and reorganize it into a unitary body. The problem for the private sector is that the very disorganization of the state reduces the ability of the private group to purchase the benefits it wants. Making an agreement with one official will not discourage another from coming forward. Such a state is very inefficient as officials compete with each other for the available rents. Individuals may be unable to create substantial rents on their own, but they compete with each other for a share of the gains produced by the dominant private firm. Facing such freelance rent seeking, however, the private firm will produce less. The activities of the corrupt officials are like taxes on outputs or inputs that reduce the firm's profit-maximizing level of output.

The Philippines since independence provides an example of a weak state dealing with a powerful oligarchy of private business interests. The legal and administrative system is unpredictable and inconsistent. Political arbitrariness inhibits the development of a productive private sector. Some business leaders obtain special favors, but the overall effect on commerce is reportedly negative. Prominent business families spend time and effort to diversify their political connections as insurance against changes in the regime (Hutchcroft 1998: 13–39).

Competitive Bribery

In the fourth case many low-level officials deal with large numbers of citizens. As in the case discussed above, this situation could occur in a democratic state with weak legal controls on corruption and poor public accountability. It might also be the way a weak autocrat dispenses public services.

The competitive corruption case is not analogous to an efficient competitive market. A fundamental problem is the possibility of an upward spiral of corruption. The corruption of some encourages additional officials to accept bribes until all but the unreconstructed moralists are corrupt. Several theoretical models produce this result along with a second equilibrium with little corruption – a low level of corruption in one period encourages even fewer to be corrupt in the next period.

To generate an upward spiral of corruption, the profitability of bribery must increase, over some range, as the incidence of corruption increases. For instance, suppose that potential bribers are ignorant about which officials are corrupt. Then the higher the proportion of corrupt officials, the easier it is to encounter a corrupt official, the lower the risk of offering a payoff, and the greater the number of individuals who expect to benefit from paying a bribe. Ordinarily, one would expect that as bribe levels increase, fewer people would be willing to pay them. However, in this case, because the proportion of corrupt officials increases with the level of bribes, an increase in the bribe level frequently *increases* the proportion of private individuals who pay bribes. Under plausible assumptions about the distribution of corruption costs across officials, both high- and low-corruption equilibria exist. Temporary changes in underlying conditions can produce long-run shifts in the level of corruption by moving the system from the high- to the low-corruption equilibrium (Andvig and Moene 1990).

This conclusion can be strengthened by several plausible extensions. As I suggested in the previous chapter, if moral scruples fall as the incidence of corruption rises, such a phenomenon would contribute to both upward and downward spirals. A similar result occurs if the probability of detection falls when the incidence of corruption rises (Andvig and

Moene 1990: 75). This might happen, for example, if there is a fixed budget for combating corruption and if those enforcing the law depend upon the cooperation of honest officials in uncovering malfeasance. Then if few officials are corrupt, anticorruption resources can be used efficiently to collect evidence, thus discouraging corruption in the future. In contrast, if a high proportion of officials are corrupt, collecting evidence is costly and relatively ineffective, thus encouraging more corruption in the next period. An even smaller percentage are caught in that period, inducing more corrupt behavior and so forth.[7]

Reform requires systemic changes in expectations and in government behavior to move such a state from a high- to a low-corruption equilibrium. Unfortunately, the nation-states that fall into this fourth category are precisely those that lack the centralized authority needed to carry out such reforms. The decentralized, competitive corrupt system is well entrenched, and no one has the power to administer the policy shock needed for reform.

Conclusions

The case for autocracy as a technically efficient form of government is weak. Kleptocracy will seldom be equivalent to private monopoly. There is no simple correspondence between the level and consequences of corruption and the organization of government. One cannot, for instance,

---

[7] Another model focuses on the principal's hiring choices (Tirole 1996). Corruption is a function of agents' behavior and the kind of tasks they are given. High government officials can engage agents to perform an efficient or a less efficient task. Each period a different agent appears at the public agency's door asking to be hired. All the agents are part of a well-defined group of people eligible for these positions. One might think of a tax collection agency hiring collectors who may accept bribes from taxpayers. The task might be either a complex tax collection system in which agents must calculate taxpayers' ability to pay or a simple fixed head tax. The group of potential tax collectors has a reputation based on the proportion who are always honest, the proportion who are always corrupt, and the proportion of opportunists. The principal also has limited information about the track record of the agent before him. Multiple equilibria exist under some conditions. In the low-corruption equilibrium, the opportunists are all honest. If they maintain an honest track record, they will be hired for the lucrative, high-efficiency task. In contrast, a high-corruption equilibrium also exists where all the opportunists are corrupt. The overall corrupt reputation of the group makes it pointless for any one opportunistic agent to become honest. Short-run attempts to control corruption may be ineffective. A one-period crackdown will not work. The possibility of a high-corruption equilibrium argues for hiring policies that permit principals to monitor individual agents from period to period rather than relying on group reputation and weak information about individual applicants.

claim with confidence that corruption at the top is less harmful than low-level corruption. The impact of corruption depends upon the strength and lack of scruples of the private firms and individuals that pay bribes. Under bilateral monopoly, powerful public and private actors divide the economic gains. A powerful kleptocrat facing weak private actors not only extracts rents but also organizes the state to create rents. In contrast, large, corrupt, private firms facing a weak state can extract high levels of benefits without paying high bribes. The incidence of corruption is high, but the size of bribes is low. The cost of tolerating payoffs is likely to be very high once one considers the benefits that flow to the powerful private actors in return for payoffs.

With multiple payers and recipients of bribes complex markets can arise. Frequently, in a competitive environment, bribery breeds more bribery until the system is permeated with corruption. Under other conditions, however, honesty breeds honesty. Reformers in competitive environments have the difficult task of encouraging beneficial spirals while avoiding destructive ones.

Democracy can help limit corruption if it gives people alternative avenues of complaint and gives incumbents an incentive to be honest. However, as I demonstrate in the next chapter it is not a panacea. To assess the role of democracy, one must go beyond simple labels to evaluate alternative democratic forms.

8

Democracy and Corruption:
Incentives and Reforms

Democracies based on strong legal foundations provide a stable framework for economic activity. For this framework to operate efficiently, however, politicians must seek reelection and must feel insecure about their prospects, but not too insecure. This leads to a "paradox of stability." Too much security of tenure can further corrupt arrangements. Too much insecurity can have the same effect.

The strength of the competitive political environment raises the stakes and reduces the likelihood of corruption. A competitive political system can be a check on corruption. For elected politicians the most immediate form of "punishment" occurs at the polls. The electorate may extract a cost even if the payoffs are kept secret. Bribes and illegal campaign donations are given in return for a benefit. Often the quid pro quo is something the corrupt politician would not have done without the payoff. If politicians vote against the interests of their constituents, they can expect to suffer at the polls.

The distinctive incentives for corruption in democracies depend on the organization of electoral and legislative processes and on the methods of campaign finance. These factors may be intertwined. Some electoral systems encourage the development of strong political parties while others encourage politicians to develop personal followings. Corrupt possibilities are related to the relationship between political structure and private wealth.

Electoral Systems
In a democracy, electoral voting rules and legislative processes interact with underlying political cleavages to affect the opportunities for corruption. Political systems provide various mixtures of both broad-based policies and narrowly focused private or group benefits. Some public

127

goods like national defense also provide benefits to firms and regions that obtain defense contracts and military bases. Incentives for corruption are higher if the state provides individualized benefits, but the connection between corruption and political structure is complex.

Corruption and Political Organization

Consider two contrasting types of political organization. The first is a democratic system that supplies narrowly focused benefits and does not need corruption to favor groups with political clout. In a district-based plurality system with weak parties, for example, the beneficiaries of government programs may be geographically concentrated population groups and local industries. Similarly, under proportional representation, narrow interests may be able to establish national political parties with pivotal influence. Thus a system might rank quite low on the scale of political corruption simply because groups that are willing to pay bribes find that they do not need to do so.

Even in such systems, not all narrow groups have direct political influence. Some may try to buy benefits either through legal campaign gifts or illegal campaign contributions and bribes. These payments might be treated more tolerantly by politicians if government is viewed by most citizens as a source of private benefits. The low expectations of the populace can fuel both legal patronage and illegal favors. Although one might expect the incidence of bribery to be inversely related to the level of legal benefits provided to narrow groups, this may not be true. Instead, society may be divided into two groups: those endowed with political clout by the structure of the political system and those obliged to buy influence through illegal payoffs.

Politicians might then try to structure policies so that these two groups are not in direct conflict. For example, a politician could support a project that benefits his or her constituents and then take bribes from those who want contracts or jobs. Although such practices may reduce the quality or raise the price of the project, this may not be obvious to most voters. Suppose, for example, that a politician obtains public money to build a port facility in his or her district. The politician might then give construction contracts to firms that make payoffs. The constituents get their pork-barrel project at the same time as corrupt firms obtain favors. Narrowly focused public projects and illegal payoffs go together.

Second, consider a political system with strong party discipline and two evenly matched national parties. Broadly speaking, this is a scenario that, in the absence of payoffs, is more likely to supply broad-based public services that benefit a majority of the population. Wealthy, but narrow, groups have no way to advance their political agenda directly without mounting a campaign that can garner broad support. Thus legal and illegal campaign contributions and corruption might be more, not less, prevalent simply because other options are closed off. Once again, those who make payoffs are likely to have more success if they can tie their gains to policies that politicians find attractive for electoral reasons. Corruptly obtained contracts or licenses to supply public services are an obvious source of payoffs. Operating against the possibility of high levels of malfeasance, however, is the likelihood that the public will favor a tough stance against corruption and money in politics generally. They will be better able to make their beliefs effective if the political scene is highly competitive – so that representatives have little freedom to act against their constituents' wishes.

In response, those who seek corrupt influence will focus on the politicians who are cheapest to purchase. Everything else equal, these will be representatives with safe seats facing little opposition, "sure losers" facing certain electoral defeat, or those who are planning to retire either voluntarily or through the operation of term limits. Term limits spur corruption by placing politicians in an end game in which they are sure that they will not be returned to office (Rose-Ackerman 1978: 15–58).

Some unpopular policies may be impossible to purchase from an elected legislature. If disclosure of corruption spells political death and if disclosure is more likely the higher the level of bribery, some politicians may be unwilling to accept large bribes (Rasmusen and Ramseyer 1994). The benefits of higher bribes are eventually outweighed by higher costs. There are two possible outcomes under these conditions. Under the first, bribes are set high enough to compensate for the expected political costs of accepting payoffs, and some deals are too expensive for bribers to undertake. Corrupt deals that occur involve payoffs to the lowest-priced legislators. Under the second, officials either reject bribe offers or accept only small ones. If bribery fails, it is not because private groups are unwilling to pay the sums needed, but because not enough politicians can be bought given the risks.

Political party leaders are not necessarily passive participants. Strong party discipline can be used to further public goals, but it can also be used to bargain for high payoffs. When wealthy organized interests exist on both sides of an issue, party leaders and agenda setters may encourage competitive bribe offers and may even threaten to introduce damaging legislation as a means of extorting payoffs.[1] If a single party or a

---

[1] Legislative committees at the state and federal level have sometimes proposed taxes and business regulations as a way of extorting payoffs and campaign contributions (McChesney 1997; Rose-Ackerman 1978: 48–51).

stable coalition controls the legislature, it may be able to extract a large share of the gains from the corrupt deal especially when organized interests are in competition.

In short, it is impossible to associate abstract political systems unproblematically with levels of corruption. The key variables in any regime are the ability of wealthy organized groups to obtain legal influence and the attitude of the general population toward the public provision of private benefits. Do people react with outrage to corrupt deals, or do they simply want a bigger share of the spoils for themselves? An exclusive focus on limiting corruption may produce policy recommendations with undesirable consequences. Outright corruption may fall as the legal influence of special interests increases with little change in the perceived legitimacy of the state. More promising directions for reform are changes in the competitiveness of the political system and in the discretion given to elected politicians. Decisions that impose costs or benefits on individuals or small groups can be removed from politics. It would be desirable to insulate the selection of contractors from the political process so that this decision is not part of the spoils available for distribution by politicians through legal or illegal means. Of course, as I have discussed previously, corruption in contracting is common even if politicians are not involved, but at least a set of techniques exists that can limit its impact within the bureaucracy. In many countries the replacement of patronage with a civil service system has limited politicians' opportunities for personal enrichment and for obtaining political favors in return for jobs.

Representation and Corruption in Divided Societies

Systems that are based on the exchange of narrow political favors cannot be cured by reforms in civil service and procurement systems. More fundamental shifts in political structure are needed, but will, of course, be difficult to produce. The problem may not be corruption per se so much as a well-entrenched system of narrowly focused patronage relations. Some political scientists, however, argue that "consociational" systems of this type are desirable because they produce stability in deeply divided societies (Lijphart 1977). Others are less concerned with stability and more focused on providing minority groups with a greater share of political power (Guinier 1994). These benefits may be achieved, however, through a series of inefficient rent-seeking deals. Even worse, the deals may benefit not ordinary people, but only the leaders of various constituencies.

Other scholars have argued, instead, that divided societies ought to organize political life to provide incentives for accommodation. Donald Horowitz, in particular, has proposed electoral systems for divided societies that reward politicians for making broad appeals across ethnic and other social groups (Horowitz 1985). The problem is not just instability but other aspects of government performance as well, including the incidence of corruption. A recent study suggests that a high level of ethnic fragmentation makes it difficult to establish a functioning, competent government (Easterly and Levine 1997), but a state can overcome the disadvantages of ethnic divisions by establishing strong, corruption-free government institutions. Where ethnic divisions have not been well handled, as in Nigeria, the result can be a state focused on sharing the spoils, not promoting overall prosperity. Governments are short-lived, and each represents a different ethnic coalition. Military rule alternates with periods of electoral politics. Political life is focused on rent seeking, not productive activity (Diamond 1993b, 1995). Corruption in such cases indicates a lack of competence and political will at the top of government. Divisions can be so severe that government can aim for no more than the avoidance of civil war.

Some divided states have a dominant group that always retains political power. In such cases, majority politicians may espouse a populist ideology that demonizes minority ethnic groups but then accept payoffs to permit them to flourish. This is a particularly common pattern if the minority group is also wealthy and active in business. Such corruption raises a difficult problem especially if combined with patronage and close personal ties that cement monopoly business relationships. One might be tempted to excuse these payoffs as a way around the narrow-mindedness of ordinary people. But the corruption scandals that come to light will only fuel ethnic prejudices, especially if bribes are paid not just to operate businesses but also to limit competition in the interest of maximizing the gains to be shared by political and business leaders. Here one question for reformers is whether the dominance of one group is inevitable or whether a different method of selecting leaders could lead to the accommodation of other groups in legitimate, noncorrupt ways (Horowitz 1985).

Even if there are no important underlying ethnic or racial divisions in a society, people may simply have widely different views about government policy. If the issue space is complex and multidimensional, unstable coalition governments are likely (Laver and Schofield 1990). Such instability may encourage corruption in much the same way as a system based on the provision of narrowly focused benefits. No coalition believes that it will retain power for long and so uses its time in office to amass personal gains instead of making policy. This result suggests that voting systems that encourage stability will limit corruption and encourage reform.

This conclusion seems directly counter to Mancur Olson's claim that stable systems permit the development of inefficient rent-seeking coalitions (Olson 1982). However, the idea is not to organize the state to give one group monopoly power, but to give incumbents an incentive to take a long-run view and to anticipate that they have a good chance of either winning or losing the next election. Incumbents should be unsure of winning, but believe that they have a good chance of returning to office. Opposition parties play the role of monitors, threatening to make corruption a campaign issue. If voters care about policy, not private spoils, such a structure will encourage honest policy making.

Conclusions

To summarize, there are three dimensions that are central in determining the incidence of political corruption. They affect politicians' willingness to accept bribes and illegal campaign financing, voters' tolerance of such payoffs, and the willingness to pay of wealthy groups. The first dimension is the existence of narrowly focused favors available for distribution by politicians. The second is the ability of wealthy groups to obtain these benefits legally. The third is the temporal stability of political alliances. Instability may arise from competition over the spoils of office, but governments in ideologically divided societies can also be unstable. Instability can induce both politicians and wealthy interests to get what private benefits they can in the short run. Reforms can focus on any or all of these dimensions. Thus, first, the system can insulate politicians from making certain personalized choices, or the electoral system can be structurally changed to give politicians a greater incentive to satisfy broad-based constituencies. Second, civic education campaigns can educate voters to require public benefits from the political system, not personal favors. This might make corruption seem the only option for narrow groups, but it also makes the acceptance of illegal payoffs a risky strategy for a career politician. Third, structural reforms can seek to produce more stability but without leading to an essentially autocratic system. Politicians should worry about losing office, but should also believe that reelection is possible. If the divisions that produce instability are based on ideological or social divisions, reforms should give politicians an incentive to accommodate a broad range of opinion or a multiplicity of social groups.

Buying Political Influence and Buying Votes

In democracies corruption scandals are frequently associated with the financing of political campaigns. Some countries have little bureaucratic corruption but suffer from a corrupt political process. However, money cannot be entirely eliminated from politics. Elections must be financed, and wealthy interests concerned with legislative outcomes and government policy may be willing to foot the bill. Financial pressures give politicians an incentive to accept payoffs, thus working against the other corruption-reducing effects of competitive elections. Observers of the U.S. political system worry that the cost of political campaigns encourages quid pro quo deals (Etzioni 1988). In France and Italy modern parties have lost ideological focus and come to be dominated by "business politicians" (della Porta 1996; Mény 1996: 314). Many of the recent scandals in those countries involved illegal campaign contributions. The same is true of the recent scandals in Korea and Japan (Park 1995; Reed 1996).

Financing Political Campaigns

Democratic political systems must find a way to finance political campaigns without encouraging the sale of politicians to contributors. Governments have drawn the line between legal and illegal gifts in quite different ways, and legal frameworks vary greatly in the limits they place on quid pro quo deals by politicians.

Even entirely legal contributions from wealthy interests are a source of concern. The worry is favoritism. Groups that give funds to elected officials expect help in the legislative process. They may also expect special treatment on individual problems in dealing with the bureaucracy or in seeking contracts and concessions. If the interests of such groups or individuals conflict with those of the general public, this undermines democratic values. The electoral process can discipline politicians to represent the interests of their constituents, and voters may penalize candidates who seem too deeply beholden to special interests. But voters cannot act unless they know both how their representatives behave and who has given them money. Legal gifts can have a corrupting effect if they need not be made public and if the quid pro quo is not itself obvious to voters.

Sometimes the expectations of a quid pro quo have been quite straightforward. In North Carolina in 1997, a construction firm that did not receive the favor it expected in return for a contribution to the incumbent governor's campaign asked for its money back.[2] In Canada in the early twentieth century firms gave kickbacks to political candidates to help finance their campaigns in return for assistance in obtaining government contracts. The resulting scandal led to a law banning such

---

[2] "A Road-Building Scandal Forces a Governor's Hand," *New York Times*, January 14, 1998.

quid pro quo arrangements, but they still allegedly occur (Qui 1996: 197, 230). In Japan, politicians who assist local firms in obtaining contracts allegedly expect a percentage of the price in return (Qui 1996: 231). In Germany in the 1980s, contributions disguised as charitable contributions were given to political parties in an effort to obtain legislative quid pro quos. At the time, paying members of Parliament for favors was not a punishable offense (Seibel 1997: 88, 94). In Spain scandals uncovered in the early 1990s involved politicians who raised funds for their political party by charging businesses and banks for fictitious consultancy work (Heywood 1996: 116–117).

At the federal level in the United States, the outright purchase of favors occurs but is muted and difficult to document. As one congressional representative put it, "it would be hard to argue that contributions don't open doors. Do I think a vote or a member can be bought by contributions? No. But there's always the subtle influence by the contributors" (quoted in Koszczuk 1997: 771). Contributions seem to be viewed by many donors as long-term investments in developing relationships of mutual trust (Snyder 1992). A recent study using American data finds that donations are made not to buy votes but to get sympathetic candidates into office. Once in office, politicians try to accommodate their supporters. In practice, however, it is difficult to distinguish between politicians who bend their positions to favor contributors and those who were elected because they share their contributors' point of view (Bronars and Lott 1997). Private contributions influence who runs for office as well as how politicians behave once in office.

The worry about undue influence would be of little concern if campaign funds were unimportant to electoral success. Then strict legal spending limits could be enforced. However, although empirical work has not conclusively determined the impact of campaign donations on electoral success, politicians and contributors certainly act as if money matters (Snyder 1992). Incumbents have a fund-raising advantage over other candidates, and those in powerful positions in the legislature are especially favored (Alexander 1991). The link between campaign funds and influence remains a persistent concern of critics of the American political system because the high cost of congressional races must be raised from private sources (Etzioni 1988).

In all democratic political systems some gifts to politicians violate domestic laws. Even when the legal restrictions on fund raising seem permissive, politicians and their wealthy patrons may prefer the anonymity of an illegal gift. Keeping a gift secret can help hide the illicit quid pro quo and will facilitate efforts to siphon off funds for personal use. Voters cannot be expected to look with tolerance on tax breaks or contracts granted in return for payoffs.

For example, the testimony of Italian political operatives in the Clean Hands investigations reveals how corrupt practices can become entrenched in nominally democratic systems. Party leaders placed would-be politicians in positions where the payment of bribes was routine. The construction industry was a particularly lucrative source of funds. Specialized "party cashiers" managed the collection of bribes and the distribution of contracts. Such people generally had no official government positions but were intermediaries for businessmen who had a problem in dealing with the government. They collected bribes for the party coffers, but some share of the gains was also kept by individuals (della Porta 1996). A study of one prominent Italian case suggests that illegal contributors had quite specific favors they wanted from the state and that much of the money could not be accounted for. There was a large discrepancy between the amount the firms reported giving and the amount the political parties reported receiving (Colazingari and Rose-Ackerman 1998).

Conflicts of Interest

Elected legislators in democracies need to be independent and publicly accountable. When the major issue was undue deference to the monarch, the ideal was an independently wealthy legislator not beholden to the sovereign. Thus in 1911 some members of the British House of Commons opposed a bill that mandated the payment of salaries to M.P.s on the ground that unpaid legislators would be more independent of the crown. In opposing pay increases in the 1970s some members argued that their pay should not be "so substantial as to make them feel beholden to the cabinet of the day with its power to dissolve Parliament, nor to the various parliamentary political parties" (Stark 1992: 433). The common French practice of civil servants taking a leave of absence to serve as members of the parliament raises similar questions about legislative independence from the executive (Rohr 1991: 287–288).

In the present day, however, the main concern is not dependence on the monarch but use of public office to further one's private financial interests. Potential conflicts of interest exist whenever a politician or a member of his or her family or staff has an ownership interest in a firm that does business with the government or that can benefit from state policy. No corrupt payoffs or campaign donations occur, but the risk of favoritism is the same.

Most mature democracies recognize the need to limit the impact of private economic interests on elected politicians and, at least, require them to report their financial interests. Within the European Union every member state except Luxembourg has such a requirement for parliamentarians. The member states differ widely, however, in exactly what must be disclosed, whether the reports are public, and what sanctions can be levied. Some states make no provision for sanctions, and some with strong sanctions do not provide public access to records (Peterson 1997). Nevertheless, in Europe concern with private financial conflicts of interest has increased in recent years. For example, in Britain the practice of private individuals paying M.P.s to ask questions in the House has come under unfavorable scrutiny, and the resulting scandals ended the careers of a number of politicians.[3]

In the United States federal legislators and their staffs face antibribery laws and conflict-of-interest rules that limit outside earnings and employment on leaving office [18 U.S.C. §§ 201, 203, 207(e)], but the section of the statute dealing with financial conflicts of interest does not apply to the legislative branch (18 U.S.C. § 208). Rules are much weaker at the state level. A recent study of the Illinois legislature, for example, concluded that existing conflict-of-interest rules are weak and poorly applied. Although legislators are forbidden from voting on legislation affecting a company that they own, they frequently propose and vote on laws affecting industries in which they have an interest. Disclosure provisions are weak, and the ethics law is rarely enforced.[4] Thus even in established democracies, the possibility exists that a politician's private business interests will collide with his or her role as a representative of the public.

Self-dealing has only recently raised questions in some countries. In new democracies, conflicts of interest have not been a high priority for reformers. Yet if uncontrolled, politicians with widespread business interests can undermine governmental legitimacy as surely as those who do the bidding of large contributors. In the former socialist countries, such as Russia and Poland, the problem is particularly acute because many newly privatized firms are controlled by their former managers who often remain active in politics (Collins 1993: 326). According to one commentator, in Russia "many government officials simply do not grasp that self-enrichment while in office is a crime" (Coulloudon 1997: 73). In the Ukraine 150 businessmen and bankers were elected to the Parliament in

[3] Stark (1992: 435); Philip Webster, "Sleaze Report Condemns Hamilton," *The Times* (London), July 4, 1997; David Hencke, "A Liar and a Cheat: Official," *The Guardian*, July 4, 1997.
[4] "Study Criticizes Illinois's Rules for Legislators," *New York Times*, March 30, 1998.

1998, many with economic interests that will be affected by the legislation they consider.[5] Although some applaud this development as a way of assuring independence from the executive, it creates obvious conflict-of-interest problems when regulatory and tax laws are at issue.

The problem is closely related to a familiar weakness of government-owned enterprises. In some developing countries, cabinet ministers chair public enterprises' boards of directors, reducing their independence and creating conflicts of interest (World Bank 1991: 28–29). If China ever moves toward a more democratic government structure, it will need to face the widespread conflicts of interest that exist in Chinese enterprises. Government officials sometimes hold multiple positions in the public and the private sectors. According to a study of the Chinese power industry, one person may be both an officer in a power corporation and an official in the power bureau (Chow 1997: 416). China has a long history of "blurring the line between government and the private sector," but this history seems inconsistent not only with the development of efficient modern enterprises but also with a more accountable government (ibid.: 418).

This is an area where it is difficult to prescribe definitive rules for all political systems. Nevertheless, at a minimum, disclosure of politicians' financial interests and those of their families seems necessary for democratic accountability. Similarly, relations with lobbyists and wealthy interests should be disclosed so that voters can judge whether their representative's behavior has been affected. Direct restrictions on outside earnings and lobbying activities are more controversial, but will be most important in those political systems where the electorate is less educated and informed.

Buying Votes

The problem of money in politics is not limited to pressures on politicians. On the other side of the equation are inducements given to voters. A particularly intractable form of political corruption occurs when politicians accept illegal campaign contributions and then use them to pay off the voters on an individual basis. These systems are nominally democratic, but they have much in common with older traditions of patronage. Voters may not object to the politicians' methods of campaign finance because they benefit from the largesse of candidates.

Direct payments to voters have a long history, going back to Great Britain and the United States in the nineteenth century. In those coun-

---

[5] "Ukraine's Businessmen – A New Political Class," *Financial Times,* April 17, 1998.

tries reforms have limited such payoffs, but they remain a feature of electoral politics elsewhere. In Italy political "bosses" attempt to get out the vote not only with campaign funds but also by mobilizing state resources, patronage jobs, and other types of government favors to create webs of obligation (della Porta 1996). Similar exchanges of favors for votes occur in Spain where party dues and donations and public subsidies are insufficient to finance campaigns, and existing laws are poorly enforced (Heywood 1996: 125–127). The 1996 election in Thailand carried on a long-standing practice of small payoffs to voters. An original twist included a post-election bonus if the candidate won.[6] Politicians accused of amassing illegal campaign war chests in Korea and Japan justified their actions by reference to the financial demands of campaigning in countries where voters expect gifts or other personalized benefits from candidates (Park 1995; Reed 1996). In such political systems, voters may approve even illegal contributions if they benefit personally from corrupt politicians' largesse. The personalized nature of the benefits given to voters by incumbents can make it particularly difficult for credible opposition candidates to arise. Of course, some might argue that if most payoffs are spent to benefit constituents, there is nothing to worry about. But this is wrong. Instead of a system based on democratic principles, the government is a structure of mutual favor giving that benefits those with the most resources and the most political power.

Politicians must be prevented from giving gifts and valuable favors to constituents. If this can be accomplished, it will level the playing field and help increase popular support for more fundamental reforms. Once payoffs are just going into the pockets and campaign advertising budgets of candidates, voters may be less inclined to accept the corrupt system. Publicity can also help. In both Korea and Italy improved information about the level of payoffs and the size of campaign war chests convinced people that few of the benefits were filtering down to them. If, in addition, the consequences of these payoffs are seen to be harmful to society, the stage is set for reform.

Reform

In a highly competitive system with informed voters who do not expect personal favors for themselves, a policy of prompt and complete disclosure might be sufficient. Any politician who relied too heavily on special interest money and voted accordingly would be defeated. More direct restrictions are needed if the system is not very competitive and if voters

---

[6] *New York Times,* November 19, 1996; *Far Eastern Economic Review,* November 28, 1996. For background on Thailand, see Pasuk and Sungsidh (1994).

are poorly informed. Without spending limits, politicians have leeway to favor large contributors, and the gifts themselves can be used to mislead voters as to the candidates' positions and behavior (Rose-Ackerman 1978: 33–45).

A basic problem in the design of a system of campaign finance is to avoid imposing restrictions that themselves encourage illegality. Although campaign finance laws in many countries are overly permissive, in others the laws are so restrictive that they practically require off-the-books transfers in order to finance campaigns.[7] Limits on donations are justified as a way to curb corrupt influences (Connolly 1996: 496), but strict legal limits can encourage unreported illegal transfers. For example, some critics of the Japanese system in force between 1975 and 1993 argue that it encouraged illegal payoffs by limiting legal business contributions (Qui 1996: 207–208). When the ban on corporate contributions in the current Japanese law comes into effect in 2000, a similar result may occur. Recent scandals in industrialized countries point to the importance both of clear rules governing the solicitation of private money and the provision of sufficient legal sources of funds. Furthermore, the impact of corporate gifts depends upon the ability of politicians to provide individualized favors to firms. If such favors are not outlawed or otherwise controlled, the difference between bribes and legal campaign contributions will be blurred and will depend, first, on reporting requirements and, second, on the reaction of voters.

An entrenched system of illegal payoffs may undermine efforts to reform the funding of political campaigns. In Italy campaign finance rules seem quite permissive. Corporate contributions are permitted so long as they are made public and approved by the firm's board of directors. Yet illegal contributions featured prominently in recent anticorruption cases (Colazingari and Rose-Ackerman 1998). Thus even if the rules seem permissive and if public funding is available, law enforcement authorities still need to check for illegal payments. Reformers will need to look beyond the details of the campaign finance law to seek ways to limit the discretion of politicians to favor gift givers.

The debate over campaign finance reform in the United States has focused mainly on the undue influence afforded to large givers (Koszczuk 1997; Tanenbaum 1995). This has led to calls for public financing and a modest attempt along these lines has been in place for presidential races since 1974 (Qui 1996: 212–216). One solution has been publicity. Firms must form Political Action Committees in order to make

---

[7] For a summary that indicates the range of options, see Law Library of Congress (1991).

donations, and all gifts must be reported. All fifty states also have legislation requiring that donations be reported, but enforcement is quite weak, and loopholes are easy to find (Alexander 1991: 76–78, 110). In many states and at the federal level contributions to political parties are not presently restrained.[8] Concerns for preserving free speech have limited the options in the United States.[9]

Solutions can approach the problem from four dimensions. First, the costs of political campaigns could be reduced by reducing the length of time for the campaign. Systems where the date of the next election is uncertain can enforce such constraints fairly well, but in all systems time limits are hard to make operational. Restrictions could also be imposed on the methods of campaigning in an effort to keep costs down. Second, stronger disclosure rules can be established. The United States already has quite strong disclosure requirements, but many records are not made public until well after the election has taken place (Alexander 1991: 76–78). Disclosure permits citizens to vote against candidates who receive too much special interest money and also makes it possible for scholars to study the impact of gifts on behavior to see how close to bribes they are. Third, laws in many countries and in the American states limit individual donations, and other laws limit candidates' spending. In the United States the Supreme Court has found contribution limits in the federal law consistent with the protection of free speech, but lower limits in some state laws have been struck down by the federal courts (Connolly 1996). The details of American constitutional jurisprudence need not detain us here, but the basic issue is important: To what extent can a democratic government interfere with its citizens' wishes to express their political interests through gifts to support political parties or individual candidates?

Fourth, alternative sources of funds can be found in the public sector. In the United States the federal government provides funds only for presidential candidates under certain conditions, and several American states provide public support for political campaigns.[10] Many other countries provide public funds for political campaigns or permit tax deductions or credits (Kaltefleiter and Naßmacher 1994: 261; Law Library of Congress 1991; Qui 1996). Germany, in particular, has experimented with various formulas in a effort to satisfy its constitutional principles.

---

[8] Koszczuk (1997); *Colorado Republican Federal Campaign Committee v. Federal Election Commission*, 116 S. Ct. 2309 (1996).

[9] Connolly (1996); Tanenbaum (1995); *Buckley v. Valeo*, 424 U.S. 1, at 37–61 (1976).

[10] See Alexander (1991); "Minnesota Steals the Spotlight on Campaign-Finance Reform," *Congressional Quarterly Weekly Report*, April 28, 1990: 1240; Tanenbaum (1995).

In Germany's strong party state, the Constitutional Court has been especially concerned with the negative impact of public funding on new or small parties. The latest law provides public funding to parties up to an overall ceiling. As a result of a 1992 decision of the Constitutional Court, the new law emphasizes the ability of parties to attract private donations as well as votes. Funds are distributed in proportion to each party's ability to attract both votes and party dues with a formula that disadvantages the largest parties relative to their vote-getting power. Contributions from businesses are permitted, but only a portion is tax deductible for a firm (Gunlicks 1995; Kaltefleiter and Naßmacher 1994).

A number of proposals have been made for more extensive public funding in United States. Those who oppose these reforms worry that public funding and spending limits will protect incumbents and unduly disadvantage nonmajor parties. Incumbents generally start with an advantage that only challengers with higher spending levels can over-come. Incumbents are also advantaged in the competition for funds (Snyder 1992). Public funding formulas could be designed to overcome the incumbency advantage, but the design of a workable system may be difficult. For example, Minnesota awarded public funds to candidates equal to one-half of the independent expenditures made against them.[11] One study concluded, however, that the Minnesota law did not succeed in helping challengers. In 1992 incumbents obtained almost $2000 more in public funds than challengers (Thompson and Moncrief 1998: 225). Notice that the Minnesota provision is the reverse of the German statute, which rewards parties in proportion to their ability to attract party dues up to an upper limit. At issue is whether public financing should build on or counteract a party or candidate's ability to tap private sources of funds. The Minnesota law has one advantage over the German law. It does not give political actors the incentive fraudulently to attract private money, use it to get matching funds, and then surreptitiously pay it back (Rudzio 1994). It is, instead, intended to dilute the impact of private funds in political campaigns.

Alternatively, public funds could be given to candidates who can demonstrate substantial public support. One way to do this is to give vouchers to voters to support the candidates of their choice. This plan would combine public funding with an egalitarian system for allocating funds (Ackerman 1993). In promoting democratic values, this plan would

---

[11] Tanenbaum (1995: 156). The provision was overturned by a federal appellate court under the free speech provisions of the United States Constitution, but the Supreme Court has not ruled on this issue (ibid.: 152).

reduce the influence of wealthy interests. If not well-monitored, however, it might increase illegal payments. Wealthy individuals and firms with strong interests in politics would find an important legal avenue to influence closed. They could lobby members of Congress but not support them financially. The result could be more under-the-table payoffs, especially to the losers in the race for vouchers. Conflict-of-interest rules might need to be strengthened and enforced more stringently because the incentive for politicians to use that route to financial gain would be increased by the introduction of a voucher system. Campaign financing reform needs to be carefully designed if it is not to introduce new incentives for malfeasance by closing off formerly legal alternatives.

Conclusions

Democratic elections are not invariably a cure for corruption. Instead, some electoral systems are more vulnerable to special interest influence than others. When narrow groups wield power, some use legal means, and others are corrupt. The choice of tactics can be influenced by the nature of the political system. In all democracies competitive elections help limit corruption because opposition candidates have an incentive to expose corrupt incumbents. However, the need to finance political campaigns introduces new incentives to favor special interests that do not exist in autocratic regimes. These incentives are especially high if electoral campaigns allocate individualized favors to voters – that is, if politicians bribe voters.

Illegal campaign contributions and the bribery of politicians can undermine democratic systems. Even though payoffs from wealthy individuals and firms benefit campaign committees, political parties, and voters, not the personal bank accounts of politicians, the distortionary impact of secret, illegal payments can be large. Payoffs are often made to obtain legislative or regulatory favors. Their effectiveness, however, depends on the organization of legislative and executive processes. Corrupt firms and individuals will focus on obtaining individual and firm-specific favors. Elections are not sufficient to check payoffs. Other means of public oversight are necessary to keep government accountable. Democratic governments must establish explicit policies to limit corrupt incentives.

9

Controlling Political Power

Public accountability is necessary for the control of corruption. Both autocracies and democracies can be deeply corrupt, and each can be held accountable in different ways. Elections can constrain politicians, but, as we have seen, they are an imperfect tool. Public accountability is possible even in countries without elections or with a dominant party that always wins the vote. These constraints may be more difficult for autocrats to accept than for elected officials, but even democratic officials resist reforms that expose them to public scrutiny and criticism. Corruption can be limited both by internal government structures and organizations that constrain malfeasance and by outside pressure from the public.

Limits on the power of politicians and political institutions combined with independent monitoring and enforcement can be potent anticorruption strategies. In a democracy, these limits include the separation of powers between the legislative and executive branches. An independent judicial and prosecutorial system and a federal structure can limit the power of political leaders. But the fragmentation of political power is not necessarily effective. Under some conditions, a system with multiple veto points is particularly subject to improper influence, and a federal system may simply give state and local political leaders leeway to enrich themselves at public expense. Independent sources of prosecutorial and judicial power are less problematic, although, of course, these institutions must themselves be largely free of corruption and patronage. Independence is necessary but not sufficient.

Another group of reforms increases the openness and accountability of government. Government collects and provides information; both the media and citizens' groups operate freely; and groups and individuals

143

have effective avenues for challenging official actions. Although such policies are likely to be more acceptable to democratically elected leaders, these reforms can also have an effect in undemocratic systems whose leaders nevertheless need public support to retain power.

Checks and Balances in the Legislative Process

In a government with strong checks and balances, no public institution is all-powerful. This reaches its most extreme form in the United States, but even parliamentary democracies usually have some power diffusion. Even seemingly unitary systems often are constrained by opposition parties and coalition dynamics. They may have an upper house based on different principles of representation, an independent judiciary, a constitution that can be amended only by special procedures, or a constitutionally protected bill of rights.

In a political system with multiple veto points, such as the U.S. federal government, the status quo has a privileged position. In the Senate two-fifths plus one of the members can threaten a filibuster, that is, they can refuse to limit debate on a bill. Thus, forty-one senators can block a bill favored by the President and a majority of each house. If a filibuster does not succeed or is not proposed, passage requires a majority vote in both the Senate and the House. The bill is then sent to the President. If he signs it, the bill becomes a law. If he vetoes it, the bill is defeated unless two-thirds of each house of Congress votes to override the veto. Just over one-third of the members of either house can block passage of a bill with majority support in Congress, but opposed by the President (Krehbiel 1998).

Can the American government structure be recommended as an anti-corruption framework? The answer depends on the goals of the corrupt. If they want to block something, the system is a poor check on corruption since it is relatively inexpensive to manipulate. Those who seek influence only need to find the weak link and corrupt that group or make conditional campaign contributions. Those with the power to set the agenda will be a focus of both corrupt payoffs and legal campaign donations because they can keep an issue out of the public eye. Agenda-setters do, in fact, have an advantage in raising legal campaign funds (Ansolabehere and Snyder 1999). They may also be the target of illegal payoffs if the giver wants the political system to stay away from a potentially popular issue. Accomplishing something affirmative is much harder than blocking a costly law. Here the complexities of the American system can be beneficial to those seeking to control malfeasance. However, the difficulty of exerting influence depends on whether the outside group wants a public or a hidden benefit.

In the case of a public benefit, some of the links in the chain may favor the policy without payoffs. Some legislators may have constituents who benefit from the policy so that one or both houses of Congress support the law without the need for payoffs. Politicians who are committed ideologues may favor the policy and be unable credibly to demand payoffs. Then in close cases only a few legislators who are swing votes may need to be influenced. The President may also support the proposal for reasons of policy or politics. The judiciary overturns only those laws that violate the constitution. Thus, those seeking to influence the outcome may be able to concentrate on only a few of the potential veto points. Corruption can have an impact in spite of the complexity of the legislative process.

For a hidden, special-interest benefit, corruption is unlikely to be successful because every decision point must be purchased. This is both expensive and risky because just one honest official can undermine the entire effort. The exposé will involve not just the bribery allegations themselves but also revelation of the special treatment they were supposed to buy.

Of course, special interest benefits need not always be obtained by secret, underhanded means. In the United States, bargains are frequently made that logroll a range of private benefits together into a single statute in a way that can gain majority support.[1] In political systems where ties of family and friendship are more salient than in the U.S. federal government, such outcomes will be even more common. Laws are structured so that most everyone gets something for his or her powerful constituents or supporters. Corruption is not necessary.

To conclude, multiple sources of authority give the status quo an advantage and imply that no one group has absolute power. Nothing can be done unless all the separate bodies agree. The constraints on legislative power in the American system imply that obtaining new benefits from government can be costly and complex. Using corruption to pass a law can be expensive and risky. A payoff will be more effective and cheaper if the goal is simply to block passage of a bill. In the United States corruption ought to be biased toward attempts to block legislation and toward close cases where only one part of government needs to be influenced. The American example suggests that, whatever its other benefits, a government with strong separation of powers is not unambiguously desirable as an anticorruption device.

---

[1] See Douglas Arnold, who argues that omnibus bills may be necessary for the passage of certain kinds of broad-based compromises in the public interest (Arnold 1990: 131–132).

Accountable Implementation

Legislatures frequently delegate implementation to the executive. I have already argued that this is a desirable way to limit political corruption. Thus it is interesting to observe that legislators often voluntarily draft statutes that limit their own control over implementation. The statutes leave the development of precise standards to government agencies, but may include detailed procedural requirements (Moe 1990; Rose-Ackerman 1992: 33–96). The traditional justifications for this technique combine a belief in the expertise of executive agencies with the claim that legislators should not be either making individual personnel and procurement choices or deciding enforcement priorities. Thus regulation writing is delegated because the legislature is not competent to carry out this essentially legislative task, and purely executive or adjudicatory functions are not appropriate for the legislature under separation-of-powers principles.

Terry Moe, however, explains the structure of American statutes as a response to uncertainty about who will control the legislature in the future. Worried that opponents will gain control, interest groups push for laws that separate politics from administration. They accept less influence for themselves as a way of shutting out their opponents as well. Opponents who wish to undermine the effectiveness of the law support the creation of dysfunctional administrative processes, and supporters go along because they are uncertain of their future political influence (Moe 1990). Moe believes that parliamentary systems are not subject to the same pressures. He and Michael Caldwell argue that the British system is superior because laws, once passed, are easy to repeal. Thus it does little good to build in rigid bureaucratic structures because they will not protect a policy from a change in regime. They hypothesize that public agencies will be less encumbered by externally imposed rules and that the bureaucratic system will be more simple, coherent, and rational (Moe and Caldwell 1994).

Moe and Caldwell's normative claims seem overblown. Whatever the explanation for constrained delegation in the United States, the results are not uniformly bad. General rules issued by agencies under enabling statutes have the force of law. Thus the process by which they are produced requires accountability because these processes may be honestly or corruptly influenced for the benefit of the narrow groups. Whether one focuses on executive branch accountability to the public or on the avoidance of corrupt payoffs, the procedural constraints of the American Administrative Procedures Act (5 U.S.C. §§ 551–559, 701–706) seem valuable. Under the American act agencies must give notice of their intent to issue a regulation, accept testimony from a broad range of individuals and groups, and issue a statement of reasons along with the final rule. The rule can be challenged in court if proper procedures are not followed or if the end result is inconsistent with the underlying statute. This process has been criticized as time-consuming and cumbersome, but inconvenience is the price of limitations on the arbitrary power of an executive (Rose-Ackerman 1995a).

By way of contrast, Germany's parliamentary system imposes fewer controls on executive branch rule making, but federal regulations administered by the states must be approved by the upper house, which represents the state governments. Otherwise, German rule making procedures are much less transparent than American ones and have been criticized for being too open to industry influence. Payoffs do not seem to be a problem, but excess influence may be (ibid.). Great Britain seems to have a less procedurally constrained administrative process than does Germany. This could imply a more rational administrative process, but there seems no good, logical reason why that should be the result. If interest groups want influence, they can get it in a much more opaque and potentially corrupt manner under the procedurally unconstrained British system. Moe (1990) may be correct in saying that the United States imposes too many controls on administrative action. However, an administrative law system that is more beholden to the current legislative majority and lacks procedural safeguards seems more prone to the ongoing influence of narrow groups. Thus from the point of view of constraining rent seeking by politicians and narrow groups, the weak administrative law constraints produced by parliamentary governments create accountability problems that are more serious than those in a system where the legislature has both the power and the incentive to constrain the bureaucracy.

Another set of problems can arise in political systems with weak legislative branches. Critics of Latin American governments argue that most have overly powerful executives. Unlike the American Congress, Latin American legislatures frequently have little influence (Mainwaring and Shugart 1997). As a consequence, incentives for rent seeking and corruption are high within the executive branch. The president has extensive decree power, may control a secret financial account that can be used to reward supporters, and is less subject to popular control while in office. Furthermore, the judiciary is generally less independent in practice and, until recently, has seldom effectively constrained the executive.[2]

---

[2] Borner, Brunetti, and Weder (1992: 28–30); Del Granado (1995: 19–20); Manzetti and Blake (1996).

Some Asian countries exhibit a similar pattern. For example, in Thailand the executive in the past controlled and limited legislative activity so that it could rule by decree (Pasuk and Sungsidh 1994). Executive rule has been accompanied by close business–government relations (Anek 1994: 208–211; Hewison: 1993). The lack of executive accountability facilitates corruption by centralizing regulatory power and giving the executive wide discretion. In many countries the judiciary is also weak. China is an extreme case where some courts have held that only the National People's Congress, not the courts, can decide on the legality of administrative rules. Furthermore, judges are not independent of the rest of government. Their budgets and the terms of their appointments are controlled by governments at all levels (Bing 1994: 6–7, 17–18). Whatever the structure of government, the interests of narrow groups can predominate if they face no credible opposition. If such groups start out in a powerful position, they may be able to block reform efforts.

These cases suggest that administrative law reform ought to be a part of any anticorruption strategy. The background conditions that determine rule making in the executive branch should be examined to assure adequate participation and transparency. The public needs avenues for appeal to the judiciary if the government has not followed its own procedures or has acted lawlessly. The goal is to make corrupt deals harder to hide by forcing review of the process and the substantive outcome. A review process aimed at achieving good substantive policy and democratic accountability can indirectly fight corruption.

However, countries with a judiciary that is both corrupt and unrestrained will obviously be reluctant to give it additional powers. Furthermore, if an independent judiciary enforces laws that are biased in favor of regulated interests, reform will be difficult without a change in underlying legal standards. For example, in the Philippines oversight of the banking industry in the 1980s was hampered by lawsuits brought by banks against both regulatory agencies and the public officials themselves. As one banker himself admitted, lawsuits were a way "of preventing officials from implementing the regulations. You intimidate the bureaucracy" (quoted in Hutchcroft 1998: 202).

Although the details of the American administrative process can surely use reform, the basic principles express the essence of accountable bureaucratic behavior. The Administrative Procedures Act requires that rule making involve public notice, public participation, and a government obligation to publicize and explain its actions. These requirements not only are consistent with democratic government but also limit the scope for corrupt deals. Even a country with a weak legislature or a unitary parliamentary system could limit the opportunities for corruption and other types of influence by adopting more transparent administrative processes.[3]

Federalism: Exit and Voice

In a federal system each governmental entity has a limited domain within which it can exercise power. It need not obtain agreement from any other unit of government so long as it stays within its jurisdiction. If it oversteps, it can expect to be challenged. The national government can constrain the states, and the states, the localities. Institutions operating internationally may provide a check on national governments. This kind of leverage has problematic aspects because higher-level power wielders can make no straightforward claim to represent the interests of the affected citizens. In the control of corruption, however, there are two cases in which intervention can be justified.

First, corrupt politicians may restrict commerce across state borders. Internationally, officials working in collaboration with corrupt business firms harm the prospects of honest international businesses. Within a country, state or provincial governments may limit interstate commerce to protect local businesses (Ma 1995). In such cases, international or national authorities can limit the protectionist actions of lower-level governments.

Second, state and local governments may be under the control of narrow elites that use the apparatus of government for personal gain. Although competition between jurisdictions for investment resources limits corrupt possibilities, it does not eliminate them. The very smallness and intimacy of local jurisdictions may make corrupt relations possible (Rodden and Rose-Ackerman 1997). Indeed, the most corrupt and patronage-ridden governments seem to be at the local level in many countries, including developed countries such as the United States and Germany. The close cooperation between public authorities and private interests limits partisan politics and the oversight it provides (Seibel 1997: 85–86).[4]

---

[3] See del Granado (1995: 19–23), who argues this point for Latin America. Bolivia, for example, has no Code of Administrative Procedures.

[4] Consider the following examples. In Italy the small size of local governments in Sicily facilitates the dominance of local politics by individual Mafia families (Gambetta and Reuter 1995: 119). In Taiwan corruption in local government contracting is an acknowledged problem, and in Japan procurement reform at the federal level has not trickled down to local governments where bid rigging and favoritism are pervasive (Prystay 1997; "Bid Rigours," *Far Eastern Economic Review*, March 23, 1995). In South Africa, state and local government institutions are weak and often under the control of rent-seeking politicians (Rubinfeld 1997) while in Spain a new policy of decentralization allegedly greatly

In such cases, intervention by higher-level government is often desirable. For example, the Federal Bureau of Investigation is active in the control of municipal corruption in the United States. Similarly, when the federal government provides grants to lower-level governments, it frequently requires them to establish systems of accountability. In the United Kingdom an Audit Commission monitors the probity of local governments (United Kingdom 1993, 1994, 1996). Sometimes the overlap in jurisdictions has an international dimension. A defector from the Colombian drug cartel chose the American justice system over the Colombian. This enabled him to reveal payoffs to Colombian politicians.[5]

Conversely, corruption control is sometimes enhanced by the limited power of the central government vis-à-vis the states. In this scenario, the threat of exit can be a method of control. Exit does not require a concerted organizational effort. In a world with many coequal governments, the corruption and ineffectiveness of government officials are limited by the ability of constituents and business firms to go elsewhere. Firms trying to decide where to locate a manufacturing plant can limit bribe demands by locating several feasible sites. Residents of a village whose officials extract large payoffs for routine services can move elsewhere. The mobility of people and businesses clearly limits the ability of officials to extract payoffs for services to which one is entitled (Montinola, Qian, and Weingast 1995; Weingast 1995).

But mobility is not always helpful if it means that individual jurisdictions find it harder to control undesirable behavior. Suppose, for example, that one city government has installed an honest police force that cracks down on illegal gambling. The gamblers may simply move to a friendly suburb that they can control and establish their business there – as has sometimes happened in the United States.[6] The ease with which

increased the spoils of office at the municipal level (Heywood 1996: 130). Corruption is common at the municipal level in Chile where government institutions are "isolated and closed to public scrutiny" (Rehren 1997: 330). In China decentralization occurred without an increase in capacity at the local level. Although some Chinese states took advantage of their new powers to promote economic growth, in other provinces the result has been massive corruption and misappropriation of government resources. This has been a particular problem in the banking sector where credit has frequently been allocated for political reasons (Burns 1993: 357).

[5] "Informant's Revelations on Cali Cartel Implicate Colombian Officials," *Washington Post*, January 28, 1996.

[6] Fort Lee, New Jersey, across the Hudson River from New York City, was one example. The wealthy organizers of illegal gambling games, however, made one mistake: They invested in Fort Lee condominium projects. These projects soon

funds can cross national borders, coming to rest in various "financial paradises," is another example of how multiple, competing jurisdictions can make control of corruption, fraud, and tax evasion more, not less, difficult. Because, in practice, it may be difficult to tell the difference between constructive and destructive competition, the decentralization of government structures can, at best, make a marginal contribution to the control of corruption.

Independent Judicial and Prosecutorial Institutions
Many countries have exemplary anticorruption statutes that are irrelevant in the real world (Singh 1997: 636; United Nations, 1990: 22–27). Even if a nation's prosecutors are actively engaged, this will mean little unless the country has an honest judicial system. In the absence of such basic institutions, specialized bodies focusing exclusively on corruption will be necessary.

The Judiciary
Because judicial decisions help determine the distribution of wealth and power, judges can exploit their positions for private gain. A corrupt or politically dependent judiciary can facilitate high-level corruption, undermine reforms, and override legal norms. When the judiciary is part of the corrupt system, the wealthy and the corrupt operate with impunity, confident that a well-placed payoff will deal with any legal problems. The impact extends beyond the public sector to purely private disputes over contracts and property. Business deals may be structured inefficiently to avoid encounters with the judicial system, and ordinary people may be systematically taken advantage of because they lack access to an impartial system of dispute resolution. Bidding wars may develop in which parties on opposing sides compete in making payoffs.[7]

An honest and well-respected judiciary has a special role to play in resisting corrupt governments and maintaining the rule of law. In Italy, for example, independent magistrates were central to the persistence of

---

filled up with reform-minded young professionals who voted in a reform mayor and city council committed to closing down the gambling industry in their town (Amick 1976: 89).

[7] An historical example from Egypt under Muhammed Ali in the 1820s illustrates the problem. According to an Englishman living in Egypt at that time, judges' decisions were influenced by the rank of the plaintiff and the defendant or a bribe from either. "On some occasions, particularly in long litigations, bribes are given by each party, and a decision is awarded in favour of him who pays the highest." Quoted by Johnson (1991: 686). MacLean (1996: 157) claims that in Jakarta, Indonesia, "justice" belongs to the high bidder. He argues that such practices occur in many countries.

the recent anticorruption investigations and prosecutions. In India, the Supreme Court pushed forward with a corruption investigation that the government had wanted to quash. The Court removed the Prime Minister from control of the federal agency investigating the issue.[8] In Spain, the Supreme Court forced officials to reveal the way secret Interior Ministry accounts were used. It held that public officials could not use state security as a defense if criminal activities are suspected.[9] In Korea an appellate court upheld the conviction of two former presidents on corruption charges (Kim and Kim 1997). In Brazil, the Supreme Court insisted that the congressional impeachment of President Collor be held in public and that each congressman's vote be fully open. These demands helped keep the process honest and led to the dismissal from office of a blatantly corrupt president (Geddes and Ribeiro Neto 1992).

The judiciary assumes particular importance in countries trying to establish democracy and the rule of law. Yet many such countries, especially in Latin America and Eastern Europe, have poorly functioning courts and legal systems.[10] Corruption is a response to underlying problems in the administration of justice, but the existence of widespread payoffs makes reform difficult. There are three kinds of difficulties: the nature of the underlying laws, weaknesses in the administration of justice, and a judiciary unable to serve as a check on other branches of government. Each demands a different kind of response.

First, in countries that have just become committed to democracy and the free market, laws governing the private market either do not exist or are vague and contradictory. Judges may have little experience or training in resolving the legal problems arising out of private business deals and in applying new regulatory and taxation statutes (Buscaglia and Dakolias 1996: 12). The law on the books may not mean much and sometimes it may be difficult even to find out what the law says. In Latin America one study refers to the "jungle of laws" governing private contracts and argues that the discretion accorded to judges creates corrupt incentives that, in turn, increase the uncertainty of the business climate.

---

[8] "Court Removes Rao as Head of Political Bribes Investigation," *The Times*, March 2, 1996.

[9] "Spanish Court Overturns Ruling on Secret Funds," *Financial Times*, February 22, 1995.

[10] For example, a survey of businesses in Latin America indicated that the judicial system was among the top ten most significant constraints to private sector development (Dakolias 1996: 3). An excellent overview of the problems facing judicial reformers in Venezuela is presented in Lawyers Committee for Human Rights and Venezuelan Program for Human Rights Education and Action (1996: 41–80) (hereinafter cited as Lawyers Committee).

"The legislature and executive produce a multitude of laws [that] make it almost impossible for anyone to know which ones are actually in force. This uncertainty makes the courts the ideal place for bargaining, corruption, and rent seeking" (Borner, Brunetti, and Weder 1992: 20, 29–30; see also Buscaglia and Dakolias 1996; Buscaglia and Ulen 1997; Dakolias 1996; Rowat, Malik, and Dakolias 1995). Often, it is hard for lawyers even to find the text of statutes and regulations. In countries in the civil law tradition, such as Latin America, uncertainty about the law is particularly ironic because the ideal is a pure set of legal norms that can be logically applied in individual cases. There is a poor fit between the formal law and the reality of private disputes (Linarelli 1996). Elsewhere, some developing countries function with laws written in the language of the colonial power or continue to use obsolete statutes borrowed from developed countries many years ago. For example, in those parts of Asia subject to British influence, some laws, including those dealing with corruption, are written in English and are thus incomprehensible to much of the population (Lee 1986: 103).

If the law on the books does not mean much and the judicial system operates poorly, people will avoid bringing disputes before the courts unless they are certain to be the high bribers. Otherwise they will find ways to circumvent the court system by hiring private arbitrators and using other methods, such as the protection provided by organized crime. The Latin American judiciary is reportedly so deficient that most business people try to avoid using the courts to resolve disputes (Buscaglia 1995; Dakolias 1996). As a result, an informal sector has arisen. In Peru, for example, one writer claims that this involves "pseudo-attorneys, false documents, forged title deeds, nonexistent identities, and virtually no legal guarantees" (Santa Gadea 1995: 185). In Indonesia the courts are ineffective because of the widespread belief that many judges are corrupt or incompetent (Das-Gupta and Mookherjee 1998: 427). Alternative private "collection agencies" are used by private creditors to extort payments. According to Roberto MacLean (1996: 158), a delinquent debtor in Jakarta may find a basket of snakes or a box of spiders in his home. In Eastern Europe and Russia murders of businessmen and bankers are common. Many appear to be execution-style killings that are part of a brutal private system of "dispute resolution."[11]

In these cases corruption is a signal of deeper problems in the legal system. The goal of reform is not just to improve the operation of the

---

[11] According to the Russian government, 269 businessmen and financiers were murdered in 1995 in execution-style slayings. "Mr. Tatum Checks Out," *The Economist*, November 9, 1996.

courts, but also to create a secure legal framework for private market activity. Corrupt incentives can be reduced by laws that are well drafted, relatively clear, and generally available. Projects, like a recent one in Costa Rica, to computerize all governing statutes and regulations, should be a high priority on corruption-fighting grounds (París Rodriquez 1995: 203). If laws are clear, not only will the cases that get into court be easier to resolve, but fewer disputes will arise. In other countries the law needs to be established at the same time as it is made public. Borrowing from successful market economies and established democracies is a commonplace occurrence however problematic it seems to scholars of comparative law. At least in some of the countries in the former Soviet bloc, such borrowings, however awkward, seem to be effective. Even in the Central Asian republic of Kazakhstan, with a history and culture far removed from Western Europe and the United States, the Foreign Investment Code, based on the work of foreign advisers, is viewed as successful by local business leaders. In interviews many of them pointed to the importance of the code in proving Kazakhstan's commitment to providing a stable and supportive environment for foreign investment (Nichols 1997b).

Second, even if laws are relatively clear, bribes can avoid some of the costs and inconveniences of a judicial proceeding. Public opinion polls in Latin America indicate a lack of confidence in the legal system. A survey carried out in Argentina in 1994 found that 49 percent thought the administration of justice was bad or very bad, and 65 percent considered the major problems to be corruption and delays (Alvarez 1995: 81). In Brazil and Peru very high percentages lacked confidence in the judicial system (Dakolias 1996: 4). A seven-country study in Latin America found that delays and backlogs had increased dramatically between 1973 and 1993 (Buscaglia and Ulen 1997: 278–280). In Argentina in 1993 the expected times to disposition for commercial, civil, and family cases, respectively, were 3, 9.5, and 12 years. Long average delays went along with a high variance across cases (Buscaglia and Dakolias 1996: 3, 13).

Payoffs can be a way to speed up decisions when delays and backlogs are high. The bribe payers go to the head of the queue, thus increasing the wait for the honest and perhaps inducing more litigants to pay for expedited service. Even if judges are not themselves corrupt, clerks in charge of assigning cases and managing files may demand or accept bribes.[12] The lack of formal court fees creates incentives for court

---

[12] MacLean (1996: 157) notes that in Poland judges are reputed to be independent and honest, but long delays in processing cases are causing corruption to arise among support personnel who accept bribes in return for expediting case processing.

employees and judges to demand unauthorized fees (Buscaglia 1995). In Venezuela, for example, informal fees are apparently common with the speed and efficiency of service depending on the size of the payoff (Lawyers Committee 1996: 57). Throughout Latin America the practice of private meetings between judges and the lawyers for individual liti- gants can be used to "motivate" court personnel, including judges (Buscaglia and Ulen 1997: 280–281; MacLean 1996: 158). Similar prac- tices are common in China where legal officials often require the parties to lawsuits "to hold lavish banquets for them before the trial begins" (Jordan 1997: 345). The system gives wealthy plaintiffs an advantage – they appear to be able to pay to speed up the process significantly and perhaps affect the outcome as well.

Bribes are more likely to be accepted or demanded by judges and their functionaries if they are underpaid and work under conditions much worse than those of private lawyers and their assistants. Furthermore, additional training may be needed for judges if they are to deal respon- sibly with the new types of disputes coming before their courts as a result of the growth in the market economy. Deciding a case on the basis of a bribe may be the easy way out for a judge unable competently to review a complex dispute.

Improvements in the professionalism, pay, and working conditions of judges appear to be necessary, but they should also be com- bined with efforts to reduce the incentives to pay bribes. Those with weak cases may have no option except bribery, but even litigants who think they will win may bribe to speed up consideration of their cases. One study of the Latin American judiciary, for example, con- cludes that improvements in the court system could be accomplished through better case-management techniques including increased com- puterization, the creation of additional courts, and the establishment of a more uniform administrative system (Buscaglia and Ulen 1997: 287–291).

This kind of judicial reform raises a paradox. If the services of the courts improve, more people will use them, leading to the need for even more resources to maintain service quality. For example, when Ecuador dramatically improved conditions for its judiciary in 1992, there was an increase in the number of cases filed (Buscaglia and Dakolias 1996: 18). Studies of a cross-section of Latin American countries found no rela- tionship between spending on personnel and court delay (Buscaglia and Dakolias 1996: 26; Buscaglia and Ulen 1997: 282–283). In most markets, prices ration the quality and quantity of services, but if congestion is a problem, each service user imposes costs on others. If the price of the service does not reflect this cost, the market will operate inefficiently. Although judges and court personnel may become less willing to take bribes, litigants and their lawyers may be no less willing to offer them to get to the head of the queue. Bribery can be used as a rationing device, but in a way that violates norms of judicial behavior and encourages court officials to introduce artificial delays to increase payoffs. To avoid this result, especially for commercial disputes, reformers should consider ways to impose the costs of the system on the litigants and to eliminate incentives to increase delay – such as payment schemes for lawyers that reward them on the basis of the complexity of the case.[13] One way to solve this problem is to give court personnel legal incentives to perform expeditiously. Reforms could provide information on delays by type of case and provide incentive payments for judges tied to improved performance.[14]

Third, a corrupt judiciary is costly for democracy because it cannot credibly play the role of watchdog on constitutional values or monitor the honesty of the other branches of government. This is an important role for the courts that is not present in authoritarian systems (Bing 1994: 5–8; Fuke 1989: 226).

If major investment deals involve the state as purchaser, privatizer, or provider of a concession, an independent court system is a necessary guarantor of impartiality to investors. If the prestige and competence of the judiciary can be established, their independence from the political branches should be assured.[15] Obviously, independence is not valuable if judges are not viewed with respect, and even respected and independent judges can produce rulings that undercut reform. For example, in Brazil the Supreme Court has delayed major privatizations as it reviewed challenges to the sales.[16] In the Philippines the Supreme Court overturned a contract to privatize a hotel and declared unconstitutional a law dereg-

---

[13] One study of a sample of commercial cases in Argentina and Venezuela concluded that an important source of delay was the strategic behavior of lawyers at the discovery stage (Buscaglia and Ulen 1997).

[14] Reforms designed to reduce corruption in the courts can be complemented with improvements in alternative methods of resolving disputes that keep many routine cases out of court (Alvarez 1995; Brandt 1995; Dakolias 1996: 37–43; Lawyers Committee 1996: 67–68).

[15] Lawyers Committee (1996: 45–55, 104–106). In Zimbabwe an independent Supreme Court upheld constitutional challenges raised by an independent cellphone entrepreneur. The entrepreneur continued in business in spite of opposition from those close to the country's rulers. See "Judgment Day," *The Economist*, October 10, 1998.

[16] "Telia-Led Group Waits for Cellphone Verdict," *Financial Times*, August 9/10, 1997; "Injunction Threatens Telebrás Sale," *Financial Times*, July 29, 1998. The Supreme Court ultimately permitted the auction of Telebrás to proceed. "Telebrás Sold for U.S. $19.1bn," *Latin American Weekly Report*, August 4, 1998.

ulating the oil industry.[17] Even in Argentina where compliant judges made no objection to President Menem's first round of economic reforms (Saba and Manzetti 1997: 363), a 1997 decision struck down a presidential decree offering a concession on the country's airports.[18] Although these rulings are inconvenient for reformers, they are the cost of an independent judiciary that can also uphold the constitution and take on cases of malfeasance by high-level officials. Furthermore, in some situations the problem is not the independence of the judiciary per se, but the unreformed character of the underlying laws and constitutional principles it must interpret.

An honest government administration will be difficult to establish if the judiciary is venal. Victims of corrupt officials have no place to turn, and the unscrupulous can bribe officials with impunity. The risk of engaging in high-level corrupt or fraudulent deals is significantly reduced if the court system is itself corrupt, incompetent, and lacking in independence. Sometimes, complex networks develop to maintain corrupt systems. Thus in Venezuela judicial "tribes" exist that are informal networks of judges, judicial personnel, private lawyers, and political officials. For a fee, these groupings guarantee the results of particular judicial proceedings (Lawyers Committee, 1996: 56–57). In the extreme, a corrupt judiciary can be part of an extortionary system where the threat of prosecution, perhaps even for paying bribes, is used as a way to gain the cooperation of private individuals and firms.

Paradoxically, however, an honest judiciary can help maintain a corrupt system under certain conditions. Suppose that private individuals and firms engage in secret corrupt deals with public officials. Private actors are willing to make payoffs because they are confident that the procurement contracts, concessions, and privatization deals they obtain will be upheld by the honest, impartial judicial system. Suppose, as in the United States, that the public prosecutor is part of the executive branch of government, not a part of the judiciary. If the government, outside of the judiciary, is organized to facilitate corruption, the private firms are confident that they will not be prosecuted. Even if a scandal does develop, only public officials may suffer politically. This may deter some public officials, but it does not constrain private individuals.

The best example of a corruption-friendly polity comes from the early years of the American Republic. A corrupt land sale approved by the

---

[17] "Oil Ruling Puts Philippine IMF Position in Doubt," *Financial Times* November 7, 1997; "Philippines Sell-off Setback," *Financial Times* December 3, 1997.

[18] "Argentine Sell-off Frozen," *Financial Times*, September 26, 1997.

legislature of Georgia in the early 1800s was upheld by the U.S. Supreme Court in the case of *Fletcher v. Peck* [3 L.Ed. 162–181 (1810)]. The Court was unmoved by the fact that all but one of the legislators had been bribed. When the scandal was revealed, the entire legislature lost office in the next election, but the Court held that the contract was a legal obligation of the state of Georgia (Magrath 1966). What better way to encourage payoffs than a legal system that upholds public contracts no matter what the underlying corrupt deals?

The case of *Fletcher v. Peck* is a warning that establishing an honest independent judiciary is not sufficient if corruption is commonplace. Deeper reforms in the political system are necessary. Judicial independence, however, does seem a valuable, if elusive, concept. In the United States life tenure and limits on congressional ability to reduce salaries help maintain the independence of the federal judiciary, but many countries have independent judiciaries without these constraints. In the United States the appointments' process is politicized with presidential appointment followed by Senate confirmation. If the Senate is controlled by a party different from that of the President, this limits the possibility of partisan appointments, but if it is not, that constraint obviously does not apply. At the state and local level, some judges are elected. In some other countries appointments to the Constitutional Court are more firmly controlled by the legal profession, and in others special committees make the choices. In most countries with a civil law tradition, the judges in the lower courts are essentially career bureaucrats who choose a judicial career on leaving law school. The judiciary is, however, generally recruited and organized separately from the rest of the civil service to maintain its independence. Thus, there does not appear to be a single blueprint available for developing countries. Nevertheless – however it is accomplished – skeptical politicians would do well to support an independent judiciary as a necessary step in creating a credible state commitment to the rule of law.

Judicial reform is politically difficult. Although surveys of citizens suggest dissatisfaction with the judiciary in many countries, the judges themselves are unlikely to be so unhappy. They may support programs to raise salaries and improve working conditions but not if these improvements are attached to stringent performance reviews. The executive may also block reform if the courts are full of patronage appointments. A recent independent report details the problems faced by the World Bank's first judicial reform project in Venezuela (Lawyers Committee 1996). Reformers face the question of whether to coopt existing judges and court personnel or try to start over with a new group. In the light of these criticisms, a World Bank paper on judicial reform recommends going ahead only if the existing judges will cooperate (Dakolias 1996). Although the World Bank may have little choice for its own projects in this area, this may not be the correct choice in countries with very corrupt systems. Changes in personnel may be necessary, but even then, they will never be sufficient. If long delays and vague legal standards create corrupt incentives, it seems unlikely that a change of faces will accomplish much. Personnel change must be joined to structural and administrative reforms.

Independent Anticorruption Agencies

Often prosecutors ignore corruption and focus on less politically sensitive issues. One response is the creation of independent anticorruption commissions or inspector generals reporting only to the chief executive or parliament.[19] The best-known examples are provided by Hong Kong and Singapore, both city states and former British colonies. In both cases, the turnaround in corruption combined commitment from the top, credible law enforcement by an independent agency operating under a strong statute, and reform of the civil service.

Corruption was endemic in Hong Kong in the sixties (Manion 1996b; Skidmore 1996). Its entrenched character is suggested by an expression popular at the time. People had the choice of "getting on the bus" (actively participating in corruption) or "running alongside the bus" (being a bystander who did not interfere with the system). "Standing in front of the bus" (reporting or resisting corruption) was not a viable option (Manion 1996b). Spurred to action by a scandal involving a high-ranking police officer, the governor established an Independent Commission Against Corruption (ICAC) in 1974. The ICAC reported only to the governor and was independent of the police force. Officials in the ICAC were paid more than other bureaucrats, and were not subject to transfer to other departments. No one in the ICAC could end up working for a more senior officer who had been subject to investigation. The ICAC was given the power to investigate and prosecute corruption cases, to recommend legal and administrative changes to reduce corrupt incentives, and to engage in a campaign of public education (Klitgaard 1988: 98–121; Manion 1996b; Quah 1995; Rahman 1986: 144–146; Skidmore 1996).

The new policy apparently succeeded in transforming citizens' beliefs and expectations. The credibility of the new institution is indicated by the increased number of complaints it received upon establishment and by the high proportion of complaints that were not anonymous. In

---

[19] Antoniou (1990) and Pope (1996: 73–78).

addition to the ICAC's independence, the government's commitment to reform was indicated by the appointment of a person of unquestioned integrity to head the ICAC and by an initial policy of investigating and prosecuting "big tigers" (Klitgaard 1988; Manion 1996b). Efforts to clean up corrupt syndicates within the police, however, met with protests, and the ICAC backed down and granted an amnesty for offenses committed before January 1, 1977. This setback was harmful, but the ICAC was able to recover with a vigorous focus on public education. Surveys of the public carried out between 1977 and 1994 indicate that public perceptions of corruption fell in the early years of the ICAC. Indirect evidence suggests that corruption did, in fact, decline along with public perceptions (Manion 1996b).

Now that Hong Kong has reunified with China, the future of the ICAC is in doubt, and business opportunities on the mainland have increased the benefits of corruption. Hong Kong risks a return to pre-ICAC corruption levels. The head of the ICAC at the time of the transfer argued in a June 1997 interview that a strong ICAC was crucial to a successful transition and claimed that the agency will continue to focus on its three arms of punishment, prevention, and education.[20] Others are not so optimistic, although the ICAC has continued to bring cases.[21]

Singapore is another success story. Among Asian countries, Singapore stands out as a relatively clean place to do business. Corruption occurs, but it is not endemic. But during the colonial era, it was a very corrupt place. How did it make the leap? Just after World War II, civil servants were poorly paid and inadequately supervised. Graft was pervasive in the police department (Quah 1989, 1994). When the People's Action Party (PAP) assumed power in 1959, it made corruption control a priority. As part of its strategy, the PAP government strengthened the powers of an existing Corrupt Practices Investigations Bureau (CPIB). Since 1970 it has been directly under the Prime Minister's office. The CPIB has been a success (Rahman 1986: 149–152), but it raises some of the same issues as the ICAC in Hong Kong. The CPIB does not seem subject to external checks, and those accused of corruption have sometimes accused the agency of heavy-handed behavior that violated their rights (Quah 1989).

Singapore also requires ministries to review their work practices with the aim of reducing corrupt incentives. Strategies include reducing delays, rotating officers, and increasing supervision. The country reduces

---

[20] "HK's Anti-Graft Chief Stakes Out Territory," *Financial Times*, June 6, 1997.
[21] "Hong Kong: Corruption Reports Increase," *Financial Times* July 9, 1998.

corrupt incentives by giving civil servants a stake in their jobs through high wages, bonuses, and favorable working conditions. The aim is to keep compensation packages in line with private sector alternatives (Klitgaard 1988: 122–133; Quah 1989, 1994, 1995).

In both Hong Kong and Singapore the turnaround in corruption combined commitment from the top, credible law enforcement by an independent agency operating under a strong statute, and reform of the civil service. Prior to Hong Kong's reunification with China, the ICAC was better constrained than the Singapore bureau by review committees and an independent judiciary. A tough, independent anticorruption agency can be a potent tool so long as it represents a credible long-term commitment and can avoid being misused for political ends.

Successes also sometimes accompany the creation of more specialized anticorruption agencies that monitor a particular government system. For example, the School Construction Authority of New York City has established an internal agency with some independence to both ferret out corrupt contractors and propose internal reorganizations that reduce corruption. This hybrid form not only focuses on after-the-fact law enforcement but also helps design internal control systems. Although some critics believe that it has been too rigid and intrusive, the School Construction Authority has apparently paid for itself by saving the city many millions of dollars.[22] This experiment suggests the value of mixing the benefits of an independent prosecutorial body with an oversight capability located inside a public agency. This option presents tricky problems of avoiding cooptation, but it promises to make possible structural reforms that would be beyond the scope of the Hong Kong and Singapore institutions.

Independent anticorruption agencies are a popular reform proposal for developing countries. In addition to Hong Kong and Singapore, a number of other jurisdictions, such as Malaysia, Botswana, Malawi, and the Australian state of New South Wales, have similar institutions (Skidmore 1996). Yet even the Hong Kong ICAC is not without problematic aspects. Under British rule, the ICAC reported only to the colonel governor. An anticorruption commission reporting to an autocratic ruler could be used as an instrument of repression against political opponents, and even the ICAC has not been immune to such charges. The widespread powers of the ICAC could be abused in systems less committed

---

[22] Thacher (1995); "New York City Builds a Better Watchdog," *New York Times*, March 14, 1996. A critical view is expressed by Anechiarico and Jacobs (1997: 129, 136–137).

to the rule of law.[23] In Hong Kong a series of oversight committees and an independent judiciary have checked the ICAC, but even so occasional scandals have surfaced (Skidmore 1996). As a check on its power, such an agency might report not to the chief executive, but to the legislature – as does the General Accounting Office in the United States.

Another potential problem is an underemphasis on structural reforms. For example, the process of obtaining a driver's license in Hong Kong had become very long and cumbersome. The ICAC discovered that bribes were paid to obtain licenses speedily. Even though the commission's mandate includes recommending ways to reduce corrupt incentives, the agency focused on enforcing the law against corrupt drivers and civil servants rather than on reforming the bureaucracy to streamline the issuance of licenses (Skidmore 1996). An anticorruption policy will not be very useful if it leaves in place the restrictive laws and cumbersome processes that produced incentives for bribery in the first place. An anticorruption agency ought to be only one part of a larger strategy that includes more fundamental reforms that supplement law enforcement programs.

Openness and Accountability
The public can be an important check on the arbitrary exercise of power by government. However, this check can operate only if the government provides information on its actions. Citizens must have a convenient means of lodging complaints and be protected against possible reprisals. Of course, government officials must also find it in their interest to respond to complaints. There are two basic routes for public pressure: collective complaints by groups of citizens concerning general failures of government and objections raised by particular individuals against their own treatment at the hands of public authorities. Both collective and individual routes can help spur the reform of governmental structures.

Information and Auditing
A precondition for either type of complaint is information. It is easy to underestimate the importance of posters, fliers, and videotapes that tell people what they can expect from honest officials and how to make a complaint. In many cases such informative material represents the first time ordinary citizens have ever heard that they have rights against abusive authority.

---

[23] For an example of an anticorruption agency being accused of undermining rather than supporting reform, see: "Arrest of Kenya Tax Officials May Hit Donor Funding," *Financial Times*, July 25–26, 1998.

In addition to basic information on official standards of behavior, citizen activists need more comprehensive information. Government must tell them what it is doing by publishing consolidated budgets, revenue collections, statutes and rules, and the proceedings of legislative bodies. Such practices are standard in developed countries, but many developing countries are seriously deficient.[24] Former colonies often use systems originally imposed by the colonizer which may or may not fit local conditions. Financial data should be audited and published by independent authorities such as the General Accounting Office (GAO) in the United States or the Audit Commission in Great Britain (United Kingdom 1993, 1994, 1996). The GAO monitors the federal executive branch but reports directly to Congress. It resolves contracting disputes, settles the accounts of the United States government, resolves claims for or against the United States, gathers information for Congress, and makes recommendations to it.[25] The British Audit Commission audits both local governments and the National Health Service and reports to the national government. Both institutions are independent of the government agencies they audit – a necessary condition for credibility. Self-monitoring is suspect because a public agency that discovers and reports wrongdoing may suffer negative consequences. Thus it has little incentive to look closely at the behavior of its employees.

In all democratic countries the legislature can play an important role in reviewing the spending of the executive. In presidential systems, congressional committees, aided in the United States by the GAO, can provide continuing oversight. In parliamentary systems on the Westminster model, Public Accounts Committees (PACs), often headed by a leading opposition member of parliament, perform a similar function.[26] In the United Kingdom, for example, the PAC issued a report in 1994 arguing that serious failures in administrative and financial systems existed that had led to money being spent wastefully or improperly (Doig 1996: 174). In contrast, the PAC in Kenya, like the parliament itself,

---

[24] For an overview and analysis of public expenditure management systems worldwide, see Premchand (1993).

[25] Abikoff (1987); Tiefer (1983). In 1980 the GAO was granted the power to bring suit against the executive branch to assure that requests for information were honored. This amendment to the statute was opposed by the Department of Justice and has proved controversial. The case of *Bowsher v. Synar*, 106 S. Ct. 3181 (1986), limiting the GAO's ability to perform "executive" functions on separation of powers grounds, did not resolve this issue.

[26] In Britain, the first Public Accounts Committee was established by the House of Commons in 1862 as a standing committee to examine the public accounts of the British government. The committee soon became an accepted feature of the British system of government (Chester 1981: 218–219, 370).

has been politically divided and unable to operate as a strong counterweight to the executive (Kibwana, Wanjala, and Okech-Owiti 1996: 76, 92–93, 157–158).

In both the United States and in Westminster democracies, the involvement of opposition politicians in oversight means that the review will have a political cast. The input may be in the form of accounting documents, but the debate will be influenced by political factors. This is as it should be in a well-functioning democracy, but it is hardly an unbiased way of uncovering malfeasance. If violations of the criminal law are uncovered, there must also be an unbiased prosecutorial and judicial system available to pursue the allegations.

In many countries outside review is hampered because unaudited, secret funds are available to the chief executives and top ministers. These funds are an invitation to corruption throughout the world.[27] In the United States the budgets of the national security agencies such as the Central Intelligence Agency are not published.[28] Oversight is provided by a special committee of Congress – a level of review that goes beyond many other countries where the executive essentially has unfettered discretion over a secret account. For example, before 1989 the United Kingdom simply refused to formally acknowledge that it had an intelligence service (Shpiro 1998). In Brazil when President Collor's impeachment was before the Congress, observers worried that his allies were seeking to use secret government funds to bribe the members to obtain a favorable verdict (Geddes and Ribeiro Neto 1992).

Sometimes governments collect a good deal of information on their own operations but do not routinely make it public. In such cases statutes that give citizens a right to gain access to this information can be an important precondition for effective public oversight. The Freedom of Information Act in the United States serves this function, and the European Union has a directive requiring member states to pass such laws with respect to environmental information.[29] These laws permit citizens to obtain government information without demonstrating a need to know. They may request the information as members of the public

---

[27] For example, in Venezuela, President Carlos Andrés Pérez resigned amid charges that he had misused $17 million in funds from such a secret account (Little and Herrera 1996: 268).

[28] As the result of a threatened Freedom of Information Act request, the United States Central Intelligence Agency released a one-sentence document in October 1997 listing their 1996 budget at $26.6 billion dollars. "For First Time US Discloses Spying Budget," *New York Times,* October 16, 1997.

[29] The American Law is 5 U.S.C. §552. The European Union Directive is 90/313/EEC, 1990 OJ (L 158) 56–58. See also Rose-Ackerman (1995a: 113–115).

without showing that their own personal situation will be affected. Exceptions protect privacy, internal memorandums, and the integrity of ongoing prosecutions.

In the United States, unless national security is at stake, legislative hearings are open to the public, as are many executive branch meetings and hearings. For multimember agencies, the Government in the Sunshine Act gives citizens access to every meeting that includes a decision-making quorum (5 U.S.C. §552b). Some critics of the act urge that open meetings be made more useful through better publicity and the provision of background materials. Others argue that the act undermines the agencies' deliberative processes (May 1997). But even critics would retain the requirement that votes and other important substantive decisions be made in open meetings.

Few other countries have copied American laws requiring disclosure of information and open meetings, but the basic need for public access arises everywhere. At issue is the public's right to present information to the executive branch, to learn the reasons for decisions, and to flag those that are most likely influenced by corruption and favoritism.[30]

But a freedom of information act has little value if government does not gather much information. Many countries must first put information systems in order, provide for the publication of the most important documents, and assure public access to other unpublished material. Similarly, an open-meeting rule is of little value if the formal law is vague so that any decision can be justified.

The Media and Public Opinion

Even a government that keeps good records and makes them available to the public may operate with impunity if no one bothers to analyze the available information – or if analysts are afraid to raise their voices. There are three routes to accountability. If the aim is to pressure government to act in the public interest, the role of both the media and organized groups is important. If the goal is government accountability to individuals, avenues for individual complaints must be established. In all

---

[30] The experience of Japan bears watching. Japan has no national freedom of information act, but many local and prefectural governments have passed information disclosure ordinances (IDOs). The IDOs permit citizens to request information from these governments and to pursue legal remedies if their requests are denied. Citizens and the media have used the process to uncover the use of public works funds to support social gatherings at which local governments entertain central government officials. As a result, 22 local governments reported cuts of 30 percent or more in the use of funds for such purposes and 14 reported cuts of 10 percent or more (Boling 1998: 8–12).

three cases – media, groups, individuals – there is the problem of fear. If government officials or their unofficial allies intimidate and harass those who speak out, formal structures of accountability will be meaningless.

The media can facilitate public discussion if it is privately owned and free to criticize the government without fear of reprisal. Even undemocratic rulers are likely to be sensitive to public opinion if they wish to avoid civil unrest. Thus a free press is an essential check, especially in undemocratic countries that lack other means of constraining politicians and bureaucrats. And if elections are important, the media is also crucial.

Nominal press freedom will be insufficient if most of the media is associated with political parties. In Italy corruption became big news only as the Italian press became increasingly independent from the political system (Giglioli 1996: 386). Government can also keep the press in line through advertising, printing contracts, and payments to journalists. Mexican newspapers, for example, have been controlled through these methods. Another subtle form of control is to overlook underpayment of taxes by editors and media companies, retaining the possibility of prosecution as a threat.[31]

In many countries restrictive libel laws give special protections to public officials (Pope 1996: 129–141; Tucker 1994; Vick and Macpherson 1997: 647). This is just the reverse of what is needed. Politicians and other public figures should be harder to libel than private citizens, not easier. They should not be immune from facing charges of corruption, and allegations of libel should be handled as civil, not criminal matters. In this at least, the United States provides an outstanding example with a law that makes it more difficult to libel public figures than private individuals and that treats libel as a civil offense. Those in the public eye have assumed the risk of public scrutiny and have access to the media to rebut accusations (Vick and Macpherson 1997: 650). In a similar vein partici-

---

[31] "It Happened in Monterrey," *The Times*, November 29, 1991, discusses the resignation of a newspaper editor after pressure was put on his paper through the cancellation of government advertising and printing contracts. "Survey of Mexico," *Financial Times*, November 10, 1993, discusses these practices, but claims that some newspapers have retained their independence. When a leading editor was arrested in Mexico City in 1996 for tax evasion, the editor claimed that the arrest occurred in response to the paper's newly asserted independence. The tax authorities claim that the editor adopted a more outspoken line only after the investigation had begun (*Mexico Business Monthly*, October 1, 1996). He was eventually acquitted of criminal wrongdoing and fined a nominal amount in 1997 (Reuters Financial Services, February 26, 1997; *Miami Herald*, August 27, 1997).

pants in political debate in Germany relinquish some of the protections of defamation law, and the Netherlands has a public figure defense (ibid.: 651). Threats of lawsuits operate as a serious deterrent elsewhere. Great Britain has no public figure defense. Some claim that its libel law deters critical reporting of issues affecting the public interest (ibid.: 627, 649–650). An especially clear example of the chilling effect of a strong libel law is Singapore where top politicans have been active in suing both the media and political opponents.[32] In Jordan a 1998 law prohibits the publication of news items judged insulting to the king or the royal family.[33] In Latin America libel is often prosecuted as a criminal instead of a civil action.[34]

But in poor countries with high levels of illiteracy the media can play only a limited role. Many people have low levels of education and little understanding of government operations. This has two implications for reformers. First, government or independent private organizations might provide educational programs to help people understand what they should expect of a legitimate government. Some low-level bribery arises because people suppose that they ought to provide gifts in gratitude for favorable decisions by superiors (Pasuk and Sungsidh 1994). Citizens may have no notion that public officials owe them anything.

Second, the government needs a means of identifying the concerns of poor and marginalized groups without making them subject to penalties for speaking out. A free media can help here if it can sponsor or publicize surveys of popular attitudes. Even if the media plays only a limited role in informing citizens about what the government is doing, it can still tell the government what people think and what difficulties ordinary people face when dealing with bureaucracies.

Private Associations and Nonprofit Organizations as Agents of Change

A free media with good access to government information is not likely to be a sufficient check, especially in an autocracy. The media may focus on lurid scandals and may have no real interest in reforms that would

[32] See "Singapore Leaders Awarded $5.6m in Libel Damages," *Financial Times,* May 30, 1997; "Singapore Leader Wins Libel Case," *Financial Times,* September 30, 1997; and "Throwing the Book: PAP Launches Legal Barrage Against Opposition Leaders," *Far Eastern Economic Review*, March 6, 1997.

[33] "Jordan: Censored," *The Economist*, September 12, 1998. The government claims that the law does not threaten freedom of expression and will be applied leniently.

[34] "Is Mexico's Press Free, or Just Taking Liberties?," *New York Times*, November 23, 1996.

reduce the flow of corruption stories. Individuals and groups must push for change. Individuals face a familiar free rider problem. Information may be available, but no one may have an incentive to look at it. The scandals uncovered by investigative journalists may provoke outrage, but no action.

Laws that make it easy to establish private associations and nonprofit corporations will help. This will facilitate the creation of watchdog groups like Transparency International, an international nonprofit organization focused on reducing corruption with national chapters in almost fifty countries (Transparency International 1998). These local organizations carry out a range of activities including participation in Integrity Work-shops organized with the help of the Economic Development Institute at the World Bank and some of the bilateral aid agencies. Workshops have been held in Tanzania, Uganda, Malawi, and Jordan. They bring together concerned people from both the public and the private sectors to discuss the problem of corruption. Some of the workshops have ended with the participants pledging to desist from corruption. The meeting in Tanzania in 1995 produced a pledge from top government officials to reveal their assets and those of their families and led to the establish-ment of a Presidential Commission of Inquiry Against Corruption (Tanzania 1996).

Some governments, worried that nongovernmental organizations (NGOs) will be used for monitoring purposes, limit such groups or make it very costly for them to organize. Formal legal constraints may be high, and members may be subject to surveillance and harassment. For example, Transparency International has found that setting up local chapters in developing countries can be difficult even if local people are eager to organize a chapter. In some countries several years have passed without the chapter obtaining a formal charter.[35] Once registered, non-profits may face onerous formal reporting requirements. However, in practice, such rules mean little in many countries because the state lacks enforcement capacity. Sometimes the very ineffectiveness of the state can be a source of freedom (Bratton 1989: 577–578).

Another problem is cooptation. Some nonprofits organize and admin-

---

[35] For example, comparing the Annual Reports of Transparency International from 1995 and 1998, several chapters listed as "in formation" in 1994 were still in that category at the spring of 1998, and a few had been demoted to the category of "national contacts" (Transparency International 1995, 1998). The Annual Reports do not distinguish between legal difficulties and lack of grass-roots support, however. Countries where the process of chapter formation has been protracted include Mongolia, Namibia, the Netherlands, South Korea, Sri Lanka, and Sweden.

ister development programs for the poor. Their financing may be provided by the state or by aid funds administered by the state. Thus their
very existence depends upon cooperation with public authorities. As a
consequence, they may be reluctant to criticize officials openly (ibid.:
1989: 578–579). To avoid such tensions, an NGO that takes on an anticorruption mandate should avoid participation in service delivery. In
both South Asia and Africa many nonprofits that deliver services to the
poor are financed in whole or in part by governments. In contrast, Latin
American nonprofits sometimes have a more adversarial relationship
with government (ibid.: 1989: 584). Thus in the first two regions, anticorruption groups will need to be newly created separate from existing
organizations, and in Latin America existing groups many be more
appropriate.

Nonprofit organizations can also usefully carry out and publish public
opinion surveys that reveal public attitudes toward government services.
Pioneering work of this sort has been carried out by the Public Affairs
Centre in Bangalore, India (Mohn 1997; Paul 1995). One of its Report
Card Studies focused on the delivery of urban services to slum dwellers
in five cities. Although the incidence of reported bribery varied across
the cities, it was widespread everywhere. Across service areas, the higher
the prevalence of corruption, the lower the capacity or willingness
of public service agencies to solve clients' problems. The Economic
Development Institute has also sponsored several surveys that provide
useful models. Such surveys are a way of isolating the impact of corruption on the poor who may otherwise have few ways of registering
complaints.

In countries with an honest and independent judicial system, another
possibility arises for the indirect control of corruption. Private individuals and groups can be given the right to bring suits to force compliance
with tax and regulatory laws. The aim of such suits is not to uncover
bribery but to obtain compliance with the underlying substantive law. No
evidence of corruption would be presented. Instead, the focus would be
on regulatory or tax law violations.

In the United States the federal bribery statute does not incorporate
a private right of action [*Ray v. Proxmire*, 581 F.2d 998 (1978)], but most
U.S. environmental statutes include explicit provisions for citizen suits
that permit private plaintiffs to sue dischargers to require compliance
with the law. If the suit is successful, the plaintiffs obtain discharger compliance with the rule; they do not obtain damages (Rose-Ackerman
1995b: 319). Under the most familiar version, private individuals and
public interest groups sue those who violate Environmental Protection
Agency rules or orders. The U.S. statutes frequently facilitate such suits

by requiring regulated firms to supply data on their own pollution discharges and by paying the legal fees of successful or "substantially prevailing" plaintiffs. Such suits lower the benefits of bribery, because outsiders may later uncover the illegal benefit.

In India, this idea extends beyond the environmental area. Citizens affected by illegal or oppressive government actions can bring Public Interest Actions to vindicate the collective rights of the public. Plaintiffs need not show a direct specific injury (Agarwala 1996: 174–184). The Indian Supreme Court has endorsed an expansive right of standing for ordinary citizens, arguing that "public spirited citizens having faith in rule of law are rendering great social and legal service by espousing causes of public nature. They cannot be ignored or overlooked on technical or conservative yardsticks . . ." [*Bangaire Medical Trust v. Mudappa*, 1991 A.I.R. 1902 (S.C.) (India)]. Citizen actions have played a role in pushing the courts to force the government to pursue corruption allegations against top officials.

In contrast, other legal systems provide no opportunity for individuals to sue to protect public values. They must demonstrate that their rights or interests were actually injured, and only then can they have standing before the courts. Of course, sometimes an individual can further public interest goals in the process of vindicating his or her individual rights, but many administrative failures are beyond the purview of the courts in such systems. The German and Japanese judicial review processes share this weakness (Fuke 1989; Rose-Ackerman 1995a). As a commentator on Japanese law notes, "certain comprehensive administrative activities may bring about irreparable damage to the public as well as specific persons in the long run, without causing any immediate, specific, personal and justiciable injury to anyone" (Fuke 1989: 232). Some types of corruption that raise the costs and lower the effectiveness of government are in that category.

Outside the United States the losing party in a law suit commonly pays the legal fees of both sides. The American innovation is one-sided fee shifting: Private plaintiffs who bring citizen suits against the government or polluters are compensated for their legal fees if they win but are not required to pay their opponents' fees if they lose. This is a valuable innovation that could be applied in the anticorruption context. Enforcement cases have clear external benefits for all who gain from more honest government. Although opponents of citizen suits worry about an excess of trivial claims, one-sided fee shifting is an appropriate response. It gives public interest groups an incentive to focus on the most worthy cases. It has the further advantage of forcing firms that gain from paying bribes to pay most of the cost of enforcing the law against them. Because accusations of corruption and malfeasance can be motivated by revenge, the law might include a provision that shifts all legal fees onto the plaintiff for suits found to be harassing or vindictive – so long as the courts can be relied upon to apply the rule sparingly. For example, the U.S. law that protects whistleblowers generally awards them their legal fees but with an exception for suits that are "frivolous, clearly vexatious, or brought primarily for purposes of harassment." [31 U.S.C.S. §3730 (d)].

In countries with weak courts and ineffective governments, reform efforts can be frustrating. A group knows that government is working poorly, can document its failure, and speaks out in protest. The media reports the group's complaints, and they are the source of widespread public debate. But the government may not react. Even if the government does not actively intimidate its critics, it may stonewall until the protest groups have exhausted their energy and resources. In a democracy, political opposition can make corruption a campaign issue. In an autocracy, political opponents are likely to be weak. An anticorruption organization can do little without some cooperation from the country's political leadership. Here corruption may be an easier issue for citizens to tackle than other controversial topics such as land reform or labor rights. Although some autocrats operate with impunity, indifferent to domestic public opinion and criticism from the outside world, others are not so self-confident or powerful. In these cases, reform may be possible with NGOs pushing the state to change and working with it to make reform happen.

Nevertheless, serious anticorruption efforts may require a radical realignment of the relationship between ordinary people and the state. Citizens may be rightly afraid that complaining will only make things worse for them personally. Greater popular voice may challenge deep-seated views about the prerogatives of rulers. However, even autocrats have been known to reform when the cost in lost investment and growth is especially obvious. Taking over the banner of reform can be one way for an autocrat to maintain power in the face of concentrated criticism.

Avenues for Individual Complaints

Fighting high-level corruption requires national attention and private organizations willing to push leaders for change. In contrast, limiting low-level bureaucratic corruption is often in the interest of top officials who may try to enlist ordinary citizens in the effort. This can be done without organized citizen activity if individuals can lodge complaints easily and without fear that corrupt officials will take revenge.

Recall the distinction made in a previous chapter between bribes made to get around the rules and bribes made to get a benefit that should have been provided for free. Facilitating complaints will help uncover only the latter type of corruption. Bribes that permit illegal activities or that soften a legal regulation or tax assessment are unlikely to be revealed by private individuals and firms unless they have been arrested and are seeking to mitigate their punishment. In contrast, if bribery demands are a condition for obtaining a legal benefit, individuals may not go along if they can appeal to an honest forum.

To make appeals worthwhile, the processes must not only be honest, but also speedy and efficient. The plaintiff must also have a right to obtain information about his case from bureaucrats. For example, land consolidation in Uttar Pradesh in India apparently was achieved with relatively low levels of corruption. The keys were an open process with real participation by those affected, time pressure, and speedy and fair appeals (Oldenburg 1987).

Complaints are unlikely if people fear reprisals. For example, in Tanzania ordinary people questioned in 1996 believed that if they complained to superior officers, their identity would be revealed to the suspects who would then harass and threaten them (Tanzania, Presidential Commission of Inquiry Against Corruption 1996: 65). Obviously, these concerns made most people unwilling to file a complaint.

Many countries have established ombudsmen to hear complaints of all kinds, not just those related to malfeasance. These offices can help increase the accountability of government agencies to ordinary citizens (Antoniou 1990: 68–78; Noorani 1997; Pope 1996). Hence they may generate a great deal of resistance from politicians and bureaucrats. In India, for example, an office similar to an ombudsman called a Lok Pal was recommended by an administrative reform commission as early as 1966 but has never been established (Noorani 1997). Although this is regrettable, one should have modest expectations for an ombudsman. These officials seldom uncover large-scale systemic corruption and generally lack authority to initiate lawsuits. For example, South Africa has a Public Protector who can investigate alleged improper behavior by public officials and make reports that are usually publicized. Its mandate includes malfeasance and corruption as well as traditional human rights abuses. Like most ombudsmen, the office cannot initiate legal actions, but it can refer cases to prosecutors. At present, the office is very small and has difficulty handling the volume of complaints. A recent United Nations report recommends not only an expansion in its capacity but a redefinition of its mission so that it can initiate large-scale investigations of general problems rather than merely respond to individual complaints (United Nations, High Commissioner for Human Rights 1996: 38–40). In contrast, an example of a strong ombudsman comes from the Pacific island country of Vanuatu (Findlay 1997: 56–59). The ombudsman, operating with "almost religious zeal," investigated a fraudulent financial scheme involving top government officials who worked with promoters from outside the country. Although the ombudsman could not bring formal charges herself, the resulting publicity played a role in undermining public support for those involved.

Some public agencies have created "hot lines" for direct citizen complaints. In Britain a number of local communities are experimenting with antifraud hotlines (United Kingdom, Audit Commission, 1993). Mexico's Program for the Modernization of Public Administration created a similar system of hotlines for businesses harassed by inspectors (Mexico, Federal Executive Power 1996). This method will be successful, however, only if complainants can preserve their anonymity or do not fear reprisals. If telephones are not widely available to people in rural areas or in poor urban neighborhoods, other methods of collecting complaints must be found. "Hot lines" must be more than just symbolic. Public officials – the ombudsman, agency oversight units, or law enforcement agent – must follow up on complaints in a visible way. At the same time, if the complaints concern individuals, the accused must have a credible way of defending against false accusations. Otherwise, an anticorruption campaign can degenerate into a collection of private vendettas with people enlisting the state to settle their private feuds.

The existence of ombudsmen and other complaint mechanisms will not work if people are unwilling to complain. One way to encourage insiders to come forward is a whistleblower statute that protects and rewards those in government agencies and private firms willing come forward. I introduced the American laws in the discussion of law enforcement, but their broader value lies in serving as catalysts. In the United States, some scholars question whether whistle blowing actually produces policy change. Although survey data suggest a skeptical response, a recent study concludes that previous work has focused too narrowly on the act of whistle blowing, ignoring the context in which it occurs (Johnson and Kraft 1990). Important factors are the role of the media, the lobbying of groups seeking change, and sympathetic legislators in key positions. Whistleblowers acting with such support can put issues on the agenda, catalyzing a larger process of change. The study includes two case studies of successful whistleblowers within the U.S. government. One revealed abuses in the hazardous waste program in the Environmental Protection Agency; the second protested policy toward people with AIDS in the Office of Civil Rights in the Department of Health and Human Services. Both whistleblowers were policy entrepreneurs who attracted widespread media coverage and used members of Congress to highlight their concerns. Both could rely on the support of organized interest groups to back up their efforts.[36] In the field of corruption control a public mobilized against corruption is essential if a whistle-blowing statute is to do more than provide formal legal protections to complaining officials and private sector employees. Thus in developing countries that lack such organized groups whistleblower protection cannot be an important feature of a reform strategy until such groups are in place.

Conclusions

Corruption can be controlled indirectly by limits on political power. I have considered two broad types of limits. The first are government structures that create veto points and independent sources of political, administrative, and judicial power. They limit corruption by making it less profitable for both officials and bribe payers. The second gives people and groups a way to complain about government and the poor services it may provide. The government supplies information about its actions, the media and the public can voice complaints, and private organizations and individuals can push for public accountability. The first type of limit is most compatible with democratic government structures, but even autocrats will sometimes favor checks on their own power as a way of creating popular legitimacy. The second type, which increases openness, leaves government vulnerable to popular discontent. Thus many regimes, even nominally democratic ones, may view such policies with suspicion. They are, nevertheless, an essential check on corruption and on other forms of self-dealing that can arise if officials are insulated from popular oversight.

---

[36] For another example of an apparently successful whistle-blowing effort, see "He Blew the Whistle and the Health Giants Quaked," *New York Times,* October 18, 1998.

PART IV

Achieving Reform

10

The Role of the International Community

Corruption is an emerging priority for the international community. The end of the Cold War has changed the balance of forces and removed any compelling need to support corrupt regimes for national security reasons. The widespread corruption and organized crime influence in the former Eastern bloc have made the problem difficult to ignore – as have similar problems in other parts of the world. The global move to privatize and deregulate requires a rethinking of the relationship between the market and the state – including a recognition of the new corrupt opportunities created by these efforts to strengthen the role of the private market.

Some observers question this new interest by international organizations. They view corruption as a domestic political problem that should be left to individual countries. To these critics, outsiders' reform efforts represent an unacceptable attempt to impose "Western" values. But many scholars from developing countries argue that this fashionable critique is based on a mischaracterization of local practices. They make it clear that traditions of gift giving do not translate into widespread acceptance of corrupt practices (Ayittey 1992). Citizen surveys and expressions of public outrage suggest that widespread tolerance of corruption is not common (Cooksey 1996; Geddes 1994: 25–26; Pasuk and Sungsidh 1994).

Some developed countries resist efforts to control corruption because they believe that payoffs in developing countries benefit their own domestic businesses. Westerners can hardly claim that their own cultures find corruption acceptable. In addition, evidence of public opposition to corruption in poorer countries should influence attitudes in richer countries as well. Corruption can be routine and commonplace without being viewed as acceptable by the population that bears its costs.

Another line of critique concerns technique. Some argue that the control of corruption should not be linked to international trade and lending policy. As in the debate over human rights and labor standards, they argue that international bodies should not tie trade policy and development assistance to "noneconomic" issues. But corruption is an economic issue. It affects the competitiveness of the global economy and the efficiency of investment and development projects worldwide. Furthermore, economic leverage may be the only effective way to bring pressure for reform.

There are five broad arenas for international involvement:

- When the funds of international organizations are at stake either as loans or grants, these organizations will have an interest in the effective use of their resources.
- If countries wish to reform, aid agencies may directly support anticorruption efforts such as the reform of the civil service and of budgetary and financial management systems. If economic and financial crises have been exacerbated by a corruption-prone institutional structure, international aid can be made conditional on reform even if the government is not eager for change.
- International efforts may be focused on reducing the willingness of multinational businesses to pay bribes and on enlisting them in the reform effort. In some developing countries, multinational investors are larger and more powerful than the states with which they deal, and even if this is not so, multinationals often have considerable leverage with governments.
- International programs to control the flow of illicit funds can check corruption by impeding the transfer of secret funds abroad where they cannot be traced. Other types of cooperation in the control of international criminal activity can also play a role.
- Reductions in corruption may require new international institutions. A number of reforms require cooperation across borders if they are to function well. This may require the creation of new bodies for review and adjudication.

Corruption control is currently a focus of international interest, but it may be just a temporary fad. The international community is at the point where rhetoric must be translated into concrete programs. There are a number of pitfalls to avoid and new initiatives to consider. One risk is that new forms of corruption and rent seeking may arise as a result of well-meant reforms designed to improve economic performance or to democratize politics. Reformers should seek to control these new "second generation" forms of malfeasance. They should also be cautious of creating pristine enclaves of virtue amidst an otherwise deeply corrupt system. The establishment of honest islands may be a good first step, but they will have limited value without more fundamental reforms.

Controlling Corruption in Development Projects

A simple example will expose the devastating impact of corruption on the efficiency of development projects. Suppose that 20 percent of aid funds is lost due to corruption. The 20 percent represents not bribes per se, but the inflated contracting costs and the loss of equipment and other inputs that result from tolerating bribery.[1] On this scenario, a $100 million project would have cost only $80 million in an honest system. Suppose further that the investment must earn a return of 10 percent one year in the future to pass muster. Then an honest project needs to generate benefits of $88 million, while the corrupt project requires $110 million, a difference of $22 million. A project that should have cost $80 million must return $110 million in order to be worthwhile – a rate of return on productively used resources of 37.5 percent. Even in developed countries, not many projects have such a high return. In short, corruption can dramatically reduce the number of projects that seem worth doing. Worse yet, if corrupt opportunities vary across projects, a country's corrupt officials will favor those with large opportunities for private gain, skewing the ranking of projects even further. An aid agency, then, will not merely support too few projects, but the wrong ones.

One recent buzz word in development circles is "ownership." Projects will fail unless the borrower feels that it "owns," or has a stake in, the enterprise. Unfortunately, one form of "ownership" is all too common. Political figures in borrower countries and firms in lender countries try to structure deals to produce personal benefits for the politicians and excess profits for the firms. They will oppose projects that spread the benefits more broadly to the poor and that assure free competition. "Ownership" is a highly questionable value in cases where a country's rulers do not seem committed to social welfare. Aid projects should not be supported that only increase the short-term value of controlling the state.

Kleptocratic states, such as the examples of Zaire, Paraguay, and Haiti outlined above, should not be helped to become more efficient at controlling and exploiting their own population. The World Bank should not

---

[1] Twenty percent may be a conservative estimate in some countries – in Nepal in the 1970s, for example, a USSR-aided project was halted when a leakage rate of 40 percent was discovered (Cariño 1986: 183).

help autocrats collect taxes more effectively, as it once tried to do in Zaire (Dia 1993). The United States should not provide military training to armies that use their new competence and organizational coherence to enrich their top brass, as happened in Haiti (Grafton and Rowlands 1996: 271–272).

Aid and lending organizations should also be wary of being used as a cover for the distribution of patronage. In the Philippines under President Ferdinand Marcos, for example, technocrats in the government worked with the IMF and the World Bank to keep aid and lending flowing. A Filipino economist claimed, however, that the technocrats provided the public rhetoric that kept loans coming in but that the regime "then allowed the *unconstrained introduction of exceptions* that made complete mockery of the spirit and letter of the plans" (quoted in Hutchcroft 1998: 114). Paul Hutchcroft claims that Marcos saw reform and plunder as complementary (ibid.: 141–142). He was attempting to establish himself as one of Mancur Olson's "stationary bandits" who could use reform to extract rents more efficiently (Olson 1993). As other evidence presented by Hutchcroft suggests, Marcos was apparently quite unsuccessful in achieving thoroughgoing reform. Arbitrariness and cronyism remained.

Until recently, the World Bank focused its analytic energies at the project approval stage. Although it has required transparency in procurement processes, there has been little effective follow-through. Procurement guidelines sought to assure some level of competitive bidding on most large contracts, but worries about corruption were implicit. In 1996, however, the Bank revised its guidelines to state explicitly that corruption and fraud would be grounds for canceling a contract if the borrower has not taken appropriate action. Section 6.03 of the General Conditions Applicable to Loan and Guarantee Agreements was expanded to allow cancellation of a loan for corruption or fraud by representatives of the borrower or by the beneficiary. The borrowing country can, however, defend itself against cancellation by taking "timely and appropriate action satisfactory to the Bank to remedy the situation." Furthermore, the *Guidelines for Procurement under IBRD Loans and IDA Credits* have been amended to add a new paragraph 1.15 stating that the Bank will reject a proposal for an award "if it determines that the bidder recommended for award has engaged in corrupt or fraudulent practices in competing for the contract in question." The Bank will also cancel a contract if corrupt or fraudulent practices are revealed later on. Firms found to have engaged in such practices will be declared ineligible for further contracts "either indefinitely or for a stated period of time." The new rules permit Bank audits of contractors and require contractors to record all payments to agents both before and after the bidding, because such payments are frequently the route by which payoffs are made (Shihata 1997). The importance of these changes will depend on how they are implemented in the field, but they represent a promising first step.

In September 1997 the procurement guidelines were further amended to permit borrowers to require potential bidders to sign a no-bribery pledge under which they pledge to refrain from fraud and corruption (paragraph 1.16). The Bank will approve this practice if it is part of a broader anticorruption program and if it will eventually be extended to all public procurement. The pledge is a variant of the prequalification processes used by procurement offices in many jurisdictions. When a no-bribery pledge is required, the number of bidders might fall, but the selective elimination of corrupt firms should enhance the competitive nature of the process, not reduce it. Although such pledges look redundant because corruption is, in any case, illegal, they have the advantage of highlighting the issue in countries where there is little respect for the formal law on the books. Transparency International (TI) has recommended this practice. Ecuador, Panama, and the province of Mendoza in Argentina have experimented with it, and a few African countries are considering putting it into effect. TI has prepared sample bidding documents and descriptions of bidding procedures that inform firms of the procedure. As part of the process, Transparency International recommends that countries express a commitment to impose sanctions (Transparency International 1998: 71–73).

If borrowers experiment with no-bribery pledges, they will need a way to process and evaluate accusations of corruption from contractors that have lost the bid. Borrower countries and the international aid and lending community need a way to make constructive use of the information contractors provide without becoming enmeshed in investigating the claims of every disappointed bidder. Because bid challenges are often costly and time-consuming, countries must decide how to balance the need for a speedy sale against a process designed to deter corruption in this and future deals. TI recommends the use of international arbitration (ibid.) – a proposal that could be part of a more general rethinking of the need for international monitoring and dispute resolution institutions discussed below.

No-bribery pledges would be implemented by individual countries. A related proposal would have industries agree among themselves not to offer bribes or excessive "commission" payments to obtain contracts anywhere in the world. Countries with political leaders who insist on payoffs would be excluded from the market (De George 1994: 5). This is an intriguing suggestion, but it would have to be enforced at the international level to be viable. One risk is that firms would cartelize the market at the same time as they agree not to accept bribes. Widespread bribery sometimes signals that companies are competing aggressively, not to provide low-cost, high-quality products, but to buy off those with influence (Strassmann 1989: 785). The solution is not to limit competition, but to redirect it in ways that benefit the citizens of developing countries.

At the World Bank, the Controllers Office is exploring ways to improve ex post monitoring so that there is more review of goods and services actually provided. Instead of relying mostly on paper records, Bank auditors are considering more physical inspections and on-site reviews. But concentrating on the Bank's own projects is not sufficient. The Operations Evaluation Department is the World Bank's own inside/outside oversight agency. A study done for its annual evaluation review found that countries with weak governments and high levels of corruption were less likely to have successful World Bank projects (Kilby 1995). This result suggests that even if the Bank is concerned only with the success of its own projects, it ought to help borrowers improve the quality of government overall.

Aid and lending organizations must acknowledge the political and organizational dynamics that make corruption control difficult. They must self-consciously review their own control institutions to isolate areas of deficiency.[2] If they do not carry out the oversight function themselves, outside observers may do it for them and in a way that undermines the credibility of these organizations. Criticism from both the left and the right of the political spectrum is a fact of life for these organizations. It needs to be met by acknowledging that a problem exists and taking steps to reduce the harm caused by corruption and self-dealing in aid and lending projects.

Supporting Reform

The World Bank, the IMF, the United Nations Development Programme (UNDP), the bilateral aid agencies, and the regional development banks are all contemplating anticorruption policies that go beyond assuring the integrity of their own projects to supporting more fundamental structural reforms. Once these organizations publicly acknowledged the

---

[2] The World Bank, for example, has been examining the behavior of its own employees and has isolated several instances of corruption and self-dealing. "World Bank in Internal Corruption Probe," *Financial Times*, July 17, 1998; "World Bank Hires Auditors to Probe Its Own Spending; Possible Kickbacks, Embezzlement Cited," *Washington Post*, July 16, 1998.

problem of corruption in Eastern Europe, the former Soviet Union, and China, it has proved difficult for them to ignore the issue elsewhere in the world. As private capital becomes more important in some traditional areas of World Bank lending, the Bank's role in institutional reform should increase. The UNDP and the United States Agency for International Development, which already provide technical support for government reform, are expanding their projects to include an explicit concern with corruption.[3] The IMF recognizes that corrupt and secretive links between government, private business, and the banking and financial sector can contribute to and exacerbate crises. Structural reforms in these areas are a condition for some recent IMF bailouts.

At the World Bank and the IMF, governance reform projects began as part of the structural adjustment lending carried out in the eighties and, at a somewhat reduced level, up to the present (Premchand 1993: 96–139). This is an awkward vehicle for institutional reform, and the Bank is now initiating free-standing projects. It has begun making loans designed to reform regulatory authorities, taxation agencies, the judiciary, and other public institutions. The Bank frequently advises countries on the privatization process. Aid agencies such as the UNDP and bilateral donors have been leaders in developing institutional reform projects. All these initiatives require a long-term commitment of funds and expertise and a realization that "output" measures will not be easy to formulate precisely. Nevertheless, the international aid and lending community can help provide a framework within which development can proceed as a partnership between the public and private sectors.

The previous chapters outlined the steps that a reform-minded government can take to reduce corruption. International aid and lending agencies should start with such a framework and work with individual countries to develop a realistic program. The priorities for reform will differ across countries, but the basic factors include reform of the underlying legal framework, changes in the substantive law to reduce corrupt incentives in particular sectors, improvements in the integrity of monitoring and law enforcement, reform of the civil service, and the strengthening of checks and balances. Existing attempts include the provision of resources and technical assistance to ease the transition to a competent, less numerous, and well-paid civil service system. The success of such efforts has been mixed and not always very durable (Nunberg and Nellis 1995), but the effort needs to be continued – especially if the World Bank

[3] United Nations Development Programme (1996, 1997). USAID programs are described on their web page at http://www.info.usaid.gov.

can learn from some of its past failures. International aid and lending organizations have also helped transitional economies and developing countries to publish timely and accurate documents about the basic operations of government and to reform their budgetary accounting processes (Premchand 1993: 98–101, 125–130; UNDP, July 1996).

Specific sectors have been the target of reform efforts. In particular, both the IMF and the World Bank targeted tax and customs systems. Some programs appear to have been successful, although others failed because of a lack of high-level support for the project (Das-Gupta and Mookherjee 1998: 302; Dia 1993). The basic problem is the enclave nature of many past efforts. Tax collectors and customs agents receive pay raises and improved working conditions and win incentive bonuses. This works for awhile but then begins to undermine morale elsewhere in government, causing resentment and risking a backlash that can leave the government in worse shape than before. Either everybody else gets a pay raise or the enclave of virtue is destroyed by resentful bureaucrats in the rest of government.

Sometimes the problem is not just reducing corruption in existing institutions, but preventing it from arising in new ones. Consider the potential pathologies of privatization. Payoffs and insider deals can tarnish the initial auction, and corruption can undermine the performance of a new regulatory agency established to oversee privatized firms. Similarly, illegal campaign contributions and vote buying can undermine a fledgling democratic process. International organizations must be especially aware of these possibilities, lest these opportunities for corruption and self-dealing discredit reforms that are otherwise beneficial.

Greater success in improving the institutional environment for development would be likely if both the international organizations and borrower governments took a more straightforward approach to controlling corruption and other forms of malfeasance. The UNDP and the World Bank try to maneuver between the economic interests of poor and wealthy states and to manage the tensions between charitable goals and the politics of aid and lending policy. The issue is a complex one, but a place to start is to acknowledge the problem. This has been done in most international organizations with the World Bank's September 1997 statement of policy, *Helping Countries Combat Corruption*, providing the most comprehensive framework (World Bank 1997a).[4] The goal should

---

[4] Following the lead of the World Bank, the Asian Development Bank has also issued an anticorruption policy. "Asian Bank Unveils Tough Corruption Policy," *Financial Times*, July 9, 1998.

not be to insulate aid projects from a country's corrupt climate or from the payoffs that have become routine in some areas of international business. Instead, the international organizations need to work with interested countries to develop an overall program. Conversely, they should be willing to cut off aid to countries that demonstrate an inability to use it effectively.

Limiting Corruption in International Business

Corruption involves a buyer and a seller. It cannot properly be described as "imported" by evil multinational firms into innocent developing countries. Conversely, the view that a culture of gift giving and patronage induces multinational firms to demonstrate their cultural sensitivity by paying bribes is unconvincing. It is quite insulting to suppose that a traditional culture of gift giving will support massive payoffs by business firms to political leaders. Multinational firms are central actors in many large-scale corrupt deals. Thus reform has more chance of success if these firms support change.

Multilateral Initiatives

Multinational firms face a dilemma when dealing with corrupt regimes. Each firm believes it needs to pay bribes, but each knows that most of them would be better off if nobody paid. The playing field is tilted toward unscrupulous, but less efficient firms who would not fare so well in an honest system. This realization has fed recent international efforts. The main issues are the criminalization of overseas bribery, the tax deductibility of bribes, and the establishment of transparent systems of competitive public procurement.

The Council of the Organization for Economic Cooperation and Development (OECD) signed an international convention in December 1997 that requires signatories to outlaw overseas bribery of foreign officials.[5] The document is in the process of ratification. The basic goal of the treaty is to extend the principles of the United States Foreign Corrupt Practices Act to the international business community.[6] Most countries will need not just to ratify the treaty but also to pass conforming legislation criminalizing overseas bribery. Even the United States has been required to make modest amendments to its own

---

[5] Convention on Combating Bribery of Foreign Public Officials in International Business Transactions, December 11, 1997. Available at www.oecd.org/daf/cmis/bribery/20novle.htm.

[6] Foreign Corrupt Practices Act, 15 U.S.C. §§ 78m(b) & (d)(1) & (g)-(h), 78dd-1, 78dd-2, 78ff (a)(c) (1988 & Supp. IV 1992); Klich (1996: 142–143); Pickholz (1997: 247–249).

statute.[7] The Convention defines both "bribery" and "foreign official" broadly and requires mutual legal assistance and adequate sanctions. It calls for the establishment of accounting and auditing standards and establishes a monitoring and follow-up process. The main weakness of the document is the exclusion of payments to political parties and party officials.

In many countries bribes paid to obtain foreign business are tax-deductible – a legal loophole that obviously encourages payoffs. Thus the OECD Council also recommends that member states "re-examine the tax deductibility of bribes to foreign public officials, with the intention of denying this deductibility in those Member countries which do not already do so."[8] The United States already forbids the tax deductibility of bribes, and several other countries are in the process of changing their laws to conform with the recommendation.

Under the auspices of the Organization for American States (OAS), the Inter-American Convention Against Corruption is now open for ratification, and fourteen countries had ratified it by the middle of 1998.[9] The Convention requires a good deal of cross-border cooperation and requires countries to prohibit and punish transnational bribery. The Convention is distinctive in including developed countries, a number in the middle range, and some poor countries.

The development of an international procurement code has proved difficult. The World Trade Organization's revised Agreement on Government Procurement entered into force on January 1, 1996, but only twenty-two countries, mostly industrialized states, have adopted its provisions.[10] Some commentators have urged the WTO to develop a more limited code that focuses only on limiting corruption in the hope that more countries will participate.

Some international professional and business organizations have put anticorruption initiatives on their agenda. The International Chamber of Commerce (1996) issued a recommendation in March 1996 urging its members to adopt rules of conduct designed to limit bribery in international trade. The rules prohibit bribery for any purpose, not just to obtain or retain business. The Council of the International Bar Association (1996) adopted a complementary resolution in June 1996. The UNDP

---

[7] The "International Anti-Bribery and Fair Competition Act of 1998" was enacted into law on November 10, 1998.

[8] OECD, Meeting of the Council at the Ministerial Level, Paris, May 21–22, 1996, Communique, SG/COM/NEWS(96)53, section 9(x).

[9] OEA/Ser.K/XXXIV.1; CICOR/doc.14/96 rev.2, March 29, 1996.

[10] See Hoekman and Mavroidis (1997), which includes the text of the agreement as an appendix.

Aid Accountability Initiative is considering working with the International Organization of Supreme Audit Institutions and the International Federation of Accountants to develop projects to strengthen accountability in developing countries (United Nations Development Programme 1996: ii). In the United States the American Bar Association has a Task Force on International Standards for Corrupt Practices, and the Business Roundtable has taken up the question of corruption, particularly as it affects government procurement processes throughout the world.

All these initiatives are encouraging, but they are very recent, and some are purely hortatory. The next few years will indicate whether they have any real meaning.

The Obligations of Multinational Firms

Although recent international efforts represent a new willingness to confront the issue of transnational bribery, they are not sufficient. Individual firms ought to consider their obligations as international actors that exceed in size and influence some of the nations with which they deal. For example, in 1995 the sales figures for the twenty largest multinational corporations ranged from $61.5 billion to $152.5 billion. The smallest of these companies had sales that exceeded the GDP of ninety-eight of the 138 countries providing data to the World Bank.[11]

A firm's leverage in relation to a nation-state depends on the nature of its dealings with government and on the size of its deals relative to the size of the government. Firms may have contracts to extract hard rock minerals or petroleum, to cut down trees, or to produce and market agricultural products. They may purchase privatizing firms or establish new manufacturing plants or service firms. If the deal represents a sizable share of a country's national income or state budget, firms cannot responsibly adopt the position that their own business interests are all that is at stake. They may claim that they ought to be under no obligation to take a broader perspective, but they cannot claim that their actions are irrelevant to conditions in the developing or transitional country.

Multinational businesses have not generally considered the impact of their behavior on the long-term prospects of the countries where they invest and trade. One still hears expressions of cynicism and resignation from business leaders and their advisors. However, in an international

---

[11] Calculated from data in the World Bank's *World Development Indicators 1997*, Table 4.2, and the United Nations, *World Investment Report 1997: Transnational Corporations, Market Structure and Competition Policy*, Table I.7.

environment with no effective means of regulating inefficient behavior, large firms have an obligation, and may have a long-term interest, in behaving responsibly. In developed countries, with their network of regulations and reasonably responsive political systems, firms can focus on profit confident that other institutions exist to worry about monopoly power, environmental externalities, and misleading business practices. A firm that operates within the laws of the United States can argue that the constraints imposed by tax, regulatory, and criminal laws are sufficient to fulfill its obligations. Such a position is controversial even in developed countries, but it is, at least, a plausible position. This view comes into question when investment and trade occur in overseas environments where legal rules are either poorly specified or overly restrictive and where the accountability of top government officials to the long-run success of their country's economic and social development is in doubt.

Of course, there are very few cases where a multinational firm can singlehandedly influence the operation of a state. Countries such as China, India, or Russia are so large that they have market power on their own. Even in those countries, however, some companies have leverage at the national level, and the regional impact of other deals is large. For example, consumer goods companies with strong international brand recognition, such as McDonald's, Disney, Levi Strauss, and Coca-Cola, may be such a symbol of modernity that they can successfully resist corrupt demands. Other companies with a strong market position in their fields of business such as Boeing or IBM can refuse to participate in corrupt arrangements. Even if such firms lose out to corrupt deals in some countries, others may be induced to operate more cleanly so as not to sacrifice the firms' business. Large, highly diversified firms such as General Electric may have a further advantage if they can credibly threaten to exit a country entirely in the face of corrupt demands in one line of business. Such a firm may also have the bargaining power to protect local subsidiaries from acquiescing to corrupt demands. Firms that successfully use the leverage they have not only will help contribute to the long-run growth prospects of the country but also will generally benefit in the short run as well.

Companies operating in a corrupt environment must decide whether to participate actively, quietly refuse to deal, or report corruption to local authorities and to those in the outside world. Keeping quiet is probably the worst option. The firm not only loses business; it also has done nothing to change the underlying situation for the better. The advantage of the current interest in corruption is that companies suffer international embarrassment if a payoff is revealed, and this possibility can induce them not only to resist corrupt demands but even to report them. Companies that claim to abhor corruption while accepting it as a necessary evil are not acting consistently. Revealing corrupt demands can have an impact if the pressure of international public opinion affects both corrupt public officials and bribe-paying business firms.

Top management needs to be involved. Survey evidence in which business students and middle managers put company goals ahead of personal morality suggests that credible leadership must come from the top. In one experiment, over 70 percent of participants were willing to pay a bribe to get a sale for their firms. For many of the test subjects ethics took second place to the fulfillment of company goals. Those willing to make payoffs were not significantly less committed to honesty and fairness in their personal lives than other participants (Rosenberg 1987). These results, if at all typical, suggest the importance of clear and well-enforced corporate codes of conduct. Because of the provisions of the Foreign Corrupt Practices Act, United States firms have a head start in developing such codes, and their experience may be useful to firms elsewhere in the world.[12]

Certain global strategies are possible today that would have been infeasible just a few years ago. Thus one could imagine a cooperative relationship between the IMF and the World Bank, on the one hand, and multinational businesses on the other, to aid reform. For example, under its new policy the IMF requires reforms in a country's public sector institutions and in the transparency of its procedures in order to limit corruption and improve the effectiveness of IMF financial assistance.[13] Such strings were successfully attached to the packages negotiated with the Philippines and Thailand; Kenya's unwillingness to reform led to an IMF pullout in the summer of 1997. One method of checking the effectiveness of a country's policies would be to permit firms that are pressured for bribes to report their experience to the IMF. The IMF would not investigate individual complaints, but a pattern of reports could induce the IMF to reopen negotiations. Similarly, top government officials who feel pressured to accept payoffs by businesses seeking favors could also report to the IMF. Such reports, passed on to the World Bank, could be

---

[12] The United States branch of Transparency International has sponsored an effort both to compile existing codes and to help companies without such codes to develop them (Transparency International – USA 1996).

[13] International Monetary Fund, "The Role of the IMF in Governance Issues – Guidance Note," issued as part of News Brief 95/15, Washington DC: IMF, August 4, 1997.

a preliminary step in implementing the World Bank's new procurement policy that explicitly contemplates actions to discipline firms by restricting access to projects supported by World Bank loans.

Becoming a clearinghouse for allegations is a way of revealing to both sides that high-level corruption is a game in which the developing country is the loser and in which neither private nor public actors can absolve themselves of responsibility. If both a top official and a firm complain about corrupt pressures exerted by the other, the stage may be set for meaningful reforms that reduce the underlying incentives for such deals to be made in the first place. Without trying to affix blame, the IMF and World Bank could begin a dialogue with a country's leaders and major investors on ways to improve the situation for the benefit of the country's citizens. If everyone thinks that everyone else is corrupt, then all but the saints will be tempted to engage in malfeasance. If expectations can be changed by clear statements on both sides followed by consistent actions and a credible commitment to report corrupt pressures, progress seems possible. The climate of world opinion may be running strongly enough against corruption to make it worthwhile for major corporations to take a stand against bribery rather than tolerating or encouraging payoffs.

Controlling Money Laundering and International Criminal Enterprise

Anticorruption efforts should be coordinated with another international campaign – the fight against organized crime. There are two reasons for this. First, both corrupt rulers and international criminal enterprise benefit if it is easy to launder money across national borders. Accepting bribes will look more attractive if it is relatively easy to deposit the funds outside the country. Thus strong international action against money laundering can help mitigate both problems. Second, the existence of large-scale illegal businesses is likely to have a corrupting influence on government, especially law enforcement and border control. Corrupt rulers and illegal businessmen feed on each other. Illegal businesses must pay bribes in order to operate. The bribe receipts, being illegal, are themselves especially likely to provide capital to illegal businesses worldwide. This reduces the cost of capital to such industries and fuels their growth relative to legal business ventures.

Money laundering is the process of disguising illegitimate income to make it appear legitimate (Paulose 1997: 257). Estimates of the volume of funds laundered ranges from $120 billion to $500 billion per year (ibid.: 261). There are many methods in use, but one common technique is the transfer of funds to countries that permit banks to conceal the identity of depositors. These funds are then transferred to international banks with access to markets worldwide. Prosecution is difficult because sophisticated money launderers react to legal changes by changing their tactics. For example, many statutes require that financial institutions be aware of the illegal origin of the funds they receive. In reaction, money launderers take additional steps to conceal the origin of their funds (ibid.: 259–262).

The United Nations Vienna Convention Against Illicit Traffic in Narcotic Drugs and Psychotropic Substances adopted in 1988 and the 1990 Council of Europe Convention on Laundering, Search, Seizure and Confiscation of Proceeds of Crime are the main international agreements (Scott 1995). The Vienna Convention calls on countries to criminalize the laundering of money from drug transactions. The European Union also issued a directive in 1991 that obligates member states to require financial institutions to maintain systems to prevent money laundering.[14] The main international body engaged in ongoing efforts to control money laundering is the Financial Action Task Force set up in 1989. It has representatives from the OECD, Hong Kong, Singapore, the Gulf States, and the European Commission (ibid.). It has developed forty recommendations for appropriate countermeasures, including the prohibition of anonymous accounts. In recent years more than fifty new laws against money laundering have been passed. In North America the United States passed a broad statute in 1986 followed soon afterward by Canada and Mexico. European countries originally focused only on money laundering as it affected drug trafficking. At present, however, many have joined North American efforts to prohibit money laundering in connection with all major offenses, including bribery and corruption (Paulose 1997: 263–280). In all of these laws the most problematic element is the requirement that the financial institution had or should have had knowledge of the illicit origin of the funds. The stronger this requirement, the easier it will be for a bank to defend itself. Clearly, it is in the interest of the depositor to conceal the origin of the funds and of the financial institution to ask as few questions as possible.

Despite the increased national and international interest in control, the problem is becoming more serious. Money laundering is becoming the specialty of small "financial paradises" and of some emerging market economies. It is not enough to keep most developed countries pure. A serious international campaign against the worst abusers, including Switzerland, is of increasing importance. At issue is both the ease with which corrupt officials in one country can hide their gains in another and

[14] Council Directive 91/308, 1991 O.J. (L 166) 77.

the possibility that money-laundering activities can undermine the credibility of a country's financial structure (Scott 1995). Money-laundering controls are only negative sanctions, however. They are unlikely to increase investment in capital-poor countries. They are not likely to have much of an impact unless combined with more direct efforts to improve government performance and accountability.

International efforts to control illegal businesses are a second important option. If corruption is combined with organized crime, the problem for international aid organizations is especially difficult. If the entire state is permeated with crime, there is probably not much outside organizations can do except wait in the wings and hope for the best. In less extreme cases, the experience of developed countries in fighting organized crime may be useful. In developing countries, unused to confronting organized crime, a combination of training and law reform is a useful first step. But such reforms are unlikely to be sufficient unless the economy is strong and competitive. The state may need to make more direct efforts to reduce the excess profits available to criminal entrepreneurs in legitimate business.

One solution is promoting the entry of well-capitalized legitimate businesses that, with some state help on the law enforcement side, can compete with mob-dominated firms. For example, the courts mandated the entry of large multinational waste management firms into the trash hauling industry in New York City. This strategy has reduced the influence of organized crime and lowered garbage removal costs for the commercial businesses not serviced by the Sanitation Department. State prosecutors estimated that garbage removal fees of $1.5 billion in 1995 were inflated by as much as $400 million. In recent years the cost of garbage removal has fallen by 30 to 40 percent for most businesses.[15]

A country's links to the broader world can either limit or expand the scope for organized crime. On the one hand, an open trading and investment regime will make it easy for both contraband and the profits of crime to flow across borders. The existence of banking havens where black money can come to rest makes domestic criminal activity less risky, because money can be easily hidden abroad. On the other hand, open borders facilitate investment by outsiders in a country. If these outsiders are not part of the domestic criminal bodies and are not associated with

---

[15] "Judge Backs Competition in Trash-Hauling Industry," *New York Times*, February 28, 1994; "The Garbage Wars: Cracking the Cartel," *New York Times*, July 30, 1995; "Monitors Appointed for Trash Haulers," *New York Times*, December 23, 1995; "Prices Plummet and Service Rises with Crackdown on Trash Cartel," *New York Times*, May 11, 1998.

such groups elsewhere, they may challenge entrenched groups. Of course, if such investments are costly and dangerous, few may make the effort, but a country's openness to foreign investment at least makes them thinkable.

One role for international organizations and for law enforcement agencies in developed countries is the compilation of information on questionable transactions, combined with the prosecution of individuals and organizations based in developed countries that do business in developing countries. For example, it is possible to compare average product prices in U.S. international trade with the average prices for the same products recorded for U.S. trade with particular countries. The data provide a way to look for over- and under-invoicing and have been used by U.S. authorities to direct investigative efforts (Pak and Zdanowicz 1994; Paul, Pak, Zdanowicz, and Curwen 1994). Obviously, price divergences cannot prove anything on their own, but they can provide a starting point for more intensive investigation. These data could point to violations of United States tax and customs laws, as well as laws of foreign countries. They can indicate where money laundering may be occurring through mispriced traded goods. This data-gathering effort should be extended to include trade records from other developed countries and could provide a way for developed countries to help poorer countries control illegal transfers of funds and tax and customs fraud.

The control of international criminal behavior is an important matter, but the lesson of this book is that a criminal-justice approach to corruption is not sufficient. Limiting money laundering and controlling illegal businesses clearly require international cooperation, but these efforts will not by themselves have much of an impact on the level of corruption if the underlying incentives arise not from illegal business activity, but from the benefits of controlling the state.

New International Institutions

If the international initiatives bear fruit, the problem of implementation will have to be taken far more seriously. Individual country reforms, such as no-bribery pledges for large-scale procurement, may also need an outside body to resolve disputes. Thus the idea of an international tribunal deserves further scrutiny. In establishing a general forum for resolving disputes, there are clearly some difficult problems of proof and standards of decision. Nevertheless, some models exist in the international legal arena that may provide ideas about how to proceed.

For example, the World Bank Group's International Center for the Settlement of Investment Disputes (ICSID) resolves disputes under contracts where it is the forum of choice (Shihata and Parra 1994). ICSID panels are not formally courts, and their use is based on the prior consent of the parties, but they do occasionally deal with issues that are indirectly related to corruption. The process has difficulties because the review mechanism lacks finality and sometimes takes an overly technical and formalistic approach. Nevertheless, these problems may have become less severe in recent years (Reisman 1992: 46–106). ICSID has not, however, heard disputes arising at the contract-awarding stage, and it may not have jurisdiction in such matters. It is also an expensive and time-consuming process that is not presently able to handle a large volume of cases. Serious reforms would be required before it could regularly be invoked as part of a broader anticorruption effort.

In 1993 the World Bank established an independent Inspection Panel that provides another model for an international dispute-resolution mechanism. Unlike the ICSID, which is open only to parties to disputed contracts, the Panel reviews complaints from groups of private persons in borrower countries. Groups must allege that they are suffering or expect to suffer from the World Bank's failure to follow its own policies and procedures (Bradlow 1996; Bradlow and Schlemmer-Schulte 1994). Thus it appears possible for the Panel to hear complaints involving corruption in World Bank projects. For example, the Panel might consider allegations that the Bank did not follow its operational policies and procedures if it overlooked evidence of corruption. In fact, corruption may be behind some recent cases brought on other grounds. Unfortunately, the Panel is a weak instrument. It cannot proceed with an investigation unless it obtains the approval of the Bank's Board of Directors, and even if the Panel finds against the Bank, it has only advisory powers. Its recommendations are forwarded to the Bank's board, which makes the final decision, and the Panel's own findings are not made public. Of the ten cases which had come to the Panel by September 1997, the Panel refused to accept two and recommended against an investigation in three. In the remaining five, the Board fully backed the Panel in only one case (World Bank 1997b). The flaws in the Panel as an accountability mechanism were revealed in case of Yacyreta Dam on the Argentine–Paraguay border. A Bank vice president characterized a Panel report from September 1997 as a vindication of the Bank's actions, but when the report was leaked to the press, it was seen to be very critical of the Bank.[16] Thus this system

---

[16] "Yacyreta Report Implies WB Panel Downgrade," *Financial Times Business Reports*, January 1, 1998; "Row Brews Over Bank Role in Dam Project," *Financial Times*, May 4, 1998; "World Bank Issues Apology," *Financial Times* May 12, 1998.

also must be reinforced and made more accountable before it can become a serious part of the emerging regime, although even in its present form it can highlight troublesome areas in Bank lending.

The Panel's experience with handling complaints from citizens' groups and nonprofit organizations is a useful first step. It is the first international forum in which individuals who do not have a contractual relationship with an international organization can attempt to hold it accountable (Bissell 1997; Bradlow and Schlemmer-Schulte 1994: 402). After analyzing the Panel's handling of complaints about the Arun III dam project in Nepal, Daniel Bradlow (1996) concludes that the Panel can help protect the interests of people affected by World Bank projects, but he raises concerns about ambiguities in the relationship between the Panel, Bank management, and the Board of Executive Directors. A key requirement, and one that will be central to any new institution, is to assure that the Panel maintains its independence and that its processes are transparent to outside observers.

Tribunals also exist in the fields of human rights, international labor standards, and nuclear energy that might be models (Barratt-Brown 1991: 548–563). NGOs can bring complaints before them and participate in the presentation of evidence. Each of the existing bodies has its own problems, and none is a perfect model for those concerned with anti-corruption efforts. Nevertheless, they do demonstrate how NGOs can play a constructive role in international review processes.

Alternatively, the international community could establish a forum to review cases of suspected corruption in privatization or contracting processes – perhaps in connection with a no-bribery pledge. Cases brought by disappointed bidders or defrauded lenders would require the country involved to make a transparent accounting of its behavior. Plaintiffs would not necessarily need to document bribes paid. The focus should instead be on the terms of the deal. If it seems to diverge significantly from what an honest process would produce, the court could require that the project be rebid. One difficulty in making the process operational, however, is that the rebid will not simply be a more transparent and honest rerun of the old one. All the players have new information as a result of the first round that will affect their behavior in the second round. Students of auction processes need to analyze the strategic aspects of this proposal carefully to avoid creating an even more unfair system.

A more serious problem with an international tribunal is to assure obedience to its decisions. One option is to use the leverage of the World Trade Organization (WTO). The advantage of WTO sanctions is that they are not imposed by the WTO itself but by a country's trading partners. However, the WTO governs relations among nations, not individuals and businesses. Thus, transnational bribery could be controlled *through* the World Trade Organization, not *by* the WTO (Nichols 1997a: 361–364). An international process of this kind would, of course, discourage some investment and privatization projects from going ahead. First, that might not be such a bad thing. If an inside deal appears inevitable, a country should delay privatization because a public firm is much easier to monitor than a private one. Similarly, corrupt leaders may design a public works project with bribes in mind, not economic development. Second, the international community might subsidize the cost of any proceeding where the developing country emerges victorious from a challenge. Third, like the WTO procurement pact, participation could be voluntary with jurisdiction limited to those countries that fulfill WTO conditions or that volunteer to establish a system of no-bribery pledges in return for World Bank or UNDP technical advice and other support. Proposals for an international dispute resolution mechanism are an example of the more general principle that one way to fight corruption is to give losers a means of lodging a complaint.

The international business community is beginning to recognize the costs of corruption to the global investment environment. Insofar as this is true, another approach becomes possible. Perhaps international businesses themselves could provide funds and technical assistance to countries interested in reform. This is already happening through professional associations such as the American Bar Association, but aid organizations might explore the possibility of collaborative projects.

Conclusions: Policy Fads and Policy Reforms
The current interest in corruption repeats an old pattern. Reformist impulses have arisen frequently in the last couple of centuries, and sometimes have led to real reform. Nonetheless, the present wave of interest is part of a more general trend. Development specialists are beginning to recognize that the traditional focus on macroeconomic policy and on large-scale infrastructure projects is not sufficient and may even backfire. If a state's political and bureaucratic institutions are weak and if the market operates very imperfectly, development aid may fail to produce positive results.

International aid and lending organizations have taken the first steps toward reform. Corruption is no longer a taboo subject. Some World Bank projects have been withdrawn because of evidence of corruption, although generally without much publicity. The IMF is requiring countries that want a bailout to agree to governance reforms including policies to reduce corruption. Yet doubts remain about the depth of these commitments. A serious attempt to deal with the subject will require confrontations with many borrowers and with lenders whose own firms pay bribes in developing countries. The World Bank's own difficulties are easy to see in their policy document *Helping Countries Combat Corruption* (1997a). No individual country is named in the entire document except for a brief reference to three that are starting to reform. Yet change cannot occur unless countries acknowledge the problem and deal with it in a way that does not have the character of a witch hunt. Too often anticorruption campaigns have floundered on the desire of those in power to undermine their opponents.

Furthermore, the World Bank ought not develop a template based on "best practice" that is usable by all countries. Culture and history – as well as current economic and social conditions – influence both the nature of the problem and the kinds of solutions that make sense. Yet this book has shown that there are many general lessons that can be derived from a basic understanding of economic incentives. These lessons cannot be codified in a "one size fits all" model, but must be applied with a sensitive appreciation of an individual country's conditions. The World Bank's present proposals reflect this view. The question is whether it will carry out a vigorous policy or only seek to mollify its loudest critics through symbolic gestures.

Similar doubts can be raised about the move to international or regional agreements. The OAS Convention and the OECD treaty are a fine start. But both must be accompanied by the creation of monitoring and enforcement institutions that give new incentives to those hurt by corruption to come forward to complain. Otherwise the international documents will be little more than statements of pious hopes.

11

Domestic Conditions for Reform

Ideas and moral commitments matter. Reforms sometimes occur simply because a charismatic and committed leader pushes them through. Strong leaders can inspire people to accept major reforms that lesser personalities could never achieve.[1] But strong leadership is generally a necessary, not a sufficient cause of political change. Past practice creates inertia. It is often easiest to go on as before – especially because the beneficiaries of the status quo will struggle against change. Choices made at one point in time foreclose other choices in the future. However, although history imposes constraints, it seldom forces one particular outcome. The challenge is to identify structural factors, apart from charismatic leadership, that create favorable conditions for reform.

We now have sufficient experience with reform efforts throughout the world to permit some well-grounded structural speculations. The argument in this chapter assumes that developing countries and those in the transition from socialism can learn from the historical experience of developed countries as well as the more recent experience of other developing countries. Of course, the lessons will have to be filtered through the particular situation of each nation, but some of the underlying political and economic incentives seem quite universal.

There are two basic models of the reform process: one based on the exercise of political power and the other based on a contractual model

[1] On the importance of moral leaders during the Antipatronage and Progressive periods in the United States, 1870–1933, see Anechiarico and Jacobs (1996: 19–21), Maranto and Schultz (1991: 44–50), Sproat (1982), and White (1958). Das-Gupta and Mookherjee (1998: 302) discuss the necessity of political will at the top as a precondition for administrative reform. They cite the example of Uruguay as a case where resistance from public officials had to be overcome by political support from the top.

of consensus. Those who expect to lose from reform can be outvoted and outmaneuvered, or they can be coopted or compensated to accept change (Grindle and Thomas 1991: 134). For example, in Great Britain in the 1980s Prime Minister Margaret Thatcher's government carried out administrative reforms through a conflictual strategy; in Australia Prime Minister Robert Hawke sought consensus (Zifcak 1994: 158). A key strategic decision for reformers is whom to include in their coalition and whom to force to accept the costs of reform. Should one buy off corrupt officials and private persons and firms, or should one shut them out of the reformed system? How much will reform goals be undermined by the process of generating a coalition to support change?

I begin with the problem of producing a political coalition. Powerful politicians must believe that reform is in their interest. This often occurs in response to pressures by powerful private groups who decide that reform will aid them. In democracies public pressure can spur reform, but even autocracies can face political incentives to reduce corruption. The exact timing may be influenced by a scandal or an economic crisis. Such triggering events may not always lead to constructive change and are costly in themselves, but they can make it possible to organize a reform coalition. Both the absolute and the relative size of government are contributing factors affecting the costs and benefits of reform to different groups.

Reforms do not always become institutionalized. If the political conditions that produced reform disappear, the reforms often disappear as well. But in other contexts, reforms persist despite quite important political shifts. The final section seeks to understand when this is likely to happen. Sometimes, however, reforms become too well entrenched, to the point of ossification. Then the problem is to push the system to change without abandoning the remaining strengths of the old system. Once again, historical experience provides some suggestive cases.

Political Structure and Reform

Realistically, reform will not occur unless powerful groups and individuals inside and outside government support it. In democracies a political coalition must develop that supports change. In autocracies the leader is sometimes under reformist pressures from the military and from portions of the private sector. A state that is overwhelmingly corrupt risks invasion and civil war. Witness the rapid fall of President Mobutu Sese Seko of Zaire once an alternative presented itself. But the causation is circular. The threat of losing power can induce high officials to become even more corrupt as a means of insuring their economic well-being once they are out of office. Corrupt leaders may find that reform is risky if it releases opposition forces that undermine the current regime. Thus successful reformers may need to buy off potential opponents. Reformers also need to worry about sequencing. If not carefully managed, the beneficiaries of the first stage of reform may become opponents of broader restructuring.

Democracy and Reform

As we have already seen, corruption can coexist with electoral politics. However, corrupt democratic governments are sometimes able to reform. In the nineteenth century the United States, Great Britain, and many urban American governments reformed their systems of public employment and procurement. Some Latin American countries with democratic structures have also had reform periods. Democratic structures can promote reform under some, but not all, conditions.

Voting Systems and Reform: Latin America: Barbara Geddes's work on civil service reform in Latin American democracies (1991, 1994) provides a useful starting point. Assume that politicians and parties want to remain in power. They may then face what Geddes calls the "politicians' dilemma" where the country as a whole would benefit from an end to patronage, but no individual politician or political party has an incentive unilaterally to institute a merit system. Anyone who did so would give up votes to the opposition with no corresponding political benefit. Geddes then postulates a case in which the public benefits of reform are recognized by voters. A politician who advocates reform gains political support that can be balanced against the losses from the reduction in patronage jobs. Obviously, a minority party, with little hope of becoming part of a future government, can support reform more easily than a majority or governing party. The minority, with little access to patronage, loses little from its advocacy of reform. In fact, it may face a paradox. If its reform position is popular enough to give it a real chance of winning the next election, that very fact may make it a less enthusiastic reformer. Once a party obtains power, it may violate its electoral promises with the result that voters do not believe subsequent promises, discouraging such promises in the future.

Although Geddes focuses on reform of the public administration, much of what she has to say applies to other aspects of a comprehensive corruption reform strategy. For example, reform of procurement systems and improvements in the transparency and openness of government both have features in common with civil service reform. Those in power benefit from corruptly obtained contracts and secretive government processes, but the legitimacy of the public sector as a whole would be improved by reform. Many anticorruption policies impose costs on the political group that proposes them that exceed the cost borne by those who simply go along with the change. Unless public outcry is very potent and sustained, there is a first-mover disadvantage. Reforming incumbent administrations gain support by advocating change, but this is balanced by their disproportionate loss of corrupt returns.

Geddes suggests that politicians and political parties in Latin America recognize the dilemma of reform. In her analysis there are two situations in which reform is possible. First, a single party may have a dominant position, but government inefficiency, caused by corruption and patronage, threatens its hold on power. Then it may support reform in spite of the costs borne by public officials. Elections, even if they always return the same party to power, have a constraining effect on the ruling party. Second, if several parties are evenly matched in their access to patronage appointments, and if they will benefit symmetrically from reform, they may be able to collaborate to legislate change. Colombia, Uruguay, and Venezuela provide examples of reforms carried out during periods of balance in access to patronage. In Colombia a further factor encouraging reform was partisan violence that threatened the democratic framework. All sitting politicians had an interest in reforms that would help end this violence. Other authors have noted similar features of reform episodes outside Latin America. For example, under much less urgent circumstances, New Zealand was able to reform its government in the 1980s in the face of economic pressures that limited political opposition to change. The reform was begun under one government and completed by another (Scott 1996: 72).

Balanced political parties are not sufficient, however. An important deterrent to reform is the personalized nature of politics. The greater the importance of personalized circles of support, the harder it will be to carry out broad-based reforms. Geddes argues that in Colombia and Uruguay voting by closed-list proportional representation facilitated the reform effort because it limited the conflicts between individual politicians and political parties. With a closed list, the party determines the order of candidates on the ballot so individual candidates must please the party hierarchy in order to succeed, and party discipline is likely to be high. With an open list, the order of candidate selection is determined by the voters who select not just a party, but also express preferences for particular candidates. Thus politicians within each party must compete with each other. In an open-list system patronage ought to be especially difficult to eliminate because individualized benefits to voters and campaign workers loom large. In fact, the two systems that did not reform, Brazil and Chile, both had open-list systems. Coalition governments in Chile, whose members had little in common, were held together by patronage.

However, Geddes's contrast between closed- and open-list proportional representation is about necessary, not sufficient conditions. Thus under a closed-list system the rank and file will not be harmed by reform, but no reform will occur if party leaders use their positions illicitly to enrich themselves or their parties. If the party leadership is corrupt, it will want a closed-list system as a means of controlling members through control of positions on the list. Even if those at the top of the system are not corrupt, the leadership may protect less powerful members to preserve the party's image. In Germany, for example, the strength of the party system helped protect individual corrupt politicians by weakening outside monitoring of individual politicians and by rewarding those who accepted donations in return for legislative quid pro quos (Seibel 1997: 95).

Gabrielle Montinola's work on Chile complements Geddes's analysis by focusing on public oversight. Chile was a very corrupt country between 1891 and 1924 but is now relatively clean by Latin American standards (Montinola 1997). In addition, the business sector does not view the state as predatory (Stone, Levy, and Paredes 1992). According to Montinola, a shift in political alignments facilitated Chile's shift to a low level of corruption. In the early part of the century Chilean democracy was a complex, multidimensional system that produced the unstable coalitions that Geddes describes. But in the aftermath of General Pinochet's regime, Montinola argues that political preferences are now aligned along a single left–right dimension. This makes it easier for citizens to hold the government accountable because each government will represent a particular position in policy space, not a compromise coalition. Such accountability will, according to her, limit corrupt opportunities and encourage reform.

The Latin American cases analyzed by Geddes all used some form of proportional representation. One might also ask how proportional representation systems compare with plurality voting systems in encouraging reform. No simple answer is possible, except to note that plurality systems often produce two parties that represent the kinds of broad coalitions favorable to reform. The parties alternate in power so that no coalition government is necessary (Cox 1997). Proportional representation systems encourage the development of multiparty systems and hence increase the probability of narrowly focused parties and unstable coalition governments. Plurality-rule systems are not invariably more stable, however – compare the recent instability in India, with its wealth of regional parties elected by plurality rule, with the stability of coalition governments in Germany since the Second World War. Nevertheless, plurality systems may be more likely to produce governments with the perspective needed to produce credible reform. For example, New Zealand has recently shifted to a mixed proportional representation system from what was an almost pure example of a Westminster parliamentary democracy. Those involved in the recent reform effort worry that if a coalition or minority government results, it will be unable to take a long-term view. The government may need to accommodate key coalition members with narrowly focused benefits (Scott 1996: 81).

The Latin American experience has generally been quite disheartening. Geddes shows that a political coalition for reform is possible, but she goes on to demonstrate its fragility. Not only do some democratic forms make reform politically difficult, but even when reform does occur, it may not last. All of her "success" stories are followed by periods of breakdown when patronage, corruption, and inefficiency reappeared. Reforms that persisted affected only a small portion of the bureaucracy, and many were undermined by subsequent governments. Politically easy reforms that improved the working conditions of bureaucrats were maintained and extended. Without merit-based recruitment and promotion, these changes hardly count as reforms on their own. Thus even if Geddes is right that closed-list proportional representation is better than open-list proportional representation in permitting reform, perhaps plurality systems that tend to limit the number of parties are even better. Those who express concern about New Zealand's shift from plurality to proportional representation may be correct.

Furthermore, as Geddes herself argues, a dominant party in control of the executive may also reform if corruption and inefficiency have begun to harm its ability to govern. In Latin America, with its many strong presidential systems, elected presidents have sometimes pushed through reforms. An ongoing study of the preconditions for general administrative reform in eight cases in Latin America, Asia, and Eastern Europe suggests that policy and political coherence in the executive are of central importance in getting reform off the ground (Heredia and Schneider 1998). In those cases some of the factors discussed below, such as crises and the growing dissatisfaction of powerful elites, are central in explaining the timing of reform.

Geddes's work leads to two basic conclusions. First, "democracy" is too broad a category to use when analyzing reform. The details of the electoral system and, in particular, the political incentives to consider broad public values are critical. As Geddes (1991: 187) notes, "it is ironic that the reforms that would improve efficiency and fairness in the provision of government services should be impeded by the same representative

institutions whose manifest purpose is to reflect constituents' interests."
Montinola's work adds a concern for the way political party ideologies
are distributed in issue space. The two factors may be related. The nature
of the voting system may have an impact on the kinds of political parties
that can survive.

Second, reforms are likely to be fragile if they are the product of
temporarily favorable political conditions. Parity of political interests can
produce reforms, but they will only persist if party parity is an enduring
feature of the system. Once again the voting system itself may help
determine the durability of political alignments. Both the underlying
cleavages in society and the way they are reflected in the structure of
government can affect the durability of reform. To be sustained, the first
stage of reform ought to be implemented to produce supporters who
push to maintain and extend the initial successes. A look at the history
of reform in the United States and Great Britain can help shed light on
this last issue.

Nineteenth-Century Reform in the United States and Great Britain:
Studies of civil service reform in the nineteenth century in both the
United States and Great Britain complement Geddes's work on Latin
America. There are two issues. Why did reform occur, and how was it
maintained?

Geddes's emphasis on the balance of political forces seems relevant
in both countries. When reform occurred, both used first-past-the-post
voting rules that typically produced two balanced parties alternating in
power. No political grouping benefited disproportionately from its access
to patronage, and all shared in the benefits of reform. Britain's parliamentary system, with strong party discipline, limited the scope for individual favor seeking. Even though members represented individual
districts, they had a limited ability to trade favors for votes. The increase
in the size of the electorate in the nineteenth century and the elimination of many small constituencies reduced the benefits of patronage
appointments (Parris 1969: 70–71).

In the United States party discipline did not prevail, a factor that discouraged reform, and, in fact, reform did come later in the United States
than in Britain. The separately elected President at the head of the executive branch, however, could view the tradeoff between patronage and
service efficiency from a national perspective. President Andrew Jackson
developed a system of patronage to reward supporters. He believed that
a spoils systems would combat corruption by democratizing government
service and eliminating entrenched officials. Instead, corruption grew
more serious. By the late nineteenth century, a bipartisan political coali-

tion that included President Chester Arthur supported the Pendleton Act that started the federal government on the road to establishing a civil service system (Maranto and Schultz 1991: 30–36, 50–55).

Both countries demonstrate the strains that arise when some constituents care about the efficiency and fairness of the services provided by the state, and others just want jobs. The strains are of two kinds: Giving out government jobs can become a political cost instead of a benefit, and managing the conflict between constituents who want jobs and those who want efficient service can be difficult. If the quality of government services begins to loom large in voters' minds, politicians – both legislators and cabinet secretaries – begin to doubt the political benefits of patronage.

In the United States and Britain politicians complained about how much time and energy they spent dealing with job seekers (Chester 1981: 155–156; Johnson and Libecap 1994; Maranto and Schultz 1991; Parris 1969: 50–79). If the number of jobs is not expanding rapidly, many applicants will be disappointed. The number of the disgruntled and their families may vastly exceed the number of satisfied patronage appointees. Even successful job seekers may think that they should have gotten better jobs. Dispensing patronage becomes a nuisance, not a privilege (Chester 1981: 155–156; Parris 1969: 71). For example, the boss of the Pennsylvania Republican party complained that he had so many friends that he faced a serious problem of whom to recommend (Blair 1989: 31). Neither the United States nor Britain experienced revenue windfalls during the reform period – so that fiscal constraints made the distribution of jobs politically costly. The situation in Venezuela provides a useful contrast. There, windfall oil profits undermined reform efforts as the state went on a hiring spree (Geddes 1994). In other countries statist policies require large numbers of state sector employees to staff state firms. The very size of the state sector lowers the political costs of patronage, as it increases the economic costs.

Reform politicians in America and England mobilized powerful business support for a more efficient public service. Nineteenth-century business interests wanted a post office that delivered the mail effectively, and they wanted their merchandise to pass through customs quickly. They might be willing to pay individual customs agents for speedy service, but they generally preferred a system that eliminated such payoffs (Johnson and Libecap 1994). In the United States business generally supported municipal reform (Stave 1972). Businessmen may tolerate a certain level of corruption, but begin to protest if the level of graft escalates, as it apparently did in urban America in the latter part of the nineteenth century. One author claims that urban reform in the United States was given a push when graft levels increased from 10 to 30 percent of the value of contracts and benefits (Calvert 1972). In developing and transition countries businesses have voiced similar objections in the present day. For example, in Brazil President Collor's downfall was hastened by his reputed decision to increase "commissions" from an average of 15 percent of the value of deals under the previous regime to 40 percent (Fleischer 1997: 302; Manzetti and Blake 1996: 676).

In the United States an additional reason for reform derived from the federal structure of government. Federal politicians supported reform because patronage was increasingly controlled by state and local party bosses whose interests were not necessarily congruent with those of federal politicians (Johnson and Libecap 1994: 97). Thus, on the one hand, the jobs that were controlled by members of Congress were becoming costly to dispense, and, on the other hand, patronage jobs in their home districts were under local control and brought them few benefits.[2] Federalism was conducive to national reform because it was a way for national politicians to reduce the power of rivals at lower levels of government.

In short, the costs of allocating jobs and contracts through patronage and payoffs may come to outweigh the benefits for political leaders. In a democracy not everyone need support reform; it can be carried out if enough voters begin to see that it will be, on balance, beneficial. Reform ought to be more likely in governments with voting rules that limit the ability of politicians to benefit from patronage and in systems where power is balanced across political groupings. In particular, in proportional representation systems, a closed-list ought to be better than an open-list system, everything else equal. A plurality rule structure that produces two strong parties can facilitate reform if it produces stable governments. A simple unidimensional set of political issues is conducive to reform because it makes it easier for citizens to hold government accountable. The United States reformed in the nineteenth century, however, in spite of the lack of strong parties. The existence of a separately elected President subject to powerful electoral pressures helped, but part of the explanation appears to be the growing importance to voters and business interests of competently provided public services.

Autocratic Reformers

Countries with a tradition of autocratic rulers or one-party rule can be corrupt with impunity, but they sometimes produce reformers as heads

---

[2] For example, in Pennsylvania the leader of Republican state machine, not the congressional delegation, was viewed as controlling access to federal jobs (Blair 1989: 81).

of state. Although outside observers might prefer a more democratic polity, it is not absurd to suppose that such rulers are genuinely concerned with reducing corruption and promoting shared growth. Indeed, even a single-minded kleptocrat would like to control the peculation of subordinates. Thus some reform strategies will be supported by autocratic rulers.

For example, reforms that improve the revenue collection capacity of the state by limiting the corrupt dealings of subordinate officers are likely to be uniformly popular with top politicians. Tax and customs reform has been supported by such autocratic rulers as Ferdinand Marcos in the Philippines (Klitgaard 1988) and Suharto in Indonesia. Suharto contracted with a Swiss company to take over Indonesia's customs service, thus cutting out corrupt local officials, at least for a time.[3] In Zaire the World Bank once loaned funds for an abortive effort to reform customs and tax collection (Dia 1993). In Mexico the Salinas administration carried out a thoroughgoing reform of the tax system with strong support from the president (Das-Gupta and Mookherjee 1998: 331).[4]

But will economic growth be furthered when a ruler operating with little popular accountability develops a more efficient revenue collection system? A military regime may simply purchase more equipment for the armed forces. An autocrat may search for expensive capital projects that can be a source of kickbacks. The Zairean case illustrates the problem. Efforts to collect taxes lacked legitimacy because the government made large expenditures on projects that promised few development benefits. In 1990 and 1991 the country planned an uneconomic power plant expansion and budgeted large sums for a francophone summit conference and a national celebration. World Bank officials were also concerned with the possibility of "large unrecorded extra budgetary outflows," that is, corruption. The World Bank project was unable to change existing patterns of fraudulent exemptions from taxes and duties. An initially successful effort to remove exemptions was soon overturned, and computers and files were destroyed. The project did not succeed in developing a cadre of professional tax collectors. Instead, it created its own opportunities for rent seeking, and aid was eventually suspended (Dia 1993).

---

[3] Das-Gupta and Mookherjee (1998: 425) and General Agreement on Tariffs and Trade (1991, 1995). The system has now reverted to Indonesian control accompanied by expressions of both optimism and concern. "Importers Adjust to Return of Indonesia Customs Office," *Financial Times,* April 11, 1997.

[4] Mexico is a constitutional democracy, but until recently has often been classified as autocratic because of the dominance of the Institutional Revolutionary Party and the strength of the executive.

A similar irony of reform can occur in procurement. Lower-level officials may sell inside information on the bidding process, and they may provide favors to winning bidders in return for bribes. Rulers of all sorts will want to reduce such low-level payoffs except to the extent that they buy the complicity of subordinate officials. In a kleptocracy, however, reducing lower-level corruption can simply shift it up the hierarchy. The benefits of reform for the country at large will be overstated if one looks no farther than the reduced corruption of subordinates. One consequence of corrupt subordinates is the kleptocrat's reduced appetite for expanding the size of the government. With that constraint eliminated, he can be expected to seek higher levels of intervention (Coolidge and Rose-Ackerman 1997).

In short, reforms that improve the operation of a kleptocratic state will be counterproductive for ordinary citizens if they just permit the ruler to extract rents more efficiently by squeezing low-level corrupt officials. A profit-maximizing kleptocrat who is operating a state-owned business will seek monopoly rents and productive efficiency, but in other cases the kleptocrat may create bottlenecks and propose unneeded projects to extract additional rents.

Autocrats, however, have sometimes made genuine attempts to achieve reform as a means of legitimating and consolidating their power. One thinks first of nineteenth-century Prussia (Raadschelders and Rutgers 1996: 76), but elsewhere the list includes Vargas in Brazil (Geddes 1994), Fujimori in Peru, Lee in Singapore (Das-Gupta and Mookherjee 1998: 356–381), Museveni in Uganda (Coolidge and Rose-Ackerman 1997), and a number of East Asian governments (Campos and Root 1996). Many of these reformers were formally elected, but they wield more power than a leader elected under more competitive conditions, and they are frequently unsympathetic to claims of individual rights. Nevertheless, their commitment to clean government seems genuine and is not just a cover for private wealth accumulation. Their concern is not only to squeeze out the rents at lower levels of officialdom but also to provide high-quality public services.

Anticorruption campaigns, however, can have political purposes that undermine attempts to develop a competitive political regime in countries with nominal democratic structures. They can be used both to blackmail supporters into maintaining the incumbent regime and to discredit and silence opponents. One study of Mexican politics, for example, argues that the threat of prosecution has been used to deter defectors from the ruling party. Even those who leave government for the private sector are kept in check by the possibility that if they raise questions about incumbents, they may be investigated for "inexplicable self-enrichment" (Cothran 1994:144). In Italy, the possession of compromising information about one's own colleagues is a source of power. As one study concludes, "blackmail becomes one invisible form of cement for a political class condemned to a lengthy and forced cohabitation" (della Porta and Vannucci 1997b: 14). The anticorruption laws are a deterrent not to corruption itself, but to the factionalization of the ruling group and the development of strong opposition groups.

The use of the anticorruption banner as a cloak for repression is an especially worrisome aspect of reform in autocracies that lack effective outside checks. In a society where corruption and self-dealing are entrenched, the law may be enforced against dissenters while the top leadership is immune from criticism. If autocratic rulers do not also open up their societies to permit more dissent and criticism, their governments may become so ossified and intolerant that they eventually collapse. Relying on the charisma and integrity of one top leader is always a risky long-term strategy.

Scandal and Crisis as Catalysts

Corruption scandals fueled by an independent press have spurred reform in a number of political systems. Economic crises that can be blamed on poor public policies can also facilitate change. Even in an otherwise inhospitable environment, a major crisis can make it obvious that reform is required. In the United States, for example, the murder of President James Garfield by a disappointed office seeker highlighted the weaknesses of the patronage system and helped spur civil service reform. Financial panics and hyperinflation have fueled economic reform efforts in many countries.[5]

Scandal and crisis can put corruption on the public agenda, but they do not always direct reform efforts in useful directions. This highlights a central dilemma of reform. When a crisis produces strong support for change, politicians must act quickly, often without sufficient planning or expert advice. In contrast, during quiet, stable periods when reform could be thoughtfully implemented, political support is lacking (Berensztein 1998). Crises can produce either real reforms or dysfunctional responses (Corrales 1997–98). If scandals erupt, the media is frequently criticized for personalizing the news by focusing on the individuals at the center of the scandal and ignoring the systemic conditions that created incen-

---

[5] Argentina is a good example. The depth of the economic crisis at the end of the Alfonsin regime in 1989 gave President Menem an opportunity to carry out both political and economic change. The President was granted strong executive authority to deal with the crisis in spite of its dubious constitutionality (Saba and Manzetti 1997: 361–362).

tives for corruption in the first place (Garment 1991). This is a fair criticism, but it hardly lets the government off the hook. Reformers must respond to scandals by doing more than punishing the guilty. The challenge is to reduce underlying corrupt incentives. Otherwise anticorruption campaigns become little more than witch hunts that will tend disproportionately to seek out the regime's political opponents (Singh 1997: 638). Scandals are an opportunity to mobilize support for institutional changes that have little glamour in themselves.

Media attention is necessary for scandals to surface, but it is not sufficient. The revelations must have credibility with the public, and the public must be sufficiently concerned to express outrage and distress – which can itself be covered by the media. This dynamic may finally induce the government to investigate the allegations and correct the underlying abuses. Unfortunately, responses tend to focus only on personalities – covering up blame, on the one hand, and searching for scapegoats, on the other. Nevertheless, if political leaders are committed to underlying reforms, clever use of scandals can generate public support for costly changes in government operations that would otherwise be unpopular.

A free press can produce the public outcry that increases pressure for reform. This pattern was common in the United States and, of course, implies a government with some measure of accountability to its citizens (Miller 1992). For example, in the United States scandals in the New York Customs House and in the Post Office, which preceded Garfield's murder, were widely reported in the press and helped create a climate favorable to reform. It did not hurt that the new President, Chester Arthur, had been Collector of Customs in New York City and could not easily defend the existing system (Josephson 1938: 95–98, 313–322). Press reports in a number of Latin American countries have helped create scandals that brought down corrupt governments (Geddes and Ribeiro Neto 1992; Manzetti and Blake 1996).

Reform of the Boston Charter in 1949 was fostered by an atmosphere of crisis and scandal surrounding the city council in 1947 (Marchione 1976: 381–383). The council's Licensing Commission had delayed licensing a water taxi operation from the airport to the railroad station. One councillor urged speedy approval because rumors were circulating that the delay was motivated by hopes of a payoff – a good example of how the hope of corrupt gains can generate inefficiencies in the public sector. Another councillor defended the delay and accused the first of being a representative of the business interests behind the water taxi venture. He went on to proclaim:

I will take a buck and who the hell does not know it, and I am probably the only one who has guts enough to say I will take a buck. I would like to see the guy who does not take a buck, let me know the guy who does not take a buck. Who does he think he is kidding? A lawyer can go out and take a fee.

This incident was widely publicized in the Boston newspapers and generated an investigation of the council by the Suffolk County District Attorney. Notice the importance of a federal structure here with overlapping law enforcement jurisdictions. Allegations were made of shakedowns of transit line operators, bribes paid to license carnivals and parking lots, and payoffs for widening sidewalks and installing driveways. Although those indicted were eventually acquitted, the District Attorney's activity, propelled by the initial scandal, helped generate support for a reform to reduce the size of the council and change to an at-large electoral system under which councillors would have "a city-wide rather than a neighborhood viewpoint." The new breed of politicians could be expected to share the views of the broader business community, not the narrower interests of particular neighborhoods (ibid.: 398).

Even nations with state-controlled media can use corruption stories to teach cautionary lessons. In the Soviet Union, for example, corruption revelations were commonplace news items. To a Western economist, they indicated the rigidities and inefficiencies of the planned economy. To the Soviet officials themselves, they were part of periodic cleanup campaigns that did not challenge the underlying organization of the economic system.[6]

Economic crises, like political scandals, can also make reform seem necessary to the majority of voters even if it implies some pain in the short run. For example, high inflation might prompt interest groups to agree on economic policy reform more quickly than under conditions of price stability (Drazen and Grilli 1993). Empirical work based on a sample of countries with external debt crises supports this claim. Some of these countries, mostly in Latin America, had high inflation; others, mostly in the franc zone in Africa, had low inflation. The study shows that countries with high inflation rates were more likely to reduce their public sector deficits. Furthermore, very high inflation in the present induced countries to lower inflation in the future (Bruno and Easterly 1996).

Democracies are sometimes viewed critically by economic reformers

---

[6] For an analysis of corruption in Soviet-type systems and some examples of corruption stories in the Soviet press, see Montias and Rose-Ackerman (1981).

who worry that populist pressures will make reform difficult. As a counterweight, an economic crisis can act like a major scandal to push reform to the top of the agenda. Thus Arindam Das-Gupta and Dilip Mookherjee (1998: 450) argue that severe fiscal crises can make reform possible for a new government that has been elected with a mandate for change. They point to the examples of Argentina, Bolivia, Colombia, and Peru in the 1980s. They argue that India missed an opportunity for reform in 1991 in the wake of a foreign exchange crisis and the election of a new government. In Great Britain, Australia, and New Zealand in the 1980s administrative reforms by newly elected governments were spurred by the stagflation of the 1970s (Scott 1996: 5–6; Zifcak 1994: 7–8, 17–18, 138–139). Economic crises have also made reform possible in the United States. For example, a case study of reform in Wisconsin in the late nineteenth century points to the salient impact of economic depression and financial panic in bringing people together across divisions of class and status to push for reform (Thelen 1972: 200).

Of course, many economic crises have no clear relationship with the level of corruption, but in countries where the public fiscal system and the profitability of business have been undermined by corruption in tax collection and public procurement, economic crises can provide a catalyst for anticorruption policies as well as macroeconomic adjustment. In fact, if underlying relationships based on corruption, family connections, and patronage are not changed, standard macroeconomic prescriptions may not succeed. For example, a study of efforts to reform tax administration in Mexico and Argentina points to the costs of corruption and inefficiency in their revenue systems as an underlying cause of the fiscal crises of the early 1980s. The weak and arbitrary aspects of the tax system in both countries contributed to a poorly functioning public sector and inefficiencies in the private sector as well. The resulting crisis persuaded political elites of the need for reform (Berensztein 1998).

Economic and political crises are costly and risky preconditions to reform. They are often preceded by long periods of slow decline in the effectiveness of the state (Corrales 1997–98; Scott 1996: 72). Crises may produce violence, chaos, and a challenge to state legitimacy (Bruno and Easterly 1996). Reform may occur but at great cost to society, or the country may descend into anarchy. One can hardly recommend the manufacture of crises as a cure for the corruption of state institutions (Corrales 1997–98). Far better is a political system subject to ongoing pressures to perform well (Scott 1996: 72). Nevertheless, reformers need to recognize that crises and scandals can sometimes be used to push reluctant public and private actors toward change.

Natural Resource Wealth and Foreign Aid

Just as economic crises can spur reform, wealth can make reform seem unimportant. Considerable evidence suggests that a strong natural resource base does not necessarily promote economic development (Gelb 1988; Sachs and Warner 1995). Developing countries such as Nigeria, Venezuela, and Indonesia that experienced oil windfalls have been able to resist reform for many years, and the mineral wealth of Zaire helped sustain Mobutu's corrupt regime (Diamond 1993b, 1995; Geddes 1991; MacGaffey 1991). Mineral-rich countries with few other sources of foreign exchange may be unlikely reformers both because the state can finance itself through royalties (Moore 1998) and because there may be few sources of alternative employment for laid-off civil servants in the private sector. The country is rich in natural resources but does not create many private sector jobs for its citizens. Instead of promoting growth, the valuable resource may simply make control of the state worthwhile. Individuals compete to rule the state in order to use it for their own benefit and for the benefit of their families and close associates. Talented people concentrate their effort on rent seeking rather than on productive activities (Krueger 1974). The private profitability of rent-seeking activities is above their social value and may crowd out productive investment (Bigsten and Moene 1996: 192–195). One observer of the Chinese case, for example, worries that young people will fail to build up their ordinary human capital and will instead focus on developing "directly unproductive human capital" including such talents as "skills in power struggles, understanding the preferences of one's superiors and ways to flatter them, knowledge about the intricate connections among some powerful officials, and so on" (Lui 1990: 124). In Kenya the government coopts educated people who could be a political threat outside government (Bigsten and Moene 1996: 186). A study of Zambia suggests that the private rewards to a public career can be large and that entrepreneurial talent may thus have been diverted into rent seeking (von der Fehr 1995: 27). Potential entrepreneurs become public officials charged with allocating rents, and private business people concentrate on the struggle for publicly provided benefits.

Natural resource businesses usually simply want to be left alone and are not much interested in an effective public sector. The countries least likely to reform would seem to be those with more natural resources than others in their region. Then corruption and patronage can extract huge economic costs without a country's citizens feeling disadvantaged compared with their more impoverished neighbors.

A secure source of foreign aid is a little like a diamond mine or an oil deposit. Countries with access to such largesse have a cushion that others lack (Moore 1998). If overseas aid lacks conditionality, it may simply postpone painful decisions by masking underlying problems that would produce a crisis in less fortunate countries. Michael Bruno and William Easterly speculate that low-inflation countries that did not adjust current-account deficits and budget deficits were able to avoid reform because of high inflows of development aid and lending (Bruno and Easterly 1996: 216).

Weak states may face a paradoxical situation where increases in resources undermine political stability and growth. So long as the state is poor, few may care about controlling the levers of power. If the state acquires a large foreign aid package or gains control over a newly valuable mineral, new political figures may arise to stake their claims. The political struggle becomes a fight for control of the state's wealth. Insiders try to prevent outsiders from benefiting except to the extent that payoffs are needed to buy their assent to the status quo. In such perverse scenarios, wealth increases do not encourage income growth and can lead to subsequent falls in the wealth of ordinary citizens. A study of the Philippines, for example, argues that rent seeking by an oligarchy of business and political leaders was sustained by foreign aid from the United States and the presence of American military bases (Hutchcroft 1998: 23). As President Fidel Ramos noted in his 1992 inaugural address, the economic system "rewards people who do not produce at the expense of those who do . . . [and] enables persons with political influence to extract wealth without effort from the economy" (quoted in ibid.).

Nigeria is an extreme example where the state has been described as "a national cake to be divided and subdivided among officeholders" (Joseph 1996: 195). The situation is exacerbated by the presence of massive petroleum deposits (Herbst 1996: 157–158; Olowu 1993: 94). Oil represents 90 percent of Nigeria's exports and most of the government's revenue (Herbst and Olukoshi 1994: 453). The oil reserves are under state control and provide huge windfall gains to those who control them and their political allies. Especially during the years of the petroleum crisis, Nigeria profited handsomely. Control of the state is a valuable prize worth fighting for. Those who seek to get rich struggle for a share of the rents, instead of engaging in productive entrepreneurship (Diamond 1993b: 220, 1995: 474; Herbst 1996; Lewis 1996: 81).

Corrupt democracies with strong resource bases may have poorer growth prospects than corrupt autocracies with similar endowments. The autocrat may have both a longer time horizon and a better ability to control competitive rent seeking by his subordinates. The risk, of course, is that an autocrat may gradually move toward a more throughly kleptocratic position as he sees the fruits of growth. Thus a more stable long-run solution for corrupt democracies is not their replacement with autocracies, but a stronger commitment both to competitive markets and to democratic institutions that can constrain both the rent seeking of elected officials and the monopoly power of private businesses.

Demands for Reform

Because efficient service delivery is presumably always of value to some members of the public, what explains the timing of reform? A major scandal or economic crisis can help, but sometimes the impetus for reform is much less dramatic. Organizational arrangements that worked well in the past are no longer satisfactory. In British and American experience two distinct organizational dysfunctions spurred reform. The first was the growing ineffectiveness of the contracting-out of public services in the early nineteenth century. The second was the inefficiency of patronage-based employment as government grew in size in the latter part of the same century (Raadschelders and Rutgers 1996).

In Great Britain the model of public office as a contracted-for benefit became unworkable during the first half of the nineteenth century as the government extended its activities. Few large private corporations existed that could have provided mass public services. Instead of contracting out for postal or customs services, the state began to employ a large number of subordinate officials who earned a salary and were often selected on the basis of loyalty to the ruling coalition. The East India Company was an exception, a private firm operating as a surrogate for the British government that as early as the late eighteenth century introduced some measure of training and merit recruitment, but its personnel system shared many of the other weaknesses of the government (Marshall 1997; Raadschelders and Rutgers 1996: 84). A similar patronage-based system of public employment developed in the United States. These systems performed poorly, and the lack of viable private sector alternatives to state provision made internal reform by the state the only plausible option. The pressure for civil service reform derived, in part, from the lack of any alternative to public provision.

Ronald Johnson and Gary Libecap (1994) argue that in the United States civil service reform was motivated by the growing absolute size of the federal bureaucracy. It is a commonplace of the organization theory literature that loss of control increases with organizational size. In the United States this happened at the federal level after the Civil War. Direct monitoring became more costly and led those at the top of the hierarchy to relinquish some discretion in return for the establishment of formal rules. Johnson and Libecap argue that the combination of large government size and the growing independence of local party leaders produced support for civil service reform in Congress. The 1883 Pendleton Act covered only the largest federal facilities, and support for the act was indeed stronger among members of Congress from districts with important post offices and customs houses (ibid.: 105–107). However, national prosperity seems to have been unaffected by reform. Neither total nor per capita measures of gross national product were significantly associated with extension of the merit system at the federal level. This, however, appears to be the wrong level of analysis because a well-functioning national state would have a different impact on businesses depending on how dependent they were on the post office and the customs service. Unlike many countries in the present day, the federal government had few regulatory and spending responsibilities.

Experience from some developing countries seems to contradict Johnson and Libecap's argument that a growth in the size of government spurs reform. Large governments appear to be especially hard to reform. If government is very large, it will employ a large proportion of the work force. In some poor countries the government sector accounts for a large share of the jobs in the modern sector.[7] If this is true, reform that requires substantial privatization and massive layoffs may be politically difficult to achieve. Even if reform will improve job opportunities and facilitate economic growth, public employees will oppose reform because of uncertainty about how they will fare (cf. Fernandez and Rodrik 1991). Furthermore, the possibility that employees can organize into unions and pressure groups will limit reformers' freedom of action. Even if Johnson and Libecap are correct that inefficiency increases as government grows, that fact may be insufficient to overcome the political clout of public employees. Johnson and Libecap emphasize the *absolute* size of government or at least of some key agencies such as the post office. In contrast, the government *share* of total employment is also relevant.

The best case for reform occurs when government employment is large in absolute numbers but a small share of the labor force. If most jobs are in the private sector, citizens, in general, will care more about whether the mail is delivered expeditiously, roads are built and maintained, and schools and hospitals function than whether jobs within government are available. Reform in the United States may have been facilitated by the

---

[7] For example, in Ghana one study reported that government accounted for about two-thirds of total employment in the organized modern sector. This was about 16 percent of total employment (Leechor 1994: 186). In Kenya the civil service employed about one-quarter of urban wage earners in 1990 (Swamy 1994: 225). In Senegal in 1986 the government employed 68,000 of the total of 131,000 employed in the modern wage sector (Rouis 1994: 294).

relatively small size of the public sector relative to the private sector. Public employees were not a potent pressure group, and the public generally supported reform. David Rosenbloom claims that when the federal civil service was reformed in the United States, most of the nation was behind the change (Rosenbloom 1971: 71–86). The same was generally true at the state level (on Wisconsin, see Thelen 1972). Before the advent of civil service systems, jobs were a benefit used to motivate campaign workers, but their relative value declined as the costs of patronage become more visible to voters (Johnson and Libecap 1994; Maranto and Schultz 1991). Furthermore, if the civil service is small enough so that reform does not imply layoffs, existing government workers may support reform. Although appointed under political criteria, they may want to stay in office with a change in government. Even with rather long terms of four to six years, patronage workers may support creation of a civil service system especially if it involves not just job security but also increases in pay and improved working conditions. Thus American public sector workers came to support the civil service once it was in place because they were grandfathered into their current positions.

There is another limitation to Johnson and Libecap's analysis. They treat the size of government agencies as given: Increased size makes it difficult to control the bureaucracy and that in turn leads to reform pressures. However, if government leaders are corrupt, causation also runs the other way. Corrupt rulers may seek an excessively large government as a means of extracting benefits for themselves. Furthermore, powerful elected leaders may favor a large government as a means of increasing patronage opportunities. In some cases, leaders use the machinery of government both to enrich themselves and to provide jobs for supporters. These joint activities often produce bloated governments. One example of this phenomenon is the machine-dominated American cities of the nineteenth and early twentieth centuries. One scholar describes a political machine "as a political party in which a boss oversees a hierarchy of party regulars who provide private favors to citizens in exchange for votes and who expect government jobs in return for their services" (Menes 1996). A statistical study of machine and nonmachine cities over the years 1900 to 1920 found that machine cities spent 18 percent more than nonmachine cities per capita and that municipal wages for lower-skilled workers were 8 percent higher (ibid.). Machine cities averaged 34 percent higher per capita spending on general administration and 17 percent more on police and fire services – all areas with many patronage jobs. To take one extreme case, the population increased by 22.7 percent in Boston between 1895 and 1907 while the number of city clerks increased by 75 percent. By 1907 salaries in the city were three times more than for comparable jobs in the state government and the private sector. The number of day laborers on the city payroll increased 50 percent between 1895 and 1907, while productivity fell by half. The impact of machine dominance seems to have been large budgets, civil service wages above the norm, and, as a consequence, excess spending on services dominated by patronage jobs such as police and fire departments (ibid.).

Yet eventually most such cities did reform, cutting expenditures and payroll (Schiesl 1977). According to Johnson and Libecap (1994: 112–113), in states and urban areas, reform was more likely as the absolute size of government increased. They point out that the large states of New York, Massachusetts, and Illinois, which presumably also had large public sectors, were the first to introduce civil service reform. Boston, New York City, and Chicago, which also employed large numbers of people, were early reformers, while some rural areas and small towns retain vestiges of patronage systems to this day. Apparently political machines sometimes contained the seeds of their own destruction as they expanded government to a point where a backlash set in. If a vigorous private sector feels constrained by an ineffective public sector, conditions may be ripe for reform.

According to one study, reformed cities not only introduced civil service systems and procurement and tax reform but also took a more long-run view. They spent proportionately more on infrastructure projects such as roads, waterways, sewers, and water supply than unreformed cities, decisions that were presumably favored by the business community (Rauch 1995).[8] Civil service reform appears to have been good for the growth of manufacturing. In one study of American cities, reform increased the manufacturing growth rate by half a percentage point – one quarter of its mean value of 2 percent (Rauch 1995). This result is consistent with the finding that manufacturing interests were frequently in the forefront of the reform effort. Manufacturing interests resented the costly special deals struck with other business interests more concerned with government contracts and franchises (Menes 1996). Construction companies and manufacturing interests were often on opposing sides if reform included not just the civil service, but the contracting process as well. Nevertheless, a coalition for reform did eventually

---

[8] In absolute per capita terms, however, another author found that nonmachine cities did not spend significantly less on highways (Menes 1996). Because automobile and truck travel were just becoming important during this period, however, it is difficult to know what the null hypothesis should be.

develop in many cities that elected reform mayors with business support (Schiesl 1977).

The strength and growth rate of the private sector should help determine the ease of reform. Perhaps reforming cities and states were those where the private sector had a relatively large share of total employment and income. In such cases private businesses would be supporters of reforms that lowered their costs, and public sector workers might not protest too much if reemployment in the private sector was not difficult. Reform occurred when the government became a large organization in absolute size while remaining small relative to the private sector. Not enough private individuals and businesses were dependent on government jobs, contracts, and favors to block reform.

Sustaining Reform

One way to assure durable reform is to compensate opponents for the losses they would otherwise suffer. Such solicitude for the losers is not always strictly necessary. The majority can override even a vocal minority, and an autocrat can simply announce a reform plan. However, in many cases reform will have a greater likelihood of success if those most affected are compensated. This may be an unpleasant necessity if the aim is to convince a corrupt ruler to cede power without bloodshed. In other situations, compensating the formerly corrupt may not seem so distasteful. The best example is civil service reform where salaries and working conditions are improved in return for officials forgoing bribery receipts. Corrupt high-level officials are relieved of their jobs, but the rest of the bureaucracy is given an incentive to be honest. Such policies are likely to be needed in poor countries that have a scarcity of educated people capable of performing some types of public sector tasks. The wholesale dismissal of corrupt officials is seldom a viable option even if it might be the most effective way to improve performance in very corrupt systems. The danger, of course, is that the concessions made to existing officials are so large that the very effectiveness of the reform is undermined (Grindle and Thomas 1991: 121–150; Polidano 1996).

Sometimes anticorruption policies include a restructuring of the state to reduce its role through privatization and deregulation. Because this reform will reduce the number of public officials needed, they can be expected to resist the change. One study recommends obtaining bureaucrats' support for such reforms by giving officials "golden handshakes" in the form of a one-time surge in bribe receipts. This gives them a financial stake in the success of the long-term reform effort and an incentive to reveal needed information to the reformers (Basu and Li 1998). The authors give two examples from China where officials benefited personally from "sponsoring" new businesses and approving stock offerings. However, as the authors recognize, toleration of corruption is a risky strategy. Corrupt officials may take it upon themselves to organize their activities to produce greater gains, thus undermining economic growth and the legitimacy of government. The government's past toleration of corruption will then make it difficult for them credibly to crack down on malfeasance. Thus better options are legal incentive bonuses, severance payments, and assistance in changing to private employment. These policies will be expensive drains on the public budget, but they are one-time charges that make serious reform possible.

Even if opponents can be pacified, reform can be fragile. The history of reform efforts is not encouraging (Geddes 1991; Grindle and Thomas 1991; Klitgaard 1997; Nunberg and Nellis 1995). As Geddes (1991, 1994) demonstrates, the new policies are likely to be reversed if they occur because of a temporary balance of political interests. Too often reformers have contented themselves with passing laws or announcing new policies without concentrating on the difficult task of translating reforms into durable changes in government operations (Grindle and Thomas 1991). If the political and bureaucratic costs of implementation are ignored in the first flush of reformist zeal, the stage is set for subsequent failure.

The durability of national civil service reform in the United States and Great Britain deserves study. Their experience suggests the possibility of a benevolent dynamic – in which partial changes evolve over time into full-scale reform. Although research has focused on civil service reform, the basic dynamic seems to be a general one. The key is a reform process in which new allies are produced by the process of change itself. Support grows over time as the reach of the reform program grows. Thus reforms, once started, become self-sustaining.

Reform started slowly at the federal level in the United States and focused at first on those parts of the bureaucracy where the marginal gains would be highest. Important constituencies outside government benefited and helped to institutionalize reform. Inside government, the first beneficiaries of civil service protection favored its preservation. Presidents about to leave office extended civil service protection to their appointees. Although newly elected presidents did return some positions to patronage, so that the share of merit employees fell during a few years, the general trend was slowly upward. The move from 10 to 80 percent took almost forty years. The proportion covered by the merit system increased when overall government employment rose. When public sector jobs were increasing, an increased proportion could be covered without great pressure on existing employees. Although some people might lose their jobs because of incompetence, no large-scale cutbacks were needed (Johnson and Libecap 1994: 109–111).

Once the number of merit employees became large, they emerged as a potent interest group in favor of maintaining the system. This could, of course, have been a mixed blessing if the underlying conditions had changed. At some point, employees with civil service protection can undermine other reforms designed to improve productivity. The worst situation is a large, well-organized body of public employees hired on the basis of patronage, but difficult to fire or reform.[9] This has proved to be a particular problem for governments seeking to contract services out to private organizations. Contracting out, however, is likely to be less viable in poor countries that lack indigenous private organizations able to take over state functions.

Progressive reform in urban America is another example of sustainable reform. Even so, in many American cities reform did not proceed in a straight line. Machine and reform administrations alternated in power. However, although some backsliding occurred, machines often maintained the reforms introduced by progressive governments. Reforms were popular with the electorate and hard to reverse. Property tax reform in some cities led to a fall in the tax bills of homeowners as businesses paid a larger share. In Jersey City, for example, taxation of railroad properties relieved the tax burdens on home owners (Schiesl 1977). Clearly, those voters who owned real estate could see the benefits of property tax rationalization, and even renters may have perceived some benefits. Reforms were maintained because the gains were obvious to a large number of voters in spite of the costs imposed on some business interests.

Other countries have also been able to carry out partial reforms, but questions remain about their evolution into a full-scale restructuring of government. The customs service in Mexico, the reinsurance system in Argentina, and the city government of La Paz have all recently experienced successful cleanups (*El Economista*, February 13, 1992; Klitgaard and Baser 1997: 65–66; Moreno Ocampo 1995). Reform in Mexico was based on simplifying procedures and improving pay and monitoring. A scandal in Argentina led to changes in accounting practices and replacement of the board of the public company. A reform mayor in La Paz introduced a composite package of projects that began with efforts to remove the worst offenders but went on to include more fundamental

---

[9] Grindle and Thomas (1991). See Peirce's (1994) discussion of present-day reform efforts in Florida and Philadelphia. Reform in Malta was undermined by opposition from public-sector unions (Polidano 1996).

changes. Nevertheless, the durability of partial reforms is questionable. For example, in La Paz after the mayor left office, reform stalled and corrupt practices reemerged (Klitgaard and Baser 1997: 65–66). Reformers need to manage both the political and bureaucratic fallout of reform and find ways to coopt or outmaneuver potential opponents (Grindle and Thomas 1991: 121–150).

In some cases, reform founders because of bad sequencing. Instead of creating a group of early winners who support continuing reform, the program's early beneficiaries fear that they will lose if reform continues. In the worst case they become a blocking coalition that prevents broad-based change. According to one study, land reform in Latin America was an example of this reverse process (De Janvry and Sadoulet 1989). The reforming countries first introduced programs to modernize medium and large farms as the quickest way to increase productivity. However, the success of these programs made these farmers more economically powerful which in turn gave them greater political power. As a consequence, they were able to engage in rent seeking and to block plans to redistribute lands to poorer households. The authors conclude that, in spite of the short-term costs, land reform should be carried out before modernization. Their analysis may have some lessons for reformers in the former socialist countries. Permitting economic liberalization without first establishing a stable political and legal framework can lead those who benefited from the first redistribution of state assets to oppose subsequent efforts to make the legal system more efficient and fair (Kaufmann and Siegelbaum 1997).

Conclusions

Reform is possible and can under some conditions become institutionalized and hard to reverse. The structure of political institutions can facilitate or hamper reform, and some systems are organized so that long-lasting reform is unlikely. Nevertheless, under other conditions reform can create new supporters who resist efforts to undo past changes. The lessons of past and present reform efforts demonstrate the importance of powerful supporters outside government as well as inside. In particular, reform is much easier if the domestic and international business communities believe that they will benefit from a reduction in corruption and patronage and if ordinary citizens see gains as well. In many cases such a broad constituency may be possible if it is not blocked by those who gain from the status quo. Political systems that facilitate the exchange of individualized favors, be they jobs, payoffs, or government contracts, are tailormade for corrupt deals. Reform of such polities will depend on a scandal or crisis or on the slow erosion of the benefits of inside deals. Sometimes an indirect approach to reform is necessary. Credible reform of the civil service, of procurement practices, and of licensing and regulatory programs cannot occur without more fundamental reforms in the way public policy is made.

Under some conditions only partial reform is politically feasible. Latin American presidents have often selected key government agencies such as the central bank or the revenue authorities and created enclaves of high integrity and professional competence (Geddes 1994). In Africa tax reform has frequently involved the creation of insulated revenue authorities that are given special resources and exempted from civil service rules (Dia 1996). As Geddes points out, this is unlikely to be a sustainable strategy. A powerful leader can create enclaves, but if they are dependent on his protection they will collapse with a change in government. Special treatment for some creates resentment. Furthermore, even government-wide reforms may founder if they do not create a growing circle of supporters. The order in which reforms are introduced matters. Logic may need to give way to political reality. Under some conditions short-term gains can generate broad public support for more difficult further steps. Under other conditions, short-term benefits for some can produce a backlash from those seeking to maintain their initial gains. These concerns suggest two paths to durable reform. The first, which will be possible only in times of great crisis and dissatisfaction with the status quo, is a "big bang" approach in which massive changes are introduced all at once. The second involves an incremental strategy in which the steps are carefully designed to build support over time. Some short-term gains may need to be sacrificed in order to get the sequencing right.

12

Conclusions

Self-interest and the public interest frequently conflict. In a corrupt relationship both the briber and the recipient are better off, but the transaction violates government policy. A criterion other than willingness to pay is supposed to prevail. Sometimes corrupt public officials claim that bribes have not influenced their behavior. They are simply "gifts of good will." Private individuals and firms may, nevertheless, believe that such gifts are, in fact, a requirement of good service up and down the government hierarchy. Even those who pay to receive something they ought to obtain for free believe that bribery is better than the alternative presented by the corrupt official. They may believe that politicians and judges will be biased against them if no money or favors have changed hands. The systemic effect of permitting such payoffs is damaging. Those with discretion will be tempted to create a large number of vaguely specified rules that create more chances for payoffs. Those who have not paid in the past may be tempted to pay in the future because it appears to be the norm.

Although individual payoffs may seem to further efficiency and even fairness, systemic corruption will seldom do so. In a repressive state, where many policies are harmful to all except a favored elite, corruption may be a survival strategy. Toleration of this practice, however, may just permit an illegitimate and inefficient system to persist. Corruption scandals can then be a sign of a country's growing political maturity. They show that citizens are beginning to recognize the difference between the public and the private spheres and to complain when the border is crossed. Citizen concerns over bribes paid in return for favors indicate that people recognize norms of fair dealing and competent administration and are beginning to demand that government serve general public purposes.

Corruption may have its roots in culture and history, but it is, nevertheless, an economic and political problem. It produces inefficiency and unfairness in the distribution of public benefits and costs. It is a symptom that the political system is operating with little concern for the broader public interest. It indicates that the structure of government does not channel private interests effectively. Political legitimacy is undermined if government permits some to obtain disproportionate private gains at the expense of others.

One of the most vexing issues for reformers is determining when incumbent politicians and bureaucrats have an incentive to change. Outside pressure can help, but abiding change is unlikely unless those who oppose reform can be either compensated or marginalized. The best case for reform is one where an initial change creates new beneficiaries who then support further reform. The worst case is one where the corruption becomes more entrenched and widespread over time. Corruption cannot be expected to wither away just because a reform government has taken power or because economic growth is vigorous. So long as officials have discretionary authority, corrupt incentives will remain and can be especially harmful for fragile new states. Reformers will have to take concrete action, not just assume that entrenched habits will change with a change in top personnel.

Corruption is not a problem that can be attacked in isolation. It is not sufficient for the criminal law to search for bad apples and punish them. Of course, the state may need to establish credibility by punishing highly visible corrupt officials, but the goal of such prosecutions is to attract notice and public support, not solve the underlying problem. Anticorruption laws can only provide a background for more important structural reforms.

The cases in which corruption enhances the efficiency of agents and improves the allocation of public services are limited. The theoretical and empirical evidence does not support widespread tolerance of corruption. The difficulty with tolerance in some areas is that it undermines efforts to reduce corruption in other areas where it is clearly harmful. The possibility that payoffs may sometimes motivate officials to work more efficiently suggests that in particular cases illegal bribes might be converted into legal incentive pay schemes. If some types of payments are viewed as acceptable tips to public officials, they should be legalized and made subject to reporting requirements. One test of the "cultural" justification for payments is the acceptability of proposals to make such payments public.

Both theory and practice suggest that there is no single, simple response that should be adopted across the board once the basic anticorruption statutes are in place. Instead, there are two different but related types of corruption: corruption involving high-level officials that often implicates multinational corporations or large domestic firms, and corruption that is endemic in the way the government carries out its routine activities such as tax collection, customs, licensing, and inspections. Within each of these categories, some payoffs facilitate illegal activities, and some are paid to obtain benefits to which one is legally entitled.

A country serious about fighting corruption must carry out a detailed assessment to determine where corruption is most harmful and where it can be most effectively attacked. A first step is to survey the public to find out how corruption affects their daily lives. This provides a way to set priorities that reflect popular grievances. However, survey evidence is not sufficient. The corruption that is most visible to the population may not be doing the most harm. Thus a second emphasis should be on high-level corruption in contracting, privatizations, and concessions that introduces serious economic distortions and undermines the fiscal health of the state. Third, people may believe that they gain from bribery that limits their taxes and reduces their regulatory burdens. Thus bribery of this type may not be reported as a problem by survey respondents. Nevertheless, the cumulative impact of such payoffs can be very harmful. Those seeking to set priorities must look behind the individual responses to consider the overall impact of a large number of attempts to circumvent the rules. In such cases the policy response might be program redesign, not increased oversight. A direct attack on corruption through enhanced law enforcement, asset disclosure requirements, and special anticorruption agencies is not sufficient and may not even be necessary. Instead, the focus under all three types of corruption should be on the underlying causes of payoffs. Thus simple generalizations are not possible, but the experiences of different countries suggests several common reform possibilities:

- Tax and customs revenues may be far below the level needed to carry out basic government services, and the pattern of payments may be very inequitable due to payoffs. The response should be both to simplify the tax laws to reduce bureaucratic discretion and to reorganize the bureaucracy to improve oversight and incentives for good performance.
- Regulation of business may be so complex, time-consuming, and intrusive that the development of a healthy private sector is affected. Here the answer is a hard look at regulatory laws to see which can be eliminated, which can be simplified, and which require improved enforcement. Many countries have both point-

less business regulation that generates bribes and ineffective regulations in socially beneficial areas such as environmental protection.

- Another costly pattern is state sponsorship of massive infrastructure projects that are too large and complex. The cost of corruption is not the bribes themselves, but the cost of the inefficient actions they encourage. Even if direct evidence of corruption is not available, evidence of the inappropriate scale and design of projects should be sufficient to cancel them. Such a change in direction must, however, be combined with improved procedures for future project approvals, or the pattern may repeat.

Basic institutional reforms may be a precondition for reform in particular sectors. Sometimes reforms that would be effective under one set of political and economic conditions will be useless in other cases where the government is very weak and arbitrary. Especially important as a background to other reforms are improvements in the checks and balances present in a political system.

Even if one holds constant a nation's constitutional structure, there are a range of reforms that may be politically difficult, but are not particularly expensive. They must, however, be institutionalized so that they will endure changes in personnel and changes in the political coalition. Policies that seem politically costly to reverse include those that increase the transparency and accountability of government operations and facilitate the organization of independent watchdog groups.

Once the problems of substantive policy and institutional structure have been tackled, most corrupt countries must still face the difficult task of civil service reform. This will be either financially expensive or politically painful, but is a necessary part of any serious reform effort. If civil service wages are allowed to deteriorate relative to the private sector and if pay differentials within the civil service are too small to give officials an incentive to seek promotions, then efforts to control official corruption are unlikely to succeed. Reform policies must reduce the size of the civil service, pay decent base salaries to the remaining officials, and establish effective incentives to induce officials both to be honest and to perform efficiently.

The lack of credible institutions capable of hearing complaints and enforcing the law is a weakness in many developing and transitional countries. Thus one area for reform should be either improvements in existing institutions such as the courts or the creation of new bodies such as independent inspectors general or anticorruption commissions. The experience of other countries should be documented – both successful experiments and those that backfired when the nominal corruption fighters became corrupt themselves.

International institutions and the international business community can help provide incentives for reform. Aid and lending institutions should take a broad-based approach. Efforts to keep aid projects clean while ignoring the rest of a government's activities will be ultimately ineffective as corrupt officials and private individuals and firms seek opportunities elsewhere. Clearly, international organizations ought not abandon efforts to keep their own projects free of corruption, but the more serious that effort becomes, the more they will need to help countries reduce corruption throughout their institutions.

Fundamental change requires commitment from the top of government and a willingness to follow through as the anticorruption effort unfolds. Serious reform can be carried out within any existing structure of government. Governments that make it very difficult for independent voices to be raised in criticism, however, will have an especially difficult time establishing a credible commitment to honest and transparent government. Such governments may be able to move quickly in the short run but pose the risk that their policies will be reversed in the future. Anticorruption campaigns can be used to undermine political opponents and discipline troublesome groups. Reformers should resist those who would use an anticorruption crusade to limit political opposition. Nominal reform efforts that become a vendetta against political opponents will lose credibility. In a highly politicized atmosphere individualized prosecutions will not produce real reform. Only structural changes in the underlying corrupt incentives built into the operation of government can accomplish credible change.

REFERENCES

Abikoff, Kevin T. 1987. "The Role of the Comptroller General in Light of Bowsher v. Synar," *Columbia Law Review* 87:1539–1562.

Ackerman, Bruce. 1993. "Crediting the Voters: A New Beginning for Campaign Finance," *The American Prospect*, Number 13, pp. 71–80.

Ackerman, Bruce, and Richard Stewart. 1988. "Reforming Environmental Law: The Democratic Case for Economic Incentives," *Columbia Journal of Environmental Law* 13:171–190.

Adamolekun, Ladipo. 1993. "A Note on Civil Service Personnel Policy Reform in Sub-Saharan Africa," *International Journal of Public Sector Management* 6:38–46.

Ades, Alberto, and Rafael Di Tella. 1995. "Competition and Corruption," *Applied Economics Discussion Paper Series No. 169*, Oxford: Oxford University.

——. 1997a. "National Champions and Corruption: Some Unpleasant Interventionist Arithmetic," *The Economic Journal* 107:1023–1042.

——. 1997b. "The New Economics of Corruption: A Survey and Some New Results," *Political Studies* 45:496–515.

Agarwala, B. R. 1996. *Our Judiciary*, second edition, India: National Book Trust.

Alam, M. Shahid. 1991. "Some Economic Costs of Corruption in LDCs," *Journal of Development Studies* 27:89–97.

——. 1995. "A Theory of Limits on Corruption and Some Applications," *Kyklos* 48:419–435.

Alexander, Herbert E. 1991. *Reform and Reality: The Financing of State and Local Campaigns*, New York: Twentieth Century Fund.

Alfiler, Ma Concepcion P. 1986. "The Process of Bureaucratic Corruption in Asia: Emerging Patterns," in Ledivina A. Cariño, eds., *Bureaucratic Corruption in Asia: Causes, Consequences and Controls*, Quezon City, the Philippines: JMC Press, pp. 15–68.

Alvarez, Gladys Stella. 1995. "Alternative Dispute Resolution Mechanisms: Lessons of the Argentine Experience," in Malcolm Rowat, Waleed H. Malik, and Maria Dakolias, eds., *Judicial Reform in Latin America and the Caribbean: Proceedings of a World Bank Conference*, World Bank Technical Paper 280, Washington DC: World Bank, pp. 78–91.

Amick, George. 1976. *The American Way of Graft*, Princeton NJ: Center for the Analysis of Public Issues.

Andreoni, James. 1988. "Privately Provided Public Goods in a Large Economy: The Limits of Altruism," *Journal of Public Economics* 35:57–73.

Andreski, Stanislav. 1968. "Kleptocracy or Corruption as a System of Government." In Stanislav Andreski, *The African Predicament: A Study in the Pathology of Modernisation*, New York: Atherton.

Andvig, Jens Chr., and Karl Ove Moene. 1990. "How Corruption May Corrupt," *Journal of Economic Behavior and Organization* 13:63–76.

Anechiarico, Frank, and James B. Jacobs. 1996. *The Pursuit of Absolute Integrity: How Corruption Control Makes Government Ineffective*, Chicago: University of Chicago Press.

Anek Leothamtas. 1994. "From Clientelism to Partnership: Business–Government Relations in Thailand," in Andrew Macintyre, ed., *Business and Government in Industrializing Asia*, Ithaca: Cornell, pp. 195–215.

Ansolabehere, Stephen, and James Snyder. 1999. "Money and Office: The Sources of the Incumbency Advantage in Congressional Campaign Finance," in D. Brady and J. Cogan, eds., *House Elections: Continuity and Change*, Palo Alto: Stanford University Press.

Antoniou, Anthony. 1990. "Institutional Devices in Dealing with Corruption in Government," in United Nations, Department of Technical Co-operation for Development and Centre for Social Development and Humanitarian Affairs, *Corruption in Government: Report of an Interregional Seminar, The Hague, the Netherlands, 11–15 December, 1989*, TCD/SEM 90/2, INT-89-R56, New York, pp. 55–83.

Arlen, Jennifer. 1994. "The Potentially Perverse Effects of Corporate Criminal Liability," *Journal of Legal Studies* 23:833–867.

Arnold, Douglas R. 1990. *The Logic of Congressional Action*, New Haven: Yale University Press.

Ayittey, George B. N. 1992. *Africa Betrayed*, New York: St. Martin's Press.

Ayres, Ian. 1997. "Judicial Corruption: Extortion and Bribery," *Denver University Law Review* 74:1231–1253.

Azabou, Mongi, and Jeffrey B. Nugent. 1988. "Contractual Choice in Tax Collection Activities: Some Implications of the Experiences with Tax Farming," *Journal of Institutional and Theoretical Economics* 144:684–705.

Bardhan, Pranab. 1993. "Symposium on Management of Local Commons," *Journal of Economic Perspectives* 7:87–92.

———. 1997. "Corruption and Development: A Review of Issues," *Journal of Economic Literature* 35:1320–1346.

Barney, J. B., and Hansen, M. H. 1994. "Trustworthiness as a Source of Competitive Advantage," *Strategic Management Journal* 15:175–190.

Barratt-Brown, Elizabeth P. 1991. "Building a Monitoring and Compliance Regime Under the Montreal Protocol," *Yale Journal of International Law* 16:519–570.

Basu, K., S. Bhattacharya, and A. Mishra. 1992. "Notes on Bribery and the Control of Corruption," *Journal of Public Economics* 48:349–359.

Basu, Susanto, and David D. Li. 1998. "Corruption and Reform," draft, Department of Economics, University of Michigan.

Bayley, David H. 1966. "The Effect of Corruption in a Developing Nation," *Western Political Quarterly* 19:719–732.

Becker, Gary. 1968. "Crime and Punishment: An Economic Approach," *Journal of Political Economy* 76:169–217.

Becker, Gary, and George Stigler. 1974. "Law Enforcement, Malfeasance, and Compensation of Enforcers," *Journal of Legal Studies* 3:1–19.

Behr, Peter. 1997. "He's Changing the Flow: The Government's Procurement Chief Is Selling a Streamlined System, but Not Everybody's Buying It," *Washington Post*, March 3, p. F18.

Berensztein, Sergio. 1998. "Empowering the Taxman: The Politics of Tax Administration Reform in Argentina and Mexico," paper presented at conference on The Political Economy of Administrative Reform: Building State Capacity in Developing Countries, CIDE, Mexico City, June 4–5.

Besley, Timothy, and John McLaren. 1993. "Taxes and Bribery: The Role of Wage Incentives," *Economic Journal* 103:119–141.

Bhagwati, Jadish N., ed. 1974. *Illegal Transactions in International Trade*, Amsterdam and New York: North-Holland–American Elsevier.

Bhaskar, V., and Mushtaq Kahn. 1995. "Privatization and Employment: A Study of the Jute Industry in Bangladesh," *American Economic Review* 85:267–273.

Bigsten, Arne, and Karl Ove Moene. 1996. "Growth and Rent Dissipation; The Case of Kenya," *Journal of African Economics* 5:177–198.

Bing, Song. 1994. "Assessing China's System of Judicial Review of Administrative Actions," *China Law Review* 8:1–20.

Bishop, D. T., C. Cannings, and J. Maynard Smith. 1978. "The War of Attrition with Random Rewards," *Journal of Theoretical Biology* 74:377–388.

Bissell, Richard E. 1997. "Recent Practice of the Inspection Panel of the World Bank," *American Journal of International Law* 91:741–744.

Blair, William Alan. 1989. "A Practical Politician: The Boss Tactics of Matthew Stanley Quay," *Pennsylvania History*, 56:77–92.

Blinder, Alan, ed. 1990. *Paying for Productivity: A Look at the Evidence*, Washington DC: The Brookings Institution.

Boling, David. 1998. "Access to Government-Held Information in Japan: Citizens' 'Right to Know' Bows to the Bureaucracy," *Stanford Journal of International Law* 34:1–38.

Borcherding, Thomas, Werner Pommerehne, and Friedrich Schneider. 1982. "Comparing the Efficiency of Private and Public Production: The Evidence from Five Countries," *Zeitschrift für Nationalökonomie* 89:127–156.

Borner, Silvio, Aymo Brunetti, and Beatrice Weder. 1992. *Institutional Obstacles to Latin American Growth*, San Francisco CA: ICS Press.

Boyard, Tony, David Gregory, and Stephen Martin. 1991. "Improved Performance in Local Economic Development: A Warm Embrace or an Artful Sidestep," *Public Administration* 69:103–119.

Bradlow, Daniel D. 1996. "A Test Case for the World Bank," *American University Journal of International Law and Policy* 1:247–293.

Bradlow, Daniel D., and Sabine Schlemmer-Schulte. 1994. "The World Bank's New Inspection Panel: A Constructive Step in the Transformation of the International Legal Order," *Zeitschrift für ausländisches öffentliches Recht und Völkerrecht* 54:392–415.

Brandt, Hans-Jürgen. 1995. "The Justice of the Peace as an Alternative Experience with Conciliation in Peru," in Malcolm Rowat, Waleed H. Malik, and Maria Dakolias, eds., *Judicial Reform in Latin America and the Caribbean: Proceedings of a World Bank Conference*, World Bank Technical Paper 280, Washington DC: World Bank, pp. 92–99.

Bratton, Michael. 1989. "The Politics of Government-NGO Relations in Africa," *World Development* 17:569–587.

Brennan, Geoffrey, and James Buchanan. 1980. *The Power to Tax*, New York: Cambridge University Press.

Bronars, Stephen G., and John R. Lott, Jr. 1997. "Do Campaign Donations Alter How a Politician Votes? Or, Do Donors Support Candidates Who Value the Same Things That They Do?," *Journal of Law and Economics* 40:317–350.

Bruno, Michael, and William Easterly. 1996. "Inflation's Children: Tales of Crises That Beget Reforms," *American Economic Review – Papers and Proceedings* 86:213–217.

Bunker, Stephen G., and Lawrence Cohen. 1983. "Collaboration and Competition in Two Colonization Projects: Toward a General Theory of Official Corruption," *Human Organization* 42:106–114.

Burki, Shahid Javed. 1997. "Governance, Corruption and Development: The Case of Pakistan." Paper presented at the Workshop on Governance Issues in South Asia, Yale University, New Haven CT, November 19.

Burns, John. 1993. "China's Administrative Reforms for a Market Economy," *Public Administration and Development* 13:345–360.

Buscaglia, Edgardo Jr. 1995. "Judicial Reform in Latin America: The Obstacles Ahead," *Journal of Latin American Affairs*, Fall/Winter, pp. 8–13.

Buscaglia, Edgardo Jr., and Maria Dakolias. 1996. *Judicial Reform in Latin American Courts: The Experience in Argentina and Ecuador*, World Bank Technical Paper No. 350, Washington DC: World Bank.

Buscaglia, Edgardo Jr., and Thomas Ulen. 1997. "A Quantitative Assessment of the Efficiency of the Judicial Sector in Latin America," *International Review of Law and Economics* 17:275–292.

Cadot, Olivier. 1987. "Corruption as a Gamble," *Journal of Public Economics*, 33:223–244.

Calvert, Monte A. 1972. "The Manifest Functions of the Machine," in Bruce M. Stave, ed., *Urban Bosses, Machines, and Progressive Reform*, Lexington MA: D. C. Heath and Co., pp. 44–45.

"Camel Through the Needle's Eye," *Newswatch*, February 3, 1991 [excerpted in *Nigeria: Issues and Options in the Energy Sector*, Report No. 11672-UNI, World Bank: Energy Sector Management Assistance Programme, July 1993].

Campos, Jose Edgardo, and Sanjay Pradhan. 1997. "Evaluating Public Expenditure Management Systems: An Experimental Methodology with an Application to Australia and New Zealand Reforms," *Journal of Policy Analysis and Management* 16:423–445.

Campos, Jose Edgardo, and Hilton Root. 1996. *East Asia's Road to High Growth: An Institutional Perspective*, Washington DC: The Brookings Institution.

Cariño, Ledivina. 1986. "Tonic or Toxic: The Effects of Graft and Corruption," in Ledivina A. Cariño, ed., *Bureaucratic Corruption in Asia: Causes, Consequences and Controls*, Quezon City, the Philippines: JMC Press, pp. 163–194.

Cartier-Bresson, J. 1995. "L'Economie de la Corruption," in D. della Porta and Y. Mény, eds., *Démocratie et Corruption en Europe*, Paris: La Découverte, pp. 149–164.

Celarier, Michelle. 1996. "Stealing the Family Silver," *Euromoney*, February, pp. 62–66.

Chakrabarti, Debasish, Markus D. Dausses, and Tiffany Olson. 1997. "Federal Criminal Conflict of Interest," *American Criminal Law Review* 34:587–616.

Chester, Norman. 1981. *The English Administrative System 1780–1870*, Oxford: Clarendon Press.

Chhibber, Pradeep K. 1996. "State Policy, Rent Seeking, and the Electoral Success of a Religious Party in Algeria," *Journal of Politics* 58:126–148.

Chow, Daniel C. K. 1997. "An Analysis of the Political Economy of China's Enterprise

Conglomerates: A Study of the Electric Power Industry in China," *Law & Policy in International Business* 28:383–433.

Clay, Karen. 1997. "Trade Without Law: Private-Order Institutions in Mexican California," *Journal of Law, Economics, and Organization* 13:202–231.

Colazingari, Silvia, and Susan Rose-Ackerman. 1998. "Corruption in a Paternalistic Democracy: Lessons from Italy for Latin America," *Political Science Quarterly* 113:447–470.

Collins, Paul. 1993. "Civil Service Reform and Retraining in Transitional Economies: Strategic Issues and Options," *Public Administration and Development* 13:325–344.

Connolly, William J. 1996. "How Low Can You Go? State Campaign Contribution Limits and the First Amendment," *Boston University Law Review* 76:483–536.

Cooksey, Brian. 1996. "Address to the Rotary Club of Dar es Salaam, October 9, 1996," edited version reprinted in Transparency International, *National Chapter Newsletter*, No. 11, November 11.

Coolidge, Jacqueline, and Susan Rose-Ackerman. 1997. *High-Level Rent Seeking and Corruption in African Regimes: Theory and Cases*, Policy Research Working Paper 1780, World Bank, Washington DC, June.

Corrales, Javier. 1997–98. "Do Economic Crises Contribute to Economic Reform? Argentina and Venezuela in the 1990s," *Political Science Quarterly* 112:617–644.

Cothran, Dan A. 1994. *Political Stability and Democracy in Mexico: The "Perfect Dictatorship"?* Westport, CT: Praeger.

Coulloudon, Virginie. 1997. "The Criminalization of Russia's Political Elite," *East European Constitutional Review* 6:73–78.

Cox. Gary. 1997. *Making Votes Count*, Cambridge UK: Cambridge University Press.

Cramton, Peter C., and J. Gregory Dees. 1993. "Promoting Honesty in Negotiation: An Exercise in Practical Ethics," *Business Ethics Quarterly* 3:360–394.

Dakolias, Maria. 1996. *The Judicial Sector in Latin America and the Caribbean: Elements of Reform*, World Bank Technical Paper No. 319, Washington DC: World Bank.

Darrough, Masako N. 1998. "Privatization and Corruption: Patronage vs. Spoils," Graduate School of Management, University of California, Davis CA, January.

Das-Gupta, Arindam, and Dilip Mookherjee. 1998. *Incentives and Institutional Reform in Tax Enforcement: An Analysis of Developing Country Experience*, New Delhi: Oxford University Press.

Deacon, Robert T. 1994. "Deforestation and the Rule of Law in a Cross-Section of Countries," *Land Economics* 70:414–430.

De George, Richard T. 1994. "International Business Ethics," *Business Ethics Quarterly* 4:1–9.

De Janvry, Alain, and Elisabeth Sadoulet. 1989. "A Study in Resistance to Institutional Change: The Lost Game of Latin American Land Reform," *World Development* 17:1397–1407.

Del Granado, Juan Javier. 1995. *Legis Imperium*, La Paz: Fondo Editorial de la Universidad Iberoamericana.

della Porta, Donatella. 1996. "Actors in Corruption: Business Politicians in Italy," *International Social Science Journal* 48:349–364.

della Porta, Donatella, and Alberto Vannucci. 1997a. "The 'Perverse Effects' of Political Corruption," *Political Studies* 45:516–538.

——. 1997b. "The Resources of Corruption: Some Reflections from the Italian Case," *Crime, Law & Social Change* 7:1–24.

De Melo, Martha, Gur Ofer, and Olga Sandler. 1995. "Pioneers for Profit: St. Petersburg Entrepreneurs in Services," *World Bank Economic Review* 9:425–450.

Derlien, Hans-Ulrich. 1991. "Historical Legacy and Recent Developments in the German Higher Civil Service," *International Review of Administrative Sciences* 57:385–401.

Dey, Harendra Kanti. 1989. "The Genesis and Spread of Economic Corruption: A Microtheoretical Interpretation," *World Development* 17:503–511.

Dia, Mamadou. 1993. *A Governance Approach to Civil Service Reform in Sub-Saharan Africa*, World Bank Technical Paper 225, Africa Technical Department, World Bank, Washington DC.

——. 1996. *Africa's Management in the 1990s and Beyond: Reconciling Indigenous and Transplanted Institutions*, Washington DC: The World Bank.

Diamond, Larry. 1993a. "Introduction: Political Culture and Democracy," in Larry Diamond, ed., *Political Culture and Democracy in Developing Countries*, Boulder CO: Lynne Rienner, pp. 1–33.

——. 1993b. "Nigeria's Perennial Struggle Against Corruption: Prospects for the Third Republic," *Corruption and Reform* 7:215–25.

——. 1995. "Nigeria: The Uncivic Society and the Descent into Praetorianism," in Larry Diamond, Juan Linz, and Seymour Martin Lipsett, eds., *Politics in Developing Countries: Comparing Experiences with Democracy*, 2d edition, Boulder CO: Lynne Rienner Publishing, pp. 417–491.

Dick, Malise. 1992. *Latin America: Trade Facilitation and Transport Reform*, Report Number 25, World Bank. Latin America and the Caribbean Technical Department, Infrastructure and Energy Division, Washington DC: World Bank.

DiIulio, John J. Jr. 1994. *Deregulating the Public Service: Can Government Be Improved?* Washington DC: The Brookings Institution.

Doig, Alan. 1996. "Politics and Public Sector Ethics: The Impact of Change in the United Kingdom," in Walter Little and Eduardo Posada-Carbó, eds., *Political Corruption in Europe and Latin America*, New York: St. Martin's Press, pp. 173–192.

Drazen, Allan, and Vittorio, Grilli. 1993. "The Benefit of Crises for Economic Reforms," *American Economic Review* 83:598–607.

Easter, Gerald. 1996. "Personal Networks and Postrevolutionary State Building: Soviet Russia Reexamined," *World Politics* 48:551–578.

Easterly, William, and Ross Levine. 1997. "Africa's Growth Tragedy: Policies and Ethnic Divisions," *Quarterly Journal of Economics* 112:1203–1250.

Economist Intelligence Unit. 1996. *Country Report: Pakistan*, London: EIU, 3rd Quarter.

Economisti Associati. 1994. *Eastern Africa – Survey of Foreign Investors*, Volumes 2 and 3. Prepared for the World Bank, September.

Environmental Investigation Agency. 1996. *Corporate Power, Corruption and the Destruction of the World's Forests: The Case for a New Global Forest Agreement*, London & Washington DC: EIA.

Etzioni, Amitai. 1988. *Capital Corruption: The New Attack on American Democracy*, New Brunswick, NJ: Transaction Publishers.

Faruqee, Rashid, and Ishrat Husain. 1994. "Adjustment in Seven African Countries," in Ishrat Husain and Rashid Faruqee, eds., *Adjustment in Africa: Lessons from Country Studies*, Washington DC, World Bank Regional and Sectional Studies, pp. 1–10.

Fernandez, Raquel, and Dani Rodrik. 1991. "Resistance to Reform: Status Quo Bias in the Presence of Individual Specific Uncertainty," *American Economic Review* 81:1146–1155.

Findlay, Mark. 1997. "Corruption in Small States: Case Studies in Compromise," in Barry Rider, ed., *Corruption: The Enemy Within*, The Hague: Kluwer Law, pp. 49–61.

Findlay, Ronald. 1991. "Is the New Political Economy Relevant to Developing

Countries?," in G. M. Meier, ed., *Politics and Policymaking in Development: Perspectives on the New Political Economy*, Washington DC: The World Bank.

Flatters, Frank, and W. Bentley MacLeod. 1995. "Administrative Corruption and Taxation," *International Tax and Public Finance* 2:397–417.

Fleischer, David. 1997. "Political Corruption in Brazil," *Crime, Law & Social Change* 25:297–321.

Fuke, Toshiro. 1989. "Remedies in Japanese Administrative Law," *Civil Justice Quarterly* 8:226–235.

Gambetta, Diego. 1993. *The Sicilian Mafia*, Cambridge MA: Harvard University Press.

Gambetta, Diego, and Peter Reuter. 1995. "The Mafia in Legitimate Industries," in Gianluca Fiorentini and Sam Peltzman, eds., *The Economics of Organised Crime*, Cambridge UK: Cambridge University Press, pp. 116–139.

Garment, Suzanne. 1991. *Scandal: The Crisis of Mistrust in American Politics*, New York: Times Books.

Geddes, Barbara. 1991. "A Game-Theoretic Model of Reform in Latin American Democracies," *American Political Science Review* 85(2): 371–392.

——. 1994. *Politician's Dilemma: Building State Capacity in Latin America*, Berkeley: University of California Press.

Geddes, Barbara, and Artur Ribeiro Neto. 1992. "Institutional Sources of Corruption in Brazil," *Third World Quarterly* 13:641–661.

Gelb, Alan, et al. 1988. *Oil Windfalls: Blessing or Curse?* New York: Oxford University Press (published for the World Bank).

General Agreement on Tariffs and Trade. 1991. *Trade Policy Review: Indonesia*, Geneva.

——. 1995. *Trade Policy Review: Indonesia*, Geneva.

Giglioli, Pier Paolo. 1996. "Political Corruption and the Media: The Tangentopoli Affair," *International Social Science Journal* 48:381–394.

Gilman, Stuart C. 1995. "Presidential Ethics and the Ethics of the Presidency," *Annals, AAPSS*, No. 537, pp. 58–75.

Goel, Rajeev, and Daniel Rich. 1989. "On the Economic Incentives for Taking Bribes," *Public Choice* 61:269–275.

Gong, Ting. 1993. "Corruption and Reform in China: An Analysis of Unintended Consequences," *Crime, Law and Social Change* 19:311–327.

Goodman, David S. 1996. "The People's Republic of China: The Party–State, Capitalist Revolution and the New Entrepreneurs," in Richard Robison and David S. G. Goodman, eds., *The New Rich in Asia*, London: Routledge, pp. 225–243.

Gordley, James. 1995. "Enforcing Promises," *California Law Review* 83:547–613.

Grafton, R. Quentin, and Dane Rowlands. 1996. "Development Impeding Institutions," *Canadian Journal of Development Studies* 17:261–277.

Gray, John. 1996. "Open-Competitive Bidding in Japan's Public Works Sector and Foreign Contractor Access: Recent Reforms Are Unlikely to Meet Expectations," *Columbia Journal of Asian Law* 10:425–460.

Grindle, Merilee S. 1996. *Challenging the State: Crisis and Innovation in Latin America and Africa*, Cambridge, England: Cambridge University Press.

Grindle, Merilee S., and John W. Thomas. 1991. *Public Choice and Policy Choice: The Political Economy of Reform in Developing Countries*, Baltimore: Johns Hopkins University Press.

Guerro Amparán, Juan Pablo. 1998. "Un Estudio de Caso de la Reforma Administrativa en México: Los Dilemas de la Instauración de un Servicio Civil a Nivel Federal," Mexico: Centro de Investigación y Docencia Económicas.

Guinier, Lani. 1994. *The Tyranny of the Majority*, New York: Free Press.

Gunlicks, Arthur B. 1995, "The New German Party Finance Law," *German Politics* 4:101–121.

Hamilton, Clive. 1997. "The Sustainability of Logging in Indonesia's Tropical Forests: A Dynamic Input/Output Analysis," *Ecological Economics* 21:183–195.

Handelman, Stephen. 1995. *Comrade Criminal*, New Haven CT: Yale University Press.

Hao, Yufan, and Michael Johnston. 1995. "Reform at the Crossroads: An Analysis of Chinese Corruption," *Asian Perspectives* 19:117–149.

Haque, Nadeem Ul, and Ratna Sahay. 1996. *Do Government Wage Cuts Close Budget Deficits? – A Conceptual Framework for Developing Countries and Transition Economies*, IMF Working Paper WP/96/19, Washington DC: International Monetary Fund, February.

Hardin, Garrett. 1968. "The Tragedy of the Commons," *Science* 162:1243–1248.

Harding, April L. 1995. *Commercial Real Estate Market Development in Russia*, Cofinancing and Financial Advisory Services (Privatization Group) Discussion Paper Number 109, Washington DC: World Bank, July.

Hepkema, Sietze, and Willem Booysen. 1997. "The Bribery of Public Officials: An IBA Survey," *International Business Lawyer*, October 1997, pp. 415–416, 422.

Herbst, Jeffrey. 1996. "Is Nigeria a Viable State?," *The Washington Quarterly*, Spring, pp. 151–172.

Herbst, Jeffrey, and Adebayo Olukoshi. 1994. "Nigeria: Economic and Political Reform at Cross Purposes," in Stephen Haggard and Steven B. Webb, eds., *Voting for Reform: Democracy, Political Liberalization and Economic Adjustment*, New York: Oxford University Press (published for the World Bank), pp. 453–502.

Heredia, Blanca, and Ben Ross Schneider. 1998. "The Political Economy of Administrative Reform: Building State Capacity in Developing Countries." Paper presented at conference on The Political Economy of Administrative Reform: Building State Capacity in Developing Countries, CIDE, Mexico City, June 4–5.

Hewison, Kevin. 1993. "Of Regimes, States, and Pluralities: Thai Politics Enters the 1990s," in Kevin Hewison, Richard Robison, and Garry Rodan, eds., *Southeast Asia in the 1990s: Authoritarianism, Democracy, and Capitalism*, St. Leonards, Australia: Allen & Unwin, pp. 161–189.

Heywood, Paul. 1996. "Continuity and Change: Analysing Political Corruption in Modern Spain," in Walter Little and Eduardo Posada-Carbó, eds., *Political Corruption in Europe and Latin America*, New York: St. Martin's Press, pp. 115–136.

Hodgkinson, Virginia Ann, and Murray S. Weitzman. 1994. *Giving and Volunteering in the United States*, Washington DC: Independent Sector.

Hoekman, Bernard M., and Petros C. Mavroidis, eds. 1997. *Law and Policy in Public Purchasing: The WTO Agreement on Government Procurement*, Ann Arbor: University of Michigan Press.

Hood, Christopher. 1996. "Control Over Bureaucracy: Cultural Theory and Institutional Variety," *Journal of Public Policy* 15:207–230.

Horowitz, Donald. 1985. *Ethnic Groups in Conflict*, Berkeley: University of California Press.

Howse, Robert, and Ronald J. Daniels. 1995. "Rewarding Whistleblowers: The Costs and Benefits of an Incentive-Based Compliance Strategy," in Ronald J. Daniels and Randall Morck, eds., *Corporate Decision-Making in Canada*, Calgary: University of Calgary Press, pp. 525–549.

Huber, Evelyn, Dietrich Rueschemeyer, and John D. Stephens. 1993. "The Impact of Economic Development on Democracy," *Journal of Economic Perspectives* 7:70–86.

Hutchcroft, Paul D. 1998. *Booty Capitalism: The Politics of Banking in the Philippines*, Ithaca: Cornell University Press.

Ingraham, Patricia W. 1993. "Of Pigs in Pokes and Policy Diffusion: Another Look at Pay-for-Performance," *Public Administration Review* 53:348–356.

———. 1996. "The Reform Agenda for National Civil Service Systems," in Hans A. G. M. Bekke, James L. Perry, and Theo A. J. Toonen, eds., *Civil Service Systems in Comparative Perspective*, Bloomington IN: Indiana University Press, pp. 247–267.

International Bar Association Council. 1996. "Resolution on Deterring Bribery in International Business Transactions," adopted Madrid, Spain, June 1.

International Chamber of Commerce. 1996. "Extortion and Bribery in International Business Transactions," Document No. 193/15, March 26.

Jadwin, Pamela J., and Monica Shilling. 1994. "Foreign Corrupt Practices Act," *American Criminal Law Review* 31:677–686.

Johnson, Paul. 1991. *The Birth of the Modern: World Society 1815–1830*, New York: Harper Collins.

Johnson, Roberta A., and Michael E. Kraft. 1990. "Bureaucratic Whistleblowing and Policy Change," *Western Political Quarterly* 43:849–874.

Johnson, Ronald N., and Gary D. Libecap. 1994. "Patronage to Merit and Control of the Federal Labor Force," *Explorations in Economic History* 31:91–119.

Johnson, Simon, Daniel Kaufmann, and Pablo Zoido-Lobatón. 1998. "Regulatory Discretion and the Unofficial Economy," *American Economic Review – Papers and Proceedings* 88:387–392.

Johnston, Michael, and Yufan Hao. 1995. "China's Surge of Corruption," *Journal of Democracy* 6:80–94.

Jordan, Ann D. 1997. "Lost in the Translation: Two Legal Cultures, the Common Law Judiciary and the Basic Law of the Hong Kong Special Administrative Region," *Cornell International Law Journal* 30:335–380.

Joseph, Richard. 1996. "Nigeria: Inside the Dismal Tunnel," *Current History* 95:193–200.

Josephson, Matthew. 1938. *The Politicos 1865–1896*, New York: Harcourt Brace.

Kahn, Mushtaq H. 1996. "A Typology of Corrupt Transactions in Developing Countries," *IDS Bulletin* 27(2):12–21 (April).

Kaltefleiter, Werner, and Karl-Heinz Naßmacher. 1994. "Das Parteiengesetz 1994 – Reform der kleinen schritte," *Zeitschrift fuer Parlamentsfragen* 25:253–262.

Kaufmann, Daniel. 1997. "The Missing Pillar of a Growth Strategy for Ukraine: Institutional and Policy Reforms for Private Sector Development," in Peter K. Cornelius and Patrick Lenain, eds., *Ukraine: Accelerating the Transition to Market*, Washington: IMF, pp. 234–275.

Kaufmann, Daniel, and Paul Siegelbaum. 1997. "Privatization and Corruption in Transition Economies," *Journal of International Affairs* 50:419–459.

Keefer, Philip, and Stephen Knack. 1995. "Institutions and Economic Performance: Cross-Country Tests Using Alternative Institutional Measures," *Economics and Politics* 7:207–227.

Kelman, Steven. 1990. *Procurement and Public Management: The Fear of Discretion and the Quality of Government Performance*, Washington DC: AEI Press.

———. 1994. "Deregulating Federal Procurement: Nothing to Fear But Discretion Itself?," in John J. DiIulio, Jr., ed., *Deregulating the Public Service: Can Government Be Improved?*, Washington DC: The Brookings Institution, pp. 102–128.

Kibwana, Kivutha, Smokin Wanjala, and Okech-Owiti. 1996. *The Anatomy of Corruption in Kenya*, Nairobi, Kenya: Center for Law and Research International (Clarion).

Kilby, Christopher. 1995. "Risk Management: An Econometric Investigation of Project-Level Factors," background paper for the *Annual Review of Evaluation Results 1994*, World Bank, Operations Evaluation Department. Vassar College, Poughkeepsie NY.

Kim, Joongi, and Jong Bum Kim. 1997. "Cultural Differences in the Crusade Against International Bribery," *Pacific Rim Law and Policy Journal* 6:549–580.

Kim, W. Chan, and Renée Mauborgne. 1995. "A Procedural Justice Model of Strategic Decision Making," *Organization Science* 6:44–61.

Kitchen, Richard. 1994. "Compensation Upgrading in Caribbean Public Services: Comparative Needs and Experience," in Shahid Amjad Chaudhry, Gary James Reid, and Waleed Haider Malik, eds., *Civil Service Reform in Latin America and the Caribbean: Proceedings of a Conference*, World Bank Technical Paper 259, Washington DC, October, 120–127.

Klich, Agnieszka. 1996. "Bribery in Economies in Transition: The Foreign Corrupt Practices Act," *Stanford Journal of International Law* 32:121–147.

Klitgaard, Robert. 1988. *Controlling Corruption*, Berkeley CA: University of California Press.

———. 1997. "Cleaning Up and Invigorating the Civil Service," *Public Administration and Development* 17:487–510.

Klitgaard, Robert, and Heather Baser. 1997. "Working Together to Fight Corruption: State, Society and the Private Sector in Partnership," in Suzanne Taschereau and Jose Edgardo L. Campos, eds., *Governance Innovations: Lessons from Experience, Building Government–Citizen–Business Partnerships*, Washington DC: Institute on Governance, pp. 59–81.

Kochanek, Stephen A. 1993. *Patron–Client Politics and Business in Bangladesh*, New Delhi: Sage Publications.

Kollock, Peter. 1994. "The Emergence of Exchange Structures: An Experimental Study of Uncertainty, Commitment, and Trust," *American Journal of Sociology* 100:313–345.

Koszcuk, Jackie. 1997. "Nonstop Pursuit of Campaign Funds Increasingly Drives the System," *Congressional Quarterly*, April 5, pp. 770–774.

Kovacic, William. 1996. "Whistleblower Bounty Lawsuits as Monitoring Devices in Government Contracting," *Loyola of Los Angeles Law Review* 29:1799–1857.

Krehbiel, Keith. 1998. *Pivotal Politics: A Theory of U.S. Lawmaking*, Chicago: University of Chicago Press.

Krishna, Vijay, and John Morgan. 1997. "An Analysis of the War of Attrition and the All-Pay Auction," *Journal of Economic Theory* 72:343–362.

Krueger, Anne O. 1974. "The Political Economy of a Rent-Seeking Society," *American Economic Review* 64:291–303.

Kurer, Oskar. 1993. "Clientelism, Corruption, and the Allocation of Resources," *Public Choice* 77:259–273.

Laffont, Jean-Jacques. 1990. "Analysis of Hidden Games in a Three-Level Hierarchy," *Journal of Law, Economics, and Organization* 6:301–324.

Langan, Patricia, and Brian Cooksey, eds. 1995. *The National Integrity System in Tanzania: Proceedings of a Workshop Convened by the Prevention of Corruption Bureau, Tanzania*, Washington DC: Economic Development Institute, World Bank.

Laurent, Anne. 1997. "Buying Smarts," *Government Executive*, April, p. 28.

Lave, Lester. 1981. *The Strategy of Social Regulation*. Washington DC: Brookings Institution.

Laver, Michael, and Norman Schofield. 1990. *Multiparty Government*, Oxford: Oxford University Press.

Law Library of Congress. 1991. *Campaign Financing of National Elections in Foreign Countries*, Washington DC: Law Library of Congress.

Lawyers Committee for Human Rights and the Venezuelan Program for Human Rights Education and Action. 1996. *Halfway to Reform: The World Bank and the Venezuelan Justice System*, New York: Lawyers Committee for Human Rights, August.

Lee, Rance P. L. 1986. "Bureaucratic Corruption in Asia: The Problem of Incongruence between Legal Norms and Folk Norms," in Ledivina A. Cariño, ed., *Bureaucratic Corruption in Asia: Causes, Consequences and Controls*, Quezon City, the Philippines: JMC Press, pp. 69–108.

Leechor, Chad. 1994. "Ghana: Frontrunner in Adjustment," in Ishrat Husain and Rashid Faruqee, eds., *Adjustment in Africa: Lessons from Country Studies*, Washington DC: The World Bank, pp. 153–192

Leff, Nathaniel. 1964. "Economic Development Through Bureaucratic Corruption," *American Behavioral Scientist* 8:8–14.

Levine, David I., and Laura D'Andrea Tyson. 1990. "Participation, Productivity, and the Firm's Environment," in Alan Blinder, ed., *Paying for Productivity: A Look at the Evidence*, Washington DC: The Brookings Institution, pp. 183–244.

Levy, Brian, and Pablo T. Spiller, eds. 1996. *Regulations, Institutions, and Commitment*, Cambridge: Cambridge University Press.

Lewis, Peter. 1996. "From Prebendalism to Predation: the Political Economy of Decline in Nigeria," *Journal of Modern African Studies* 34:79–103.

Lien, Da-Hsiang. 1990a. "Competition, Regulation and Bribery: A Further Note," *Managerial and Decision Economics* 11:127–130.

Lien, Da-Hsiang Donald. 1990b. "Corruption and Allocation Efficiency," *Journal of Development Economics* 33:153–164.

Lijphart, Arend. 1977. *Democracy in Plural Societies*, New Haven: Yale University Press.

Linarelli, John. 1996. "Anglo-American Jurisprudence and Latin America," *Fordham International Law Journal* 20:50–89.

Lindgren, James. 1988. "The Elusive Distinction Between Bribery and Extortion: From the Common Law to Hobbs," *UCLA Law Review* 35:815–908.

Little, Walter, and Antonio Herrera. 1996. "Political Corruption in Venezuela," in Walter Little and Eduardo Posada-Carbó, eds., *Political Corruption in Europe and Latin America*, New York: St. Martin's Press, pp. 267–286.

Longenecker, Justin G., Joseph A. McKinney, and Carlos W. Moore. 1988. "The Ethical Issue of International Bribery: A Study of Attitudes Among U.S. Business Professionals," *Journal of Business Ethics* 7:341–346.

Low, Patrick. 1995. *Preshipment Inspection Services*, World Bank Discussion Paper 278, Washington DC.

Lui, Francis. T. 1985. "An Equilibrium Queuing Model of Bribery," *Journal of Political Economy* 93:760–781.

——. 1986. "A Dynamic Model of Corruption Deterrence," *Journal of Public Economics* 31:1–22.

——. 1990. "Corruption, Economic Growth and the Crisis of China," in Roger Des Forges, Luo Ning, and Wu Yen-bo, eds., *China: The Crisis of 1989: Origins and Implications*, Buffalo NY: Council on International Studies and Programs, State University of New York at Buffalo.

Lundahl, Mats. 1997. "Inside the Predatory State: The Rationale, Methods, and Economic

Consequences of Kleptocratic Regimes," *Nordic Journal of Political Economy* 24:31–50.

Ma, Jun. 1995. *Macroeconomic Management and Intergovernmental Relations in China*, Policy Working Paper 1408, Washington DC: The World Bank.

McChesney, Fred S. 1997. *Money for Nothing: Politicians, Rent Extraction, and Political Extortion*, Cambridge MA: Harvard University Press.

MacGaffey, Janet. 1991. *The Real Economy of Zaire: The Contribution of Smuggling and Other Unofficial Activities to National Wealth*, Philadelphia: University of Pennsylvania Press.

MacLean, Roberto. 1996. "The Culture of Service in the Administration of Justice," *Transnational Law & Contemporary Problems* 6:139–164.

Madron, Roy. 1995. "Performance Improvement in Public Services," *Political Quarterly* 66:181–194.

Magrath, C. Peter. 1966. *Yazoo: Law and Politics in the New Republic: The Case of* Fletcher v. Peck, Providence RI: Brown University Press.

Mainwaring, Scott, and Matthew S. Shugart, eds. 1997. *Presidentialism and Democracy in Latin America*, Cambridge: Cambridge University Press.

Mamiya, Jun. 1995. "Government and Contractors Prove: It Takes Two to Dango," *Tokyo Business Today*, July 1995, pp. 28–31.

Manion, Melanie. 1996a. "Corruption by Design: Bribery in Chinese Enterprise Licensing," *Journal of Law, Economics, and Organization* 12:167–195.

——. 1996b. "Policy Instruments and Political Context: Transforming a Culture of Corruption in Hong Kong," prepared for the Annual Meeting of the Association for Asian Studies, Honolulu, Hawaii, April 11–14. A shortened version has been published as "La experiencia de Hong Kong contra la corrupción. Algunas lecciones importantes," *Nueva Sociedad* no. 145:126–137 (September–October 1996).

Mans, Darius. 1994. "Tanzania: Resolute Action," in Ishrat Husain and Rashid Faruqee, eds., *Adjustment in Africa: Lessons from Country Studies*, Washington DC: The World Bank, pp. 352–426.

Manzetti, Luigi. 1999. *Privatization South American Style*, Oxford: Oxford University Press.

——. 1997. "Regulation in Post-Privatization Environments: Chile and Argentina in Comparative Perspective," *North–South Center Agenda Papers*, University of Miami.

Manzetti, Luigi, and Charles Blake. 1996. "Market Reforms and Corruption in Latin America: New Means for Old Ways." *Review of International Political Economy* 3:662–697.

Maranto, Robert, and David Schultz. 1991. *A Short History of the United States Civil Service*, Lanham MD: University Press of America.

Marchione, William P. Jr. 1976. "The 1949 Boston Charter Reform," *New England Quarterly* 49:373–398.

Marshall, P. J. 1997. "British Society in India under the East India Company," *Modern Asian Studies* 31:89–108.

Mauro, Paolo. 1995. "Corruption and Growth." *Quarterly Journal of Economics* 110:681–712.

——. 1998. "Corruption and the Composition of Government Expenditure," *Journal of Public Economics* 69:263–279.

May, Randolph. 1997. "Reforming the Sunshine Act," *Administrative Law Review* 49:415–419.

Mbaku, John Mukum. 1994. "Africa After More Than Thirty Years of Independence: Still Poor and Deprived," *Journal of Third World Studies* 11:13–58.

Mehmet, Ozay. 1994. "Rent-Seeking and Gate-Keeping in Indonesia: A Cultural and Economic Analysis," *Labour, Capital and Society*, 27:56–89.

Menes, Rebecca. 1996. "Public Goods and Private Favors: Patronage Politics in American Cities During the Progressive Era, 1900–1920," Ph.D. Thesis, Department of Economics, Harvard University, Cambridge MA.

Mény, Yves. 1996. " 'Fin de Siécle' Corruption: Change, Crisis and Shifting Values," *International Social Science Journal*, No. 149:309–320.

Mexico, Federal Executive Power. 1996. *Program for the Modernization of Public Administration 1995–2000*, Mexico City.

Miller, Nathan. 1992. *Stealing from America: A History of Corruption from Jamestown to Reagan*, New York: Paragon House.

Miller, Terry. 1997a. "Kelman's Latest Proposal and Past Performance Explored," *Federal Computer Market Report* 21(11): 7 (June 9).

——. 1997b. "Unnecessary Surgery," *Federal Computer Market Report* 21(7): 4 (April 14).

Mitchell, Daniel J. B., David Lewin, and Edward E. Lawler III. 1990. "Alternative Pay Systems, Firm Performance, and Productivity," in Alan Blinder, ed., *Paying for Productivity: A Look at the Evidence*, Washington DC: The Brookings Institution, pp. 15–94.

Moe, Terry. 1990. "The Politics of Structural Choice: Towards a Theory of Public Bureaucracy," in Oliver Williamson, ed., *Organization Theory: From Chester Barnard to the Present and Beyond*, New York: Oxford University Press, pp. 116–153.

Moe, Terry, and Michael Caldwell. 1994. "The Institutional Foundations of Democratic Government: A Comparison of Presidential and Parliamentary Systems," *Journal of Institutional and Theoretical Economics* 150:171–195.

Moene, Karl Ove, and Sheetal K. Chand. 1997. "Breaking the Vicious Circle of the Predatory State," *Nordic Journal of Political Economy* 24:21–30.

Mohn, Carel. 1997. " 'Speedy' Services in India," *TI Newsletter*, March, p. 3.

Monroe, Kristen Renwick. 1996. *The Heart of Altruism*, Princeton: Princeton University Press.

Montias, J. M., and Susan Rose-Ackerman. 1981. "Corruption in a Soviet-Type Economy: Theoretical Considerations," in Steven Rosefielde, ed., *Economic Welfare and the Economics of Soviet Socialism: Essays in Honor of Abram Bergson*, Cambridge: Cambridge Univ. Press, pp. 53–83.

Montinola, Gabriella R. 1997. "The Efficient Secret Revisited," paper presented at the Latin American Studies Association, Guadalajara, Mexico, April.

Montinola, Gabriella, Yingyi Qian, and Barry R. Weingast. 1995. "Federalism, Chinese Style: The Political Basis for Economic Success in China," *World Politics* 48:50–81.

Moody-Stuart, George. 1997. *Grand Corruption in Third World Development*, Oxford: Worldview Publishing.

Moore, Michael. 1998. "Death Without Taxes: Democracy, State Capacity, and Aid Dependency in the Fourth World," in Mark Robinson and Gordon Whites, eds., *The Democratic Developmental State: Politics and Institutional Design*, Oxford: Oxford University Press.

Moreno Ocampo, Luis Gabriel. 1995. "Hyper-Corruption: Concept and Solutions." Presented at the Latin American Studies Association, Washington DC, September 29.

Morris, Stephen. 1991. *Corruption and Politics in Contemporary Mexico*, Tuscaloosa: University of Alabama Press.

Murray-Rust, D. Hammond, and Edward J. Vander Velde. 1994. "Changes in Hydraulic Performance and Comparative Costs of Lining and Desilting of Secondary Canals in Punjab, Pakistan," *Irrigation and Drainage Systems* 8:137–158.

Nellis, John, and Sunita Kikeri. 1989. "Public Enterprise Reform: Privatization and the World Bank," *World Development* 17:659–672.

Nichols, Philip M. 1997a. "Outlawing Transnational Bribery Through the World Trade Organization," *Journal of Law & Policy in International Business* 28:305–381.

———. 1997b. "The Viability of Transplanted Law: Kazakhstani Reception of a Transplanted Foreign Investment Code," *University of Pennsylvania Journal of International Economic Law* 18:1235–1279.

Nickson, R. Andrew. 1996. "Democratisation and Institutional Corruption in Paraguay," in Walter Little and Eduardo Posada-Carbó, eds., *Political Corruption in Europe and Latin America*, New York: St. Martin's Press, pp. 237–266.

Nissanke, Machiko. 1991. "Mobilizing Domestic Resources for African Development and Diversification," in Ajay Chhibber and Stanley Fischer, eds., *Economic Reform in Sub-Saharan Africa*, Washington DC: World Bank, pp. 137–147.

Nobles, James C. Jr., and Christina Maistrellis. 1995. "The Foreign Corrupt Practices Act: A Systemic Solution for the U.S. Multinational," *NAFTA: Law and Business Review of the Americas* 1(2):5–30, Spring.

Noelker, Timothy F., Linda Shapiro, and Steven E. Kellogg. 1997. "Procurement Integrity Revisions Ease Burdens," *National Law Journal*, May 19, p. B7.

Nogués, Julio. 1989. *Latin America's Experience with Export Subsidies*, Policy, Planning and Research Working Papers on International Trade, WPS 182, Washington DC: International Economics Department, World Bank.

Noorani, A. G. 1997. "Lok Pal and Lok Ayuki," in S. Guhan and Samuel Paul, eds., *Corruption in India: An Agenda for Reform*, New Delhi: Vision Books, pp. 189–217.

Novitzkaya, Irina, Victor Novitzky, and Andrew Stone. 1995. "Private Enterprise in Ukraine: Getting Down to Business," World Bank Private Sector Development Division, unprocessed.

Nunberg, Barbara, and John Nellis. 1995. *Civil Service Reform and the World Bank*, World Bank Discussion Paper 161, Washington DC: World Bank.

Oldenburg, Philip. 1987. "Middlemen in Third World Corruption: Implications for an Indian Case," *World Politics* 39:508–535.

Olowu, Dele. 1993. "Ethical Violations in Nigeria's Public Services: Patterns, Explanations and Remedies," in Sadig Rasheed and Dele Olowu, eds., *Ethics and Accountability in African Public Services*, African Association for Public Administration and Management, pp. 93–118.

Olson, Mancur. 1982. *The Rise and Decline of Nations*, New Haven: Yale University Press.

———. 1993. "Dictatorship, Democracy, and Development," *American Political Science Review* 87:567–575.

———. 1996. "Big Bills Left on the Sidewalk: Why Some Nations Are Rich and Others Poor," *Journal of Economic Literature* 10:3–24.

Organisation for Economic Cooperation and Development. 1997. "OECD Actions to Fight Corruption," Note by the Secretary General to the OECD Council at Ministerial Level, Paris, May 26.

Ostrom, Elinor. 1996. "Incentives, Rules of the Game, and Development," in Michael Bruno and Boris Pleskovic, eds., *Annual World Bank Conference on Development Economics*, Washington DC: The World Bank, pp. 207–234.

Ostrom, Elinor, and Roy Gardiner. 1993. "Coping with Asymmetries in the Commons:

Self-Governing Irrigation Systems Can Work," *Journal of Economic Perspectives* 7:93–112.

Painter, Chris. 1994. "Public Service Reform: Reinventing or Abandoning Government?," *Political Quarterly* 65:242–262.

Painter, Joe. 1991. "Compulsory Competitive Tendering in Local Government: The First Round," *Public Administration* 69:191–210.

Pak, Simon J., and John S. Zdanowicz. 1994. "A Statistical Analysis of the U.S. Merchandise Trade Data Base and Its Uses in Transfer Pricing Compliance and Enforcement," *Tax Management Transfer Pricing Report* 3:50–57, May 11.

París Rodriquez, Hernando. 1995. "Improving the Administration of Justice in Costa Rica," in Malcolm Rowat, Waleed H. Malik, and Maria Dakolias, eds., *Judicial Reform in Latin America and the Caribbean: Proceedings of a World Bank Conference*, World Bank Technical Paper 280, Washington DC: World Bank, pp. 199–208.

Park, Byeong-Seog. 1995. "Political Corruption in South Korea: Concentrating on the Dynamics of Party Politics," *Asian Perspectives* 19:163–193.

Parris, Henry. 1969. *Constitutional Bureaucracy: The Development of British Central Administration Since the Eighteenth Century*, London: George Allen & Unwin.

Pasuk Phongpaicht and Sungsidh Piriyarangsan. 1994. *Corruption and Democracy in Thailand*, Bangkok: The Political Economy Centre, Faculty of Economics, Chulalongkorn University.

Paul, Karen, Simon Pak, John Zdanowicz, and Peter Curwen. 1994. "The Ethics of International Trade: Use of Deviation from Average World Price to Indicate Possible Wrongdoing," *Business Ethics Quarterly* 4:29–41.

Paul, Sam. 1995. "Evaluating Public Services: A Case Study on Bangalore, India," *New Directions for Evaluation*, American Evaluation Association, Washington DC, No. 67, Fall.

Paulose, Matthew Jr. 1997. "*United States v. McDougald*: The Anathema to 18 U.S.C. § 1956 and National Efforts Against Money Laundering," *Fordham International Law Journal* 21:253–307.

Peirce, Neal. 1994. "Is Deregulation Enough? Lessons from Florida and Philadelphia," in John J. DiIulio, Jr., *Deregulating the Public Service: Can Government Be Improved?*, Washington DC: The Brookings Institution, pp. 129–155.

Pendergast, William F. 1995. "Foreign Corrupt Practices Act: An Overview of Almost Twenty Years of Foreign Bribery Prosecutions," *International Quarterly* 7–2:187–217.

Perry, James L. 1988–89. "Making Policy by Trial and Error: Merit Pay in the Federal Service," *Policy Studies Journal* 17:389–405.

Peterson, John. 1997. "The European Union: Pooled Sovereignty, Divided Accountability," *Political Studies* 45:559–578.

Pickholz, Marvin G. 1997. "The United States Foreign Corrupt Practices Act as a Civil Remedy," in Barry Rider, ed., *Corruption: The Enemy Within*, The Hague: Kluwer, pp. 231–252.

Piggott, Charles. 1996. "Emerging Markets Boost Ratings," *Euromoney*, March, pp. 160–165.

Pinches, Michael. 1996. "The Philippines' New Rich: Capitalist Transformations Amidst Economic Gloom," in Richard Robison and David S. G. Goodman, eds. *The New Rich in Asia*, London: Routledge, pp. 105–133.

Pivovarsky, Alexander. 1997–1998. "Multinational Enterprise Entry Under Unstable Property Rights: The Case of Ukraine, *Ukranian Economic Review*, no. 4–5.

Polidano, Charles. 1996. "Public Service Reform in Malta, 1988–96: Lessons to Be Learned," *Governance* 9:459–480.

Pope, Jeremy, ed. 1996. *National Integrity Systems: The TI Source Book*, Berlin: Transparency International.

Premchand, A. 1993. *Public Expenditure Management*, Washington DC: International Monetary Fund.

Prince, Carl E. 1997. *The Federalists and the Origins of the U.S. Civil Service*, New York: New York University Press.

Pritchett, Lant, and Geeta Sethi. 1994. "Tariff Revenue, and Tariff Reform: Some New Facts," *World Bank Economic Review* 4:1–16.

Prystay, Cris. 1997. "Season of Uncertainty," *Asian Business* 33 (3):44–50, March.

Przeworski, Adam, and Fernando Limongi. 1993. "Political Regimes and Economic Growth," *Journal of Economic Perspectives* 7:51–69.

Quah, Jon S. T. 1989. "Singapore's Experience in Curbing Corruption," in Arnold J. Heidenheimer, Michael Johnston, and Victor T. LeVine, eds., *Political Corruption: A Handbook*, New Brunswick, NJ: Transaction Publishers, pp. 841–853.

——. 1994. "Culture Change in the Singapore Civil Service," in Shahid Amjad Chaudhry, Gary James Reid, and Waleed Haider Malik, eds., *Civil Service Reform in Latin America and the Caribbean: Proceedings of a Conference*, World Bank Technical Paper 259, Washington DC, October, pp. 205–216.

——. 1995. "Controlling Corruption in City-States: A Comparative Study of Hong Kong and Singapore," *Crime, Law and Social Change* 22:391–414.

Qui, Allison R. 1996. "National Campaign Finance Laws in Canada, Japan and the United States," *Suffolk Transnational Law Journal* 20:193–245.

Raadschelders, Jos. C. N., and Mark R. Rutgers. 1996. "The Evolution of Civil Service Systems," in Hans A. G. M. Bekke, James L. Perry, and Theo A. J. Toonen, eds., *Civil Service Systems in Comparative Perspective*, Bloomington IN: Indiana University Press, pp. 67–99.

Rahman, A. T. Rafique. 1986. "Legal and Administrative Measures Against Bureaucratic Corruption in Asia," in Ledivina A. Cariño, ed., *Bureaucratic Corruption in Asia: Causes, Consequences and Controls*, Quezon City, the Philippines: JMC Press, pp. 109–162.

Rashid, Salim. 1981. "Public Utilities in Egalitarian LDCs," *Kyklos* 34:448–460.

Rasmusen, Eric. 1990. *Games and Information: An Introduction to Game Theory*, Oxford: Basil Blackwell.

Rasmusen, Eric, and Mark Ramseyer. 1994. "Cheap Bribes and the Corruption Ban: A Coordination Game Among Rational Legislators," *Public Choice* 78:305–327.

Rauch, James. 1995. "Bureaucracy, Infrastructure, and Economic Growth: Evidence from U.S. Cities During the Progressive Era," *American Economic Review* 85:968–979.

Reed, Steven R. 1996. "Political Corruption in Japan," *International Social Science Journal* 48:395–405.

Rehren, Alfredo. 1997. "Corruption and Local Politics in Chile," *Crime, Law & Social Change* 25:323–334.

Reid, Gary J., and Graham Scott. 1994. "Public Sector Human Resource Management in Latin America and the Caribbean," in Shadid Amjad Chaudhry, Gary James Reid, and Waleed Haider Malik, eds., *Civil Service Reform in Latin America and the Caribbean*, World Bank Technical Paper 259, World Bank: Washington DC, pp. 39–81.

Reisman, W. Michael. 1992. *Systems of Control in International Adjudication and Arbitration*, Durham NC: Duke University Press.

Reuter, Peter. 1987. *Racketeering in Legitimate Industries: A Study in the Economics of Intimidation*, Santa Monica CA: RAND Corporation.

Rhodes, R. A. W. 1994. "The Hollowing Out of the State: The Changing Nature of the Public Service in Britain," *Political Quarterly* 65:138–151.

Roberts, Robert N., and Marion T. Doss, Jr. 1992. "Public Service and Private Hospitality: A Case Study in Federal Conflict-of-Interest Reform," *Public Administration Review* 52:260–270.

Robinson, Marguerite S. 1992. "Rural Financial Intermediation: Lessons from Indonesia, Part One," Development Discussion Paper No. 434, Harvard Institute for International Development, Harvard University, Cambridge MA.

Robison, Richard. 1986. *Indonesia: The Rise of Capital*, North Sydney, Australia: Allen & Unwin.

——. 1996. "The Middle Class and the Bourgeoisie in Indonesia," in Richard Robison and David S. G. Goodman, eds., *The New Rich in Asia*, London: Routledge, pp. 79–101.

Rodden, Jonathan, and Susan Rose-Ackerman. 1997. "Does Federalism Preserve Markets?," *University of Virginia Law Review* 83:1521–1572.

Rodrik, Dani. 1994. "King Kong Meets Godzilla: The World Bank and *The East Asian Miracle*," in A. Fishlow, C. Gwin, S. Haggard, D. Rodrik, and R. Wade, *Miracle or Design? Lessons from the East Asian Experience*, ODC Policy Essay 11, Washington DC: Overseas Development Council, pp. 13–53.

Rogers, Glenn, and Sidi Mohammed Iddal. 1996. "Reduction of Illegal Payments in West Africa: Niger's Experience," in *Good Governance and the Regional Economy in Francophone Africa*, College Park MD: IRIS (University of Maryland).

Rohr, John A. 1991. "Ethical Issues in French Public Administration," *Public Administration Review* 51:283–297.

Roodman, David Malin. 1996. *Paying the Piper: Subsidies, Politics, and the Environment*, Worldwatch Paper 133, Washington DC, December.

Rose-Ackerman, Susan. 1978. *Corruption: A Study in Political Economy*, New York: Academic Press.

——. 1983. "Social Services and the Market," *Columbia Law Review* 83:1405–1438.

——. 1986. "Reforming Public Bureaucracy through Economic Incentives?," *Journal of Law, Economics, and Organization* 2:131–161.

——. 1989. "Law and Economics: Paradigm, Politics, or Philosophy," in Nicholas Mercuro, ed., *Law and Economics*, Boston: Kluwer Academic Pub., pp. 233–258.

——. 1992. *Rethinking the Progressive Agenda: The Reform of the American Regulatory State*, New York: The Free Press.

——. 1994. "Reducing Bribery in the Public Sector," in Duc V. Trang, ed., *Corruption and Democracy: Political Institutions, Processes and Corruption in Transition States in East-Central Europe and in the Former Soviet Union*, Budapest: Institute for Constitutional and Legislative Policy, pp. 21–28.

——. 1995a. *Controlling Environmental Policy: The Limits of Public Law in the United States and Germany*, New Haven: Yale University Press.

——. 1995b. "Public Law versus Private Law in Environmental Regulation: European Union Proposals in the Light of United States Experience," *Review of European Community & International Environmental Law* 4:312–320.

——. 1996a. "Altruism, Nonprofits and Economic Theory," *Journal of Economic Literature* 34:701–728.

——. 1996b. "Democracy and 'Grand' Corruption," *International Social Science Journal* 48:365–380.

——. 1996c. "Is Leaner Government Cleaner Government?" Published in Spanish as

"¿Una Administracion Reducida Significa una Administracion Mas Limpia?," *Nueva Sociedad*, No. 145, September–October, pp. 66–79.

———. 1997a. "Corruption, Inefficiency, and Economic Growth," *Nordic Journal of Political Economy* 24:3–20.

———. 1997b. "The Political Economy of Corruption," in Kimberly Ann Elliott, ed., *Corruption and the Global Economy*, Washington: DC: Institute for International Economics, pp. 31–60.

———. 1997c. "The Role of the World Bank in Controlling Corruption," *Law and Policy in International Business* 29:93–114.

———. 1998a. "Bribes and Gifts," in Avner Ben-Nur and Louis Putterman, eds., *Economics, Values, and Organization*, New York: Cambridge University Press, pp. 296–328.

———. 1998b. "Corruption and Development," in Boris Pleskovic and Joseph Stiglitz, eds., *Annual World Bank Conference on Development Economics, 1997*, Washington DC: World Bank, pp. 35–57.

Rose-Ackerman, Susan, and Andrew Stone. 1998. "The Costs of Corruption for Private Business: Evidence from World Bank Surveys," draft working paper, World Bank, Washington DC.

Rosenberg, Richard D. 1987. "Managerial Morality and Behavior: The Questionable Payments Issue," *Journal of Business Ethics* 6:23–36.

Rosenbloom, David. 1971. *Federal Service and the Constitution: The Development of the Public Employment Relationship*, Ithaca: Cornell University Press.

Ross, Randy. 1988. *Government and the Private Sector: Who Should Do What?* New York: Crane, Russak & Co.

Rouis, Mustapha. 1994. "Senegal: Stabilization, Partial Adjustment, and Stagnation," in Ishrat Husain and Rashid Faruqee, eds., *Adjustment in Africa: Lessons from Country Studies*, Washington DC: The World Bank, pp. 286–351.

Rowat, Malcolm, Waleed H. Malik, and Maria Dakolias, eds. 1995. *Judicial Reform in Latin America and the Caribbean: Proceedings of a World Bank Conference*, World Bank Technical Paper 280, Washington DC: World Bank.

Rubinfeld, Daniel. 1997. "On Federalism and Economic Development," *Virginia Law Review* 83:1581–1592.

Rudzio, Wolfgang. 1994. "Das Neue Parteienfinanazierungsmodell und seine Auswirkungen," *Zeitschrift fuer Parlamenentsfragen* 25:390–401.

Ruzindana, Augustine. 1995. "Combating Corruption in Uganda," in Petter Langseth, J. Katorobo, E. Brett, and J. Munene, eds., *Uganda: Landmarks in Rebuilding a Nation*, Kampala: Fountain Publishers, pp. 191–209.

Saba, Roberto, and Luigi Manzetti. 1997. "Privatization in Argentina: The Implications for Corruption," *Crime, Law & Social Change* 25:353–369.

Sachs, Jeffrey D., and Andrew M. Warner. 1995. "Natural Resource Abundance and Economic Growth," Development Discussion Paper No. 517a, Harvard Institute for International Development, Cambridge MA, October.

Santa Gadea, Fernando Vega. 1995. "Judicial Reform in Peru," in Malcolm Rowat, Waleed H. Malik, and Maria Dakolias, eds., *Judicial Reform in Latin America and the Caribbean: Proceedings of a World Bank Conference*, World Bank Technical Paper 280, Washington DC: World Bank, pp. 184–191.

Savona, Ernesto U., and Laura Mezzanotte. 1997. "Double Standards in Public Life: The Case of International Corruption," in Barry Rider, ed., *Corruption: The Enemy Within*, The Hague: Kluwer, pp. 105–111.

Scalapino, Robert. 1989. *The Politics of Development: Perspectives on Twentieth-Century Asia*, Cambridge MA: Harvard University Press.

Schiesl, Martin J. 1977. *The Politics of Efficiency: Municipal Administration and Reform in America, 1800–1920*, Berkeley: University of California Press.

Schmid, A. Allan, and Lindon J. Robison. 1995. "Applications of Social Capital Theory," *Journal of Agriculture and Applied Economics* 27:59–66.

Schultze, Charles. 1977. *The Public Use of the Private Interest*, Washington DC: Brookings Institution.

Schwarz, Adam. 1994. *A Nation in Waiting: Indonesia in the 1990s*, Boulder: Westview Press.

Scott, David. 1995. "Money Laundering and International Efforts to Fight It," *Viewpoints*, No. 48, Financial Sector Development Department, Vice Presidency for Finance and Private Sector Development, World Bank, Washington, May.

Scott, Graham. 1996. *Government Reform in New Zealand*, IMF Occasional Paper 140, Washington DC: International Monetary Fund.

Seibel, Wolfgang. 1997. "Corruption in the Federal Republic of Germany Before and in the Wake of Reunification," in Donatella della Porta and Yves Mény, eds., *Democracy and Corruption in Europe*, London: Pinter, pp. 85–102.

Seligson, Mitchell A., and John A. Booth. 1993. "Political Culture and Regime Type: Evidence from Nicaragua and Costa Rica," *Journal of Politics* 55:777–792.

Sen, A. K. 1977. "Rational Fools: A Critique of the Behavioral Foundations of Economic Theory," *Philosophy and Public Affairs* 6:317–344.

Shaw, Keith, John Fenwick, and Anne Foreman. 1994. "Compulsory Competitive Tendering for Local Government Services: The Experiences of Local Authorities in the North of England 1988–1992," *Public Administration* 72: 201–217.

Shelley, Louise. 1994. "Post-Soviet Organized Crime," *Demokratizatsiya* 2:341–358.

Sherman, Lawrence W. 1974. *Police Corruption: A Sociological Perspective*, Anchor Books: New York.

Shihata, Ibrahim F. I. 1997. "Corruption – A General Review With an Emphasis on the Role of the World Bank," *Dickinson Journal of International Law* 15:451–486.

Shihata, Ibrahim F. I., and Antonio R. Parra. 1994. "Applicable Law in Disputes Between States and Private Foreign Parties: The Case of Arbitration under the ICSID Convention," *ICSID Review: Foreign Investment Law Journal* 9:183–213.

Shirk, Susan L. 1994. *How China Opened Its Door: The Political Success of the PRC's Foreign Trade and Investment Reforms*, Washington DC: The Brookings Institution.

Shleifer, A., and Vishny, R. 1993. "Corruption," *Quarterly Journal of Economics* 108:599–617.

Shpiro, Shlomo. 1998. "Parliamentary and Administrative Reforms in the Control of Intelligence Services in the European Union," *Columbia Journal of European Law* 4:545–578.

Singh, Gurharpal. 1997. "Understanding Political Corruption in Contemporary Indian Politics," *Political Studies* 45:626–638.

Skidmore, Max J. 1996. "Promise and Peril in Combating Corruption: Hong Kong's ICAC," *Annuals of the American Academy of Political Science and Sociology* 547:118–130.

Smith, Warrick, and Ben Shin. 1995. *Regulating Brazil's Infrastructure: Perspectives on Decentralization*, Economic Notes No. 6, Country Dept. I: Latin American and Caribbean Region, Washington DC: World Bank, September.

Snyder, James M. Jr. 1992. "Long-Term Investing in Politicians: Or, Give Early, Give Often," *Journal of Law and Economics* 35:15–43.

Sproat, John. 1982. "'The Best Men': Liberal Reformers in the Gilded Age," Chicago: University of Chicago Press.

Stark, Andrew. 1992. "Public Sector Conflict of Interest at the Federal Level in Canada and the U.S.: Differences in the Understanding and Approach," *Public Administration Review* 52:427–437.

Stasavage, David. 1996. "Corruption and the Mozambican Economy," second draft, OECD Development Centre, Paris, August.

Stave, Bruce, ed. 1972. *Urban Bosses, Machines, and Progressive Reform*, Lexington MA: D.C. Heath and Co.

Stella, Peter. 1992. *Tax Farming – A Radical Solution for Developing Country Tax Problems?* IMF Working Paper, WP/92/70, Washington DC: IMF.

Stigler, George. 1971. "The Theory of Regulation," *Bell Journal of Economics and Management Science* 2:3–21.

Stone, Andrew, Brian Levy, and Ricardo Paredes. 1992. "Public Institutions and Private Transactions: The Legal and Regulatory Environment for Business Transactions in Brazil and Chile," Policy Research Working Paper 891, Washington DC: World Bank.

Strassmann, W. Paul. 1989. "The Rise, Fall, and Transformation of Overseas Construction Contracting," *World Development* 17:783–794.

Sultan, Nabil Ahmed. 1993. "Bureaucratic Corruption as a Consequence of the Gulf Migration: The Case of North Yemen," *Crime, Law and Social Change* 19:379–393.

Swamy, Gurushri. 1994. "Kenya: Patchy, Intermittent Commitment," in Ishrat Husain and Rashid Faruqee, eds., *Adjustment in Africa: Lessons from Country Studies*, Washington DC: The World Bank, pp. 193–237.

Tanenbaum, Adam S. 1995. "*Day v. Holahan*: Crossroads in Campaign Finance Jurisprudence," *Georgetown Law Journal* 84:151–178.

Tanzania, Presidential Commission of Inquiry Against Corruption. 1996. *Report of the Commission on Corruption – Volume 1*, Dar Es Salaam, November.

Tanzi, Vito, and Hamid Davoodi. 1997. "Corruption, Public Investment, and Growth," IMF Working Paper WP/97/139, Washington DC: International Monetary Fund, October.

Tendler, Judith. 1979. "Rural Works Programs in Bangladesh: Community, Technology and Graft." Prepared for the Transportation Department of the World Bank, Washington DC.

Tenenbaum, Bernard. 1996. "Regulation: What the Prime Minister Needs to Know," *Electricity Journal* 9(2):28–36 (March).

Terkper, Seth E. 1994. "Ghana's Tax Administration Reforms (1985–1993)," *Tax Notes International* 94:1393–1400, May 23.

Thacher, Thomas D. II. 1995. "The New York City School Construction Authority's Office of the Inspector General: A Successful New Strategy for Reforming Public Contracting in the Construction Industry," draft, New York NY, June.

Thelen, David. 1972. *The New Citizenship: Origins of Progressivism in Wisconsin, 1885–1900*, Columbia MO: University of Missouri Press.

Thompson, Joel A., and Gary F. Moncrief. 1998. *Campaign Finance in State Legislative Elections*, Washington DC: Congressional Quarterly.

Tiefer, Charles. 1983. "The Constitutionality of Independent Officers as Checks on Abuses of Executive Power," *Boston University Law Review* 63:59–103.

Tierney, John. 1995. "Holiday Bribery," *New York Times Magazine*, December 17, pp. 42–44.

Tirole, Jean. 1986. "Hierarchies and Bureaucracies: On the Role of Collusion in Organizations," *Journal of Law, Economics, and Organization* 2:181–214.

Tirole, Jean. 1996. "A Theory of Collective Reputations (with Applications to the Persistence of Corruption and to Firm Quality)," *Review of Economic Studies* 63:1–22.

Titmuss, Richard. 1970. *The Gift Relationship*, London: Allen and Unwin.

Transparency International. 1995. *Building a Global Coalition Against Corruption*, TI Annual Report, Berlin.

——. 1998. *Combating Corruption: Are Lasting Solutions Emerging?*, TI Annual Report. Berlin.

Transparency International–USA. 1996. "Corporate Anti-Corruption Programs: A Survey of Best Practices," Washington DC, June.

Tucker, Lee. 1994. "Censorship and Corruption: Government Self-Protection Through Control of the Media," in Duc V. Trang, ed., *Corruption and Democracy: Political Institutions, Processes and Corruption in Transition States in East-Central Europe and in the Former Soviet Union*, Budapest: Institute for Constitutional and Legislative Policy, pp. 185–189.

United Kingdom, Audit Commission. 1993. *Protecting the Public Purse: Probity in the Public Sector: Combating Fraud and Corruption in Local Government*, London: HMSO.

——. 1994. *Protecting the Public Purse 2: Ensuring Probity in the NHS*, London: HMSO.

——. 1996. *Bulletin*, November.

United Nations, Department of Technical Co-operation for Development and Centre for Social Development and Humanitarian Affairs. 1990. *Corruption in Government: Report of an Interregional Seminar, The Hague, The Netherlands, 11–15 December, 1989*, TCD/SEM 90/2, INT-89-R56, New York.

United Nations Development Programme. 1996. *Aid Accountability Initiative, Bi-Annual Report, 1 January-June 30, 1996*, New York, July.

——. 1997a. "Corruption and Good Governance," Discussion Paper 3, Management Development and Governance Division, Bureau for Policy and Programme Support (prepared by Susan Rose-Ackerman).

——. 1997b. *Governance for Sustainable Human Development*, UNDP policy document, New York, January.

United Nations, High Commissioner for Human Rights. 1996. Centre for Human Rights, Programme of Technical Cooperation in the Field of Human Rights, *Report of the Needs Mission to South Africa (6–25 May 1996)*.

Vander Velde, Edward J., and Mark Svendsen. 1994. "Goals and Objectives of Irrigation in Pakistan – A Prelude to Assessing Irrigation Performance," *Quarterly Journal of International Agriculture* 33:222–242.

Van de Walle, Nicholas. 1989. "Privatization in Developing Countries: A Review of the Issues," *World Development* No. 17, pp. 601–615.

Van Rijckeghem, Caroline, and Beatrice Weder. 1997. "Corruption and the Rate of Temptation: Do Low Wages in the Civil Service Cause Corruption?," working paper 97/93, International Monetary Fund, Washington DC.

Varese, Federico. 1994. "Is Sicily the Future of Russia? Private Protection and the Rise of the Russian Mafia," *Archives of European Sociology* 35:224–258.

Verheijen, Tony, and Antoaneta Dimitrova. 1996. "Private Interests and Public Administration: The Central and East European Experience," *International Review of Administrative Sciences* 62:197–218.

Vermeulen, Gert. 1997. "The Fight Against International Corruption in the European Union," in Barry Rider, ed., *Corruption: The Enemy Within*, The Hague: Kluwer, pp. 333–342.

Vick, Douglas W., and Linda Macpherson. 1997. "An Opportunity Lost: The United Kingdom's Failed Reform of Defamation Law," *Federal Communications Law Journal* 49:621–653.

Vincent, Jeffrey R., and Clark S. Binkley, "Forest-Based Industrialization: A Dynamic Perspective," in Narendra P. Sharma, ed., *Managing the World's Forests*, Dubuque, IA: Kendall/Hunt Publishing, pp. 93–139.

von der Fehr, Nils-Henrik Morch. 1995. "The African Entrepreneur: Evidence on Entrepreneurial Activity and Firm Formation in Zambia," Discussion Paper 15095, Regional Program on Enterprise Development, Washington DC: The World Bank.

Wade, Robert. 1982. "The System of Administrative and Political Corruption: Canal Irrigation in South India," *Journal of Development Studies* 18:287–328.

———. 1984. "Irrigation Reform in Conditions of Populist Anarchy," *Journal of Development Economics* 14:285–303.

Webster, Leila M. 1993. *The Emergence of Private Sector Manufacturing in Hungary*, World Bank Technical Paper 229, Washington DC: World Bank.

———. 1993b. *The Emergence of Private Sector Manufacturing in Poland*, World Bank Technical Paper 237, Washington DC: World Bank.

Webster, Leila M., and Joshua Charap. 1993. *The Emergence of Private Sector Manufacturing in St. Petersburg*, World Bank Technical Paper 228, Washington DC: World Bank.

Webster, Leila, with Juergen Franz, Igor Artimiev, and Harold Wackman. 1994. *Newly Privatized Russian Enterprises*, World Bank Technical Paper Number 241, Washington DC: World Bank.

Wedeman, Andrew. 1997. "Looters, Rent-Scrapers, and Dividend-Collectors: Corruption and Growth in Zaire, South Korea and the Philippines," *The Journal of Developing Areas* 31:457–478.

Wei, Shang-Jin. 1997. "How Taxing Is Corruption on International Investors?," National Bureau of Economic Research Working Paper 6030, Cambridge MA, May.

Weingast, Barry R. 1995. "The Economic Role of Political Institutions: Market-Preserving Federalism and Economic Development," *Journal of Law, Economics, and Organization* 11:1–31.

Weitzman, Martin L., and Douglas L. Kruse. 1990. "Profit Sharing and Productivity," in Alan Blinder, ed., *Paying for Productivity: A Look at the Evidence*, Washington DC: The Brookings Institution, pp. 95–142.

White, Leonard D. 1958. *The Republican Era: 1869–1901: A Study in Administrative History*, New York: Macmillan.

Wiehan, Michael H. 1997. "Reform of Government Procurement Procedures: Principles and Objectives," paper presented at the 8th Conference of the International Public Procurement Association, Kuala Lumpur.

Williamson, Oliver. 1975. *Markets and Hierarchies: Analysis and Antitrust Implications*, New York: Free Press.

———. 1979. "Transaction-Cost Economics: The Governance of Contractual Relations," *Journal of Law and Economics* 22:233–261.

World Bank. 1991. *The Reform of Public Sector Management*, Policy and Research Series 18, Country Economics Department, Washington DC.

———. 1993. *Nigeria: Issues and Options in the Energy Sector*, Report No. 11672-UNI, Energy Sector Management Assistance Programme, World Bank Western Africa Department and Industry and Energy Division, July.

———. 1994a. *Nigeria: Structural Adjustment Program* Washington DC: World Bank.

World Bank. 1994b. *Paraguay: Country Economic Memorandum*, Report 11723, World Bank: Washington DC, June 29.

——. 1995. *Ghana Country Assistance Review*, Report No. 14547, Operations Evaluation Department. Washington DC: World Bank, June.

——. 1997a. *Helping Countries Combat Corruption: The Role of the World Bank*, Poverty Reduction and Economic Management Network. Washington DC.

——. 1997b. *The Inspection Panel: Overview September 1997 Update*, http://www.worldbank.org/html/ins-panel/overview.html.

——. 1997c. *World Development Report 1997: The State in a Changing World*, New York: Oxford University Press.

Yabrak, Isil, and Leila Webster. 1995. *Small and Medium Enterprises in Lebanon: A Survey*, World Bank, Private Sector Development Department and Industry and Energy Division, Middle East and North Africa Country Department II, final report, January 28.

Yotopoulos, Pan A. 1989. "The (Rip)Tide of Privatization: Lessons from Chile," *World Development* 17:683–702.

Zelizer, Viviana A. 1994. *The Social Meaning of Money*, New York: Basic Books.

Zifcak, Spencer. 1994. *New Managerialism: Administrative Reform in Whitehall and Canberra*, Buckingham: Open University Press.

NAME INDEX

SUBJECT INDEX

accountability, public: of government in
Chile, 202; in implementation of limits
on corruption, 146–9; with openness of
government, 162–74, 184; routes to,
165–7; World Bank Inspection Panel as
mechanism for, 194
accounting, provisions in Foreign Corrupt
Practices Act, 57
administration, public: competitive
pressures in, 49–52; effect of
dysfunctional, 1; public information
systems in, 162–5, 184; using contracts to
separate politics from, 84–7; *see also*
accountability, public; administrative
law; auditing; civil service systems
administrative law, reform as
anticorruption strategy, 146–8
Administrative Procedures Act, United
States, 146–8
African countries: conflicts of interest in,
75; corruption in taxation and customs
in, 19–20; crisis of institutions, 109;
decline in civil service wages, 72; need
for career civil service, 70–1; nonprofits
in, 169; performance of development
finance institutions, 109n26; structural
adjustment lending, 30n13; *see also
specific African countries*
American Bar Association: assistance to
countries interested in reform, 196; Task
force on International Standards for
Corrupt Practices, 187
anticorruption agencies, Hong Kong and
Singapore, 159–62
anticorruption laws: deterrent effect of,
52–9; rewards for evidence of bribery,
56–7

anticorruption policies: proposed by
international institutions, 182–3
Argentina: bribes by insurance companies
for favors, 16; costs of corruption and
inefficiency, 212; crisis as catalyst, 209n5;
experimentation with no-bribery
pledges in Mendoza, 181; fraudulent
plan to develop underdeveloped
regions, 40; highway privatization
bidding, 36; judicial system, 157; legal
system in, 154; privatization, 37; reform
of reinsurance system, 221; Yacyreta
Dam, 194
Asian countries: corruption in, 3; effect of
weak legislatures in, 148; mechanisms to
deter rent seeking, 120; *see also specific
Asian countries*
Asian Development Bank, anticorruption
policy, 184n4
Audit Commission, United Kingdom, 150,
163
auditing: of government laws and financial
records, 162–5; international initiatives,
186–7
Australia: administrative reform strategy,
199; bids from private sector for
government services, 85
autocracy, reform strategies in, 206–9,
214–15

Bangladesh: Grameen Bank, 110n27;
international agency loans as
patronage, 109n26; as patrimonial state,
105
banking system: corruption and patronage, 10–11, 109–10; high-risk lending,
10–11

259